ON PAUL RICOEUR

D1590025

This book examines the later work of Paul Ricoeur, particularly his major work, *Time and Narrative*. The essays, including three pieces by Ricoeur himself, consider this important study, extending and developing the debate it has inspired.

Time and Narrative is the finest example of contemporary philosophical hermeneutics and is one of the most significant works of philosophy published in the late twentieth century. Paul Ricoeur's study of the intertwining of time and narrative proposes and examines the possibility that narrative could remedy a fatal deficiency in any purely phenomenological approach. He analysed both literary and historical writing, from Proust to Braudel, as well as key figures in the history of philosophy: Aristotle, Augustine, Kant, Hegel, Husserl and Heidegger. His own recognition of his limited success in expunging aporia opens onto the positive discovery of the importance of narrative identity, on which Ricoeur writes here. Other contributors take up a range of different topics: tracing Ricoeur's own philosophical trajectory; reflexively applying the narrative approach to philosophy, or to his own text; reconstructing his dialectic of sedimentation and tradition.

An essential companion to *Time and Narrative*, this collection also provides an excellent introduction to Ricoeur's later work and to contemporary works in philosophical hermeneutics. It will be of major interest to literary theorists, narratologists, historians and philosophers.

David Wood teaches philosophy at the University of Warwick, where he is Director of the Centre for Research in Philosophy and Literature. He is the author of *The Deconstruction of Time* and *Philosophy at the Limit*.

WARWICK STUDIES IN PHILOSOPHY AND LITERATURE
General editor: Andrew Benjamin

It used to be a commonplace to insist on the elimination of the 'literary' dimension from philosophy. This was particularly true for a philosophical tradition inspired by the possibilities of formalization and by the success of the natural sciences. And yet even in the most rigorous instances of such philosophy we find demands for 'clarity', for 'tight' argument, and distinctions between 'strong' and 'weak' proofs which call out for a rhetorical reading. Equally, modern literary theory, quite as much as literature itself, is increasingly looking to philosophy (and other theoretical disciplines such as linguistics) for its inspiration. After a wave of structuralist analysis, the growing influence of deconstructive and hermeneutic readings continues to bear witness to this. While philosophy and literature are not to be identified, even if philosophy is thought of as 'a kind of writing', much of the most exciting theoretical work being done today, in Britain, Europe and America, exploits their tensions and intertwinings.

The University of Warwick pioneered the undergraduate study of the theoretical coition of Philosophy and Literature, and its recently established Centre for Research in Philosophy and Literature has won wide acclaim for its adventurous and dynamic programme of conferences and research. With this Series the work of the Centre is opened to a wider public. Each volume aims to bring the best scholarship to bear on topical themes in an atmosphere of intellectual excitement.

Books in the series:

*available in paperback

Paul Ricoeur at the University of Warwick in 1986.
By kind permission of the Photographic Department, University of
Warwick Library.

ON PAUL RICOEUR
NARRATIVE AND INTERPRETATION

edited by
DAVID WOOD

London and New York

First published 1991
by Routledge
11 New Fetter Lane, London EC4P 4EE

Simultaneously published in the USA and Canada
by Routledge
a division of Routledge, Chapman and Hall, Inc.
29 West 35th Street, New York, NY 10001

© 1991 The University of Warwick

Phototypeset by Intype, London
Printed in Great Britain by
Clays Ltd, St Ives plc

British Library Cataloguing-in-Publication Data
On Paul Ricoeur: narrative and interpretation.
(Warwick studies in philosophy and literature)
I. Wood, David   II. Series
121.68

Library of Congress Cataloging-in-Publication Data
On Paul Ricoeur: narrative and interpretation / edited by David Wood.
p.   cm.—(Warwick studies in philosophy and literature)
Includes bibliographical references and index.
1. Ricoeur, Paul. 2. Narration (Rhetoric) 3. Time—History—20th
century. I. Wood, David. II. Series.
B2430.R55406 1991
194—dc20   91–28657

ISBN 0–415–07406–1.—ISBN 0–415–07407–X (pbk)

CONTENTS

CONTENTS

THE CONTRIBUTORS

David Wood is Senior Lecturer in Philosophy at the University of Warwick. He is the author of *The Deconstruction of Time* (1988) and *Philosophy at the Limit* (1990) and is the editor of many collections of essays in continental philosophy.

Paul Ricoeur is John Nuveen Professor Emeritus at the Divinity School, University of Chicago, where he is also Professor of Philosophy and a member of the Committee on Social Thought. He was for many years dean of the Faculty of Letters and Human Sciences at the University of Paris X (Nanterre). He is Associate Fellow of the Centre for Research in Philosophy and Literature at the University of Warwick. His *Time and Narrative* appeared in English translation in three volumes from 1984–8, and he is the author of *From Text to Action* (1991).

Richard Kearney is Professor of Philosophy at University College, Dublin. He studied with Paul Ricoeur and received his doctorate from the University of Paris X (Nanterre) in 1981. He is the author of *Poétique du Possible* (1984), *Dialogues with Contemporary Continental Thinkers* (1984), *Modern Movements in Continental Philosophy* (1986) and *Transitions: Narratives in Contemporary Irish Culture* (1987), as well as *The Wake of Imagination* (1987).

Don Ihde is Professor of Philosophy and Dean of Humanities and Fine Arts at SUNY Stony Brook. He wrote *Hermeneutic Phenomenology: The Philosophy of Paul Ricoeur* (1971) and his recent books include *Consequences of Phenomenology* (1986), and *Technology and the Lifeworld* (1990).

J. M. Bernstein is Reader in Philosophy and Chairman of the Philosophy Department at the University of Essex. He is the

ix

author of *The Philosophy of the Novel: Lukacs, Marxism and the Dialectic of Form* (1984).

Kevin J. Vanhoozer is Lecturer in Theology at the University of Edinburgh, where he specializes in Paul Ricoeur, contemporary hermeneutics and questions of theological method. He is the author of *Biblical Narrative in the Philosophy of Paul Ricoeur* (1990) and several essays on hermeneutics.

Jonathan Rée is Reader in Philosophy and the History of Ideas at Middlesex Polytechnic, London. He is the author of *Proletarian Philosophers* (1984) and *Philosophical Tales* (1987).

Rhiannon Goldthorpe teaches French at St Anne's College, Oxford. She has written extensively on Sartre and Proust, and she is the author of *Sartre: Literature and Theory* (1984), and *Sartre: La Nausée* (1990).

Hayden White is Presidential Professor of Historical Studies of the Board of Studies in History of Consciousness at the University of California, Santa Cruz, and the author of numerous books including *Metahistory* (1973). He published *The Content of the Form* in 1987.

David Carr is Professor of Philosophy at the University of Ottawa. He is the author of *Phenomenology and the Problem of History: A study of Husserl's Transcendental Philosophy* (1984) and *Time, Narrative and History* (1986).

Charles Taylor is Professor of Philosophy and Political Science at McGill University. He is the author of *Human Agency and Language* (1985), *Philosophy and the Human Sciences* (1985) and *Sources of the Self* (1989).

ACKNOWLEDGEMENTS

I am grateful to various people who in different ways contributed to this volume: Tamra Wright and Heather Jones for editorial and secretarial assistance, Anita Roy and Adrian Driscoll for their continuing support and encouragement at Routledge, two anonymous reviewers for constructive comments, Iain Grant for his translation of the Round Table discussion and Leslie Hill for making substantial improvements to my own translations of Ricoeur. I would like to thank the contributors to the volume, particularly Paul Ricoeur, for their contributions and their patience. Many of these papers were presented in earlier versions at a Warwick Workshop in Continental Philosophy in 1986, and have since been revised and reworked, and supplemented by other material. We are particularly fortunate not only to have had Paul Ricoeur with us on the first occasion, but to have been able to welcome him back subsequently to Warwick as Senior Visiting Fellow of the Centre for Research in Philosophy and Literature for further lectures and discussion, from which in part this volume is drawn.

I would also like to thank the editors of *Esprit* for permission to translate Paul Ricoeur's 'Identité narrative' which appeared in the journal in 1988; Mr Jack Goellner of Johns Hopkins University Press, for permission to reprint Hayden White's 'The metaphysics of narrativity' from his *The Content of the Form* (Johns Hopkins University Press, 1987); and the University of Ottawa Press for permission to translate and reprint parts of the Round Table discussion published in *In Search of Meaning* (University of Ottawa Press, 1985, pp. 285–99).

I have Iain Grant to thank for compiling the index.

LIST OF ABBREVIATIONS

BT Martin Heidegger, *Being and Time*, translated by John Macquarrie and Edward Robinson, Oxford, Blackwell, 1962.

CJ Immanuel Kant, *Critique of Judgment*, translated by J. H. Bernard, London, Collier Macmillan, 1951.

CPR Immanuel Kant, *Critique of Pure Reason*, translated by Norman Kemp Smith, London, Macmillan, 1933.

NT Paul Ricoeur, 'Narrative time', *Critical Inquiry*, vol. 7, no. 1, 1980.

PC Jean-François Lyotard, *The Postmodern Condition; a Report on Knowledge*, translated by Geoff Bennington and Brian Massouri, Minneapolis, University of Minnesota Press, 1984.

TN Paul Ricoeur, *Time and Narrative*, translated by Kathleen McLaughlin and David Pellauer, Chicago, University of Chicago Press, 1984–8. Originally published as *Temps et récit*, Paris, Editions du Seuil, 1983–5.

1

INTRODUCTION

Interpreting narrative

David Wood

And the source of coming to be for existing beings is that into which destruction, too, happens, according to necessity, for they pay penalty and retribution to each other for their injustice according to the assessment of Time.

Anaximander
according to Theophrastus, preserved by Simplicius[1]

Ricoeur's *Time and Narrative* is one of the most impressive attempts ever made to address and resolve the paradoxical nature of time, one which gives us an original and illuminating reading of many of the important way-stations, from Aristotle to Heidegger, and one which sets out to test a hypothesis – that the resources of narrative remedy a fatal deficiency in any purely phenomenological approach to time.

No philosopher need justify an interest in time. The greatest thinkers, from Anaximander onwards, have known that time is not merely an important topic, but a pervasive and hydra-headed problem. So much so that much philosophy reads like the construction of sea-walls against it. For time is the destroyer not just of all that we are proud of, even pride itself, it threatens the realization of many a philosophical ideal.[2] Time is the possibility of corruption at the deepest level. And yet without organized temporal extension, there would be nothing to be corrupted. Time makes as well as breaks. Time giveth and it taketh away.

The pervasiveness of time is an intuition that can strike us on occasion at ..e everyday ontic level. The Heraclitean vision that all is in flux is not uncommon, even if the force of this intuition wanes like everything else. But the pervasiveness of time in philosophy does not arise simply at the level of intuition – that all

things, and all experiences are in time. It is near to the surface
of most of the central problems of philosophy, and has a major
impact on how we think of identity, of truth, of meaning, of reason,
of freedom, of language, of existence, of the self. The list is endless.
And even to talk of a major impact on these problems is too
weak a verdict. It would be wrong to imagine there being happy
respectable problems visited by the scourge of time. Without time,
these would not be the problems that they are at all. Sometimes
this is obvious as for example, in the case of the self, sometimes we
need to unpack the temporal freight with more patience. In brief,
time is not just a problem in itself, the proper object of research
on the philosophy of time. The idea of limiting it as an *object of
research* is, I am claiming, deeply implausible. The ubiquity and
pervasiveness of time does not, however, as tidy minds might hope,
make it discountable. If everything, in addition to its natural
colour, were tinted by a peculiar shade of blue, we could discount
the fact, because we could neither detect the colour, nor understand the meaning of this condition. But time is not the name of
a simple predicate or homogeneous condition. Nor is it simply the
name of a neutral dimension on which independently identifiable
things can be ranged. If the terms were not in as great a need of
explication as time itself, we could say that time is the economy
of being.

These claims about the pervasiveness of time – not just in the
world, but as a vital dimension of all our philosophical reflections
on the world – are quite as consequential as the contemporary
recognition of the pervasiveness of language. It is tempting to
suppose that some sort of deconstruction of our ordinary assumptions about the unity, unidirectionality and unidimensionality of
time could lead to a wilder, more pluralistic account of the
structures of time, one that recognized, for example, the relative
autonomy of different time-frames or *shelters*. And the observer of
discrete natural processes can suppose that much of this description involves language only in the task of faithfully reflecting the
contours of the real, rather than having much of an independent
synthetic or constitutive role. It is clearly a matter for dispute
about whether such a line can ever be drawn. I believe that, with
certain provisos, it can. And if, as is not implausible, what we
commonly call language is already caught up in certain temporal

valuations, then bringing language onto the scene is not quite as innocent as it seems.

But if there is an expository advantage to distinguishing what, following Kant, we could call an aesthetic approach to time from an analytical one, it is both possible and important to give a full run to the positive articulation of time and language, and I would like now to consider the contribution to such a project made by that remarkable intellectual adventure with which Paul Ricoeur presents us in his *Time and Narrative*. His eventual Kantian demarcation of the limits of narrative has a significance he only partly recognizes.

The locus of Augustine's perplexity about time was the act of reflection. One might think that there was something about reflection that doomed our thinking about time not just to initial confusion but to final failure. In *Time and Narrative* Ricoeur takes up the challenge and singles out as the persistent difficulty in the history of philosophy that of reconciling, of doing equal justice, to both phenomenological and cosmological time. In the story he tells, Aristotle's understanding of time as 'the number of movement with respect of the "before" and "after" ' gives us no way of thinking about time as experienced, even if an apprehending subject is actually required on Aristotle's model. Augustine's account of the distention of the soul, while it answers that problem, does not offer us any basis on which to think of objective time, which he needs to be able to account for, because he wants to say that time began at the point at which the world was created. Kant, according to Ricoeur, may give to the mind the role of being the condition of worldly time, but gives us no phenomenology of experience. And Husserl on the other hand has great difficulty in reconstituting objective time after the *epoché*. Finally, Heidegger's attempt to think of world-time as a levelled-off authentic time is a failure, because even this world-time, he claims, is specific to individual Daseins.

I will not, here, comment on the details of this story, which is taken up in different ways by the papers collected in this volume. What it indicates is the scope of Ricoeur's concern about time. His suggestion seems to be not merely that time is pervasive, as I have claimed, but that Augustine's perplexity about time reflects a deeper failure to *think time*: not just Augustine's failure, but the failure of a tradition. *Time and Narrative* is structured around a hypothesis – which in mock-Heideggerean idiom Ricoeur sums up at one point as the claim that narrative is the guardian of time. More carefully expressed, it is the claim that the phenomenology of time, 'the most exemplary attempt to express the lived experience of time', leads to the multiplication of aporias. And these tangles only get unravelled through 'the mediation of the indirect discourse of narrative'. One can almost hear Kant's claim that intuitions without concepts are blind and Ricoeur is clearly saying that phenomenology must embrace the conceptual resources of language. But he is going further and saying that what Kant called schematism in his Analytic of Principles, the application of a concept to an instance by a productive rule-governed imagination, need not be thought of as 'an art concealed in the depths of the human soul whose real modes of activity nature is hardly likely ever to allow us to discover and to have open to our gaze' (*CPR*, A141 / B180–1) as Kant put it, but can be found 'writ large' in narrative. Through narrative successive events are subjected to configuration, which generalizes Aristotle's account of plot in his *Poetics*. Narrative heals aporia. But Ricoeur's extraordinary power and virtues as a thinker emerge most strongly in the 'Conclusions' chapter to *Time and Narrative* volume III. Here he reviews the argument of the book, and as if the ravages of time and reviews could not be relied on to do it for him, he begins to unravel his own knitting. The hypothesis that narrative relieves us of the aporetics of time is seen to have limits. One of the central products of narrative is to allow us to construct a narrative identity – both at the level of history (and e.g. the identity of a nation),[3] and at the level of the individual life. This represents a considerable advance over accounts based on substance, or bodily continuity, or memory. But it is open to the objection that it makes identity somewhat unstable, insofar as many stories can be woven from the same material. Ricoeur treats this not as an objection but as a limitation – a distinction to which I shall return. But we might equally regard it as an advantage to have a model which can accommodate the contingency and revisability of identity, a model which is not an all-or-nothing model. Ricoeur also admits another, perhaps more worrying problem. Narrative identity stresses the intelligible organization of events at the expense of the will, the ethical moment, the moment of decision, of impetus. He alludes to Levinas on promising, but he could equally have cited Heidegger. In each of these examples, narrative does not just heal, it opens new rifts – first, the irresolvable plurality of stories, and then the opposition between the organizing power of imagination, and the will. Ricoeur's account of the significance of these difficulties is classic. Narrative does not resolve aporias, it makes them *productive*, which suggests that a formal or logical solution to our problems (e.g. McTaggart's proof of the dependence of the B-series (cosmic time) on the A-series (lived time)) may not be required, even if it were possible. His second, Kantian, gloss on these difficulties is to say that the limits of his account of narrative can be seen not as a defect but as 'circumscribing its domain of validity' (*TN* vol. III, p. 261). But another reading of the appearance of these limits is possible: that they represent the return of the repressed, the re-emergence of the aporetic dimension that narrative was hired to keep under control. Limits of validity mean: beyond this point, unintelligibility, contradiction, aporia. Is not Ricoeur putting a brave face on time's reassertion of its power to disrupt all attempts at conceptual domestication?

As if this were not bad enough, Ricoeur discovers that the aporia generated by the gulf between cosmic and phenomenological time, a gulf bridged by narrative, the aporia that has been centre stage in *Time and Narrative* is in fact only one of many aporias to which our thinking about time is subject. The second is precisely that – of time as one and as many, not in the sense of local time-frames that we discussed earlier, but rather that we think of time as one, and yet as divided between past, present and future. Without rehearsing the argument here – he makes a subtle deployment of the idea of the unity of history – suffice it to say that Ricoeur finds narrative even less able to deal with this difficulty. The third and last aporia he designates the inscrutability of time, by which he refers to the various ways in which time continually breaks through our attempts to constitute it, to clarify its meaning, to show us its deep archaic enveloping mystery.

> What fails is not thinking, in any acceptation of this term, but the impulse – or to put it a better way, the *hubris* – that impels our thinking to posit itself as the master of meaning. . . . Time, escaping our will to mastery, surges forth on the side of what . . . is the true master of meaning.
>
> (*TN* vol. III, p. 261)

Now in my judgement, the true master here is Ricoeur himself, who, after the fact, has recast the plot of *Time and Narrative* as a confession, in which the presumption of synthesizing thought is confronted by a power that exceeds it. If time ever seems to be acquiescing in our configuring plots, you can be sure it is silently gathering its forces for revenge. Of course the oddest paradox now arises. For we have made time into the hero of a story of confinement and release. Has not narrative finally closed the trap, and triumphed?

In the account we have given so far, we have followed the path of Ricoeur's own reflections on his attempt to both bind and illuminate time through narrative. But the third aporia he discusses – the inscrutability of time, its power to reassert its envelopment – surely opens another front: the wider relation between time and language. One response to the breakdown, or the coming up against limits, of the power of narrative to tame time, might be to reassess the specific theory of language to which Ricoeur is committed in discussing narrative. To put it very simply: might it not be that narrative is committed to the possibility of a *certain closure of meaning*, which will inexorably be breached. In other words, narrative selects from but does not exhaust the power of language to resolve the aporias of time. Its particular forte is synthesis.

But it has no monopoly on linguistic synthesis, and, more particularly, it may be just such a strength that is its weakness. If time is not essentially captured by the effects of closure narrative facilitates, then we must either find time showing through in the very pathos of narrative's failure, or we must look elsewhere. Donning for the moment a veil of ignorance, we might expect that resources for such an expansion could be found in metaphor and metonomy, which might seem to allow us to think the non-linear, creative interruption of that articulation of sense through time that we call narrative. When we lift the veil however, we find Ricoeur's *The Rule of Metaphor* in front of us, and we recall that the study of metaphor and narrative are for Ricoeur integral parts of a general poetics, 'one vast poetic sphere', both instances of the productive imagination. We have already seen him describe narrative in terms of production; we know that Ricoeur, following Aristotle who thought of plot as the mimesis of an action, allows the poetic a role in the narrative refiguring of action; we know that Ricoeur ultimately seeks to harness the poetic for speculative and eventually practical ends. Without undertaking here a full-scale review of *The Rule of Metaphor* it would not misrepresent Ricoeur to conclude that his deployment of metaphor and narrative separately and in harness is subordinated to a law of productivity, in which, I would say, the moment of synthesis has the last word. If this is right, then we will not be able to find in metaphor a countervailing force that would interrupt narrative, or set up different trails of connectedness.

There are resources for such interruption in Derrida, Heidegger, Blanchot, Levinas and others. I would like to consider an attempt at a synthesis of these resources in a recent book by Herman Rapaport called *Heidegger and Derrida: Reflections on Time and Language*.[4]

First a brief overview. Rapaport does not claim to be doing philosophy, but intellectual history. And if he had nothing new to say philosophically, his tracing out of the relation of Derrida's deconstruction to Heidegger's own accounts of the need for the destruction of the history of ontology supplies an excellent map of the Derrida/Heidegger connection. But Rapaport does in fact have a philosophical claim to make, one of the highest importance: 'the question of time is far more fundamental to a philosophical understanding of deconstruction than one might at first suppose.'[5] It is tempting but mistaken, for example, to associate Heidegger's *Kehre* with a turn towards language and away from time. Rapaport shows how wrong this is, and in presenting Heidegger as continuing to pursue 'the temporal clue', and Derrida as responding constructively to the failure of these efforts, Rapaport does a great service to Heidegger scholarship and to our appreciation of Derrida.

One of the distinctive aspects of Rapaport's reading of Derrida is his emphasis on the importance of Blanchot in accounting for the shift in Derrida's reading of Heidegger from the essays of the sixties to those of the late seventies and eighties. Erasmus Schöfer had described as *paronomasia* Heidegger's habit of 'stringing of different word types which . . . belong to the same word stem'.[6] Rapaport finds in Blanchot – especially *Le livre a venir* (1959) and *Le pas au-dela* (1973) – a way of developing or interpreting this rhetorical principle into one that offers a way of setting up not new forms of temporal synthesis, but what I would call trails, a form of temporal organization not overlaid by what Ricoeur calls configuration, and hence escaping the mimetic imperative. In his *La parole sacrée de Hölderlin*, Blanchot writes

Hölderlin is credited as comprehending the poet as one who, in announcing his arrival in the wake of his being-there (or

7

Dasein), brings into proximity a *sacred disseminating temporality* by means of reflectively holding together in an *à venir, avenir,* or *advenir* that is literature.[7] (my emphasis)

Rapaport devotes a long chapter – 'Paronomasia' – to the impact of Blanchot's elaboration of such disseminating temporalities on Derrida, instanced in his deployment of *Viens,* in, for instance 'On an apocalyptic tone recently adopted in philosophy'.[8] Rapaport's discussion is extended in a series of acute commentaries on later Derrida essays, and on the temporal dimensions of *The Post Card, Shibboleth,* 'Geschlecht II' and so on in the chapter 'Anticipations of Apocalypse'.[9]

Much work is done by such rhetorical categories as metalepsis – chained metonymy – and paronomasia, but what remains to be decided is their status and scope. It may be that the twists and disguises undergone by Heidegger's pursuit of 'the temporal clue' cannot be thought either through narrative or through a productive metaphorics. And it may be that the same can be said of certain literary constructions. But if this book is successful in showing that deconstruction is intimately entangled with the project of rethinking time, then we would have to formulate the book's claims in a more general way. Narrative is presented by Ricoeur as a rule of linguistically mediated temporal synthesis. But what this book suggests, minimally, is that there are other ways of thinking temporal connectedness which are creative, and linguistically mediated, but do not involve synthesis or configuration. If they are to be given practical exemplification I would revert to Heidegger's account of *besinnliche denken,* meditative thinking, which he claims has its own rigour, which breaks both with simple linear form, and with ordinary means–ends orientation. But it may be that what is crucial is that these other ways of thinking time break the mimetic arc that Ricoeur insists on, between temporal articulation and action. Perhaps the best way of reading such trails is as an involuntary counterpoint, in the musical sense, to the melodies of narrative organization. It is hard to defend the claim that paronomasia or metalepsis supply a new general and complete approach to thinking time, but they do suggest that narrative might have a shadow time no less important for being less visible.

My discussion of narrative has been framed by the problem of the aporias of time. Ricoeur introduced narrative poetics as an antidote to the multiplication of aporias in a pure phenomenology of time divested of these resources of linguistic synthesis. But as if by a process of selective mutation, new aporias continued to erupt. Should we not treat Ricoeur's analysis, and his extraordinary confession, as evidence of time's recursive power of interruption of our best-laid plots and plans?

Ricoeur, you will recall, hoped that narrative time would heal the aporias of time, in particular its diremption into phenomenological and cosmological time, in which the subject/object opposition flourishes unhindered. It is my suspicion that it is the a priori that leads to aporia, and that what we have to question ever more forcibly are the a priori assumptions about unity common to both phenomenological and cosmological time.[10]

Ricoeur's account of *Time and Narrative* confirms such an approach, even as it runs up against limits. I too would now like to turn to the question of limits, to take up again the way Ricoeur presents the issue, and to attempt a somewhat different formulation.

The thesis of the inevitable return of aporia, which Ricoeur does not formulate, but which is not too difficult to erect on the evidence of his work, might be thought to have a simple explanation. If references to phenomenological and cosmic time are not just two partial models of the real, but two discrete and autonomous dimensions of the real, then any being subject to double mapping, subject to constitution by both of these forms of time, would face not just an intellectual difficulty in reconciling two partial descriptions of the same thing – like the Evening Star and the Morning Star; such a being would suffer diremption, and the wound could never finally be healed. Such a being, it might be said, is man. The quest for reconciliation following, most notably, Kant, typically involves the subordination of causality (cosmological time) to self-legislation (phenomenological time), or at least the establishment of the independence of the latter from the former. But this account of diremption rests on an opposition which the setting aside of the unity of time thesis would dramatically weaken. This makes things worse, however, not better.

Time can be thought of plurally and structurally, in various complex ways. But this entire approach, though valid, has its limits. The accounts to which we have alluded, of the economy of local time-shelters, and those of Ricoeur we have relayed of narrative and of narrative identity, have their analytical, neutral side – I claimed that this was an advantage – and, however much the arc of interpretation returns to human action, they involve a certain distance. They are concerned with time as knowable, as thinkable, as constitutive of objects, identities, events, as invisible but nonetheless influential. It is possible to think Time positively, constructively, economically, and some such account as this seems to be indispensable. But what Ricoeur never loses sight of is the question of what it is *to be* a being described in this way – as managing by the construction of narratives the maintenance of fragile and permeable boundaries? *To be* such a being is to be open to both human torture and cosmic terror, to be able to be carried away by Bach's fugues, to be able to act decisively and to suffer – on top of being able to reflect about these matters. Ricoeur's last aporia centred on the inscrutability of time. What perhaps we should remember here is that time is not just an enveloping beyond to all our little bubbles of narrative order, it is more like the weather, capable of gentle breezes and violent storms. For all our ability to breed domestic forms of time, it also holds in reserve the apocalyptic possibility of dissolving any and all of the horizons of significance we have created for ourselves. I allude here to Husserl's discussion of the possibility of the end of the world, the destruction of all sense.[11]

The papers in this volume, Ricoeur's included, address these issues, and many more, in an exemplary way. There is a great deal going on at the end of *Time and Narrative*; I have only touched on some of what Ricoeur discusses in his 'Conclusion'. In the essay with which this collection begins, 'Life in quest of narrative', Ricoeur takes a critical look both at the common-sense linking of life and narrative suggested by the idea of a life-story, and at the equally common distinction between real life and fiction. Ricoeur seeks to rework the Socratic claim that the unexamined life is not worth living.

For his own approach to narrative, Ricoeur returns to Aristotle's *Poetics* and develops a general dynamic sense of 'emplotment', which he defines as a synthesis of heterogeneous elements. This turns out to have many dimensions: the plot's mediation between a plurality of events and a unified story, the primacy of concordance over discordance, and the configuration of a succession. For Ricoeur, however, much more is at stake. The *intelligibility* of this configuring activity is quite distinct from theoretical understanding, and is best described (after Aristotle) as *phronetic*. And for all the virtues of a science of narrative, Ricoeur's concern is not such second order discourse, but a primary narrative understanding. This is not fixed for all time, but has itself a life, a dynamic tradition governed by both sedimentation and innovation.

To bridge the apparent gap between narrative and life what we need to do is to rework our sense of each term. Narratives are not just configurations out there; they are completed only in the act of reading. Moreover *life* is not simply a biological phenomenon but symbolically mediated. And Ricoeur argues that human experience is already riddled with stories in a way that suggests a demand for narrative immanent to experience itself. Indeed, psychoanalysis suggests that we might think of lives in terms of untold or virtual stories; recounting a life would merely be articulating these, rather than imposing them on an alien content. Ricoeur suggests we think of the examined life as a narrated life, characterized by a struggle between concordance and discordance, the aim of which is to discover, not to impose on oneself, a narrative identity. This process allows one to develop a sense of oneself as a subject, not as a narcissistic ego but as a self 'instructed by cultural symbols'. The question of narrative identity, one of the fruits of *Time and Narrative*, is taken up in Ricoeur's second essay at the end of this book.

Kevin Vanhoozer's 'Philosophical antecedents to Ricoeur's *Time and Narrative*', offers a double-stranded introduction to Ricoeur's narrative theory. First, as an attempt, as he puts it, 'to think time and imagination together', which for Ricoeur means thinking Kant's productive imagination and Heidegger's existential temporality together. And second, he locates Ricoeur's theory in the context of his earlier philosophical anthropology, his Philosophy of the Will, the tripartite organization of which affords a further parallel with Kant's three critiques.

Kant gives to the imagination a mediating role, which is achieved by its production of schematic figures that shape time, the workings of which are for Kant hidden. Ricoeur could be said to complete Kant's project here by claiming that narrative gives an essential linguistic articulation to this schematization. Similarly, Kant's treatment of 'genius' or creative imagination in his third critique, suggests a rule-generating capacity exemplified by stories. And the reflective judgment to which Kant also refers there anticipates Ricoeur's grasp of the configurational aspect of narrative, its capacity to synthesize heterogenous parts into a whole.

Narrative also functions for Ricoeur as a corrective supplement to Heidegger's account of human temporality. If Heidegger could be said to have replaced Husserl's direct inspection of essential structures of consciousness with a detour through the fundamental structures of Dasein's existence, Ricoeur argues that Heidegger's own route is in need of a further mediating detour, through narrative. The narrative approach not only allows greater analytical rigour, it allows us to turn away from the monadic concerns of Being-towards-death to a more fully public and social sense of our temporality. Moreover, fictional narrative draws in the creative imagination, by offering us textually elaborated possibilities of existences.

In these various ways, according to Vanhoozer, Ricoeur's work constitutes a significant advance on both Kant and Heidegger, one which takes up and extends their central concerns.

The theme of creativity is taken further by Richard Kearney in 'Between tradition and utopia', in which he pursues the task announced by Ricoeur after the publication of *Time and Narrative*, of bringing tradition and utopia into a creative relationship. Ricoeur opposes to Hegel's model a relationship of open-ended mediation, one which avoids the extremes of both totalizing closure and utopian escape from all determination by a critical hermeneutics. Against romantic hermeneutics, Ricoeur argues for a *presumption of truth* at the level of our primary encounter with the past, a presumption that can of course be overturned. If Ricoeur laments the schism between past and future, Kearney points out that, paradoxically, Ricoeur's own insights about their connectedness may rest on it. Kearney pursues the theme of critical hermeneutics by taking a long look at Ricoeur's treatment of myth from *The Symbolism of Evil* (1960) onwards. Myth embodies both the aspect of tradition – sedimenting a society's 'social imaginary' – and also a utopian anticipation of the future. However, myth can become corrupted as ideological distortion. A critical hermeneutics would allow the creative functions of myth to be salvaged from its mystifying entanglements. The hermeneutics of suspicion is itself suspect. Myths have an eschatological, emancipatory side to them as well as their more obvious archaeological side. Ricoeur, Kearney argues, is insisting on the bringing together of *logos* and *muthos*. *Only connect . . .*

Jonathan Rée's 'Narrative and philosophical experience' takes a more reflexive turn. It is one thing to talk about the philosophical treatment of narrative and time. But if philosophy were not just a matter of deductive proof but involved the presentation of a journey of experience from error to enlightenment, considerations of narrative would become central to philosophical form itself, and not just a privileged object of its concern. Rée makes this claim about narrative in the very specific sense of storytelling.

He begins by recounting a range of perverse assessments of the status of narrative in philosophy. Hegel, for example, who seeks to rescue us from Descartes's deductive mathematical form, ignores the fact that Descartes's most influential writings are written in narrative form. And not only are Mill's anti-narrative pronouncements contradicted by his positive valuation of illusions, as distinct from delusions (a distinction which could be thought to prefigure Ricoeur's own distinction between positive and negative functions of myth), Mill's actual literary practice is soaked in narrative and in the narrative voice, a pattern of inconsistency shared by Bentham. And these special cases give way to a general requirement in presenting philosophical arguments to distinguish between different views and voices. At this point, the resources of narrative come powerfully into their own; moreover, through 'narrative personality' the animating experiences of the 'author' (and his characters) can be conveyed. Reflexively applied to philosophy itself, Ricoeur's work on narrative continues to illuminate the difficulties of giving voice to philosophical experience.

While Jonathan Rée discusses the literary dimension of philosophy, Rhiannon Goldthorpe's 'Ricoeur, Proust and the aporias of time' reviews Ricoeur's treatment of a literary work exemplary in its treatment of these themes: Proust's *A la recherche du temps perdu*, arguing that Ricoeur's recognition of the limits of narrative at the end of volume III of *Time and Narrative* reflects his confrontation with Proust. The echoes of *Le Temps retrouvé* (the last volume of Proust's work) in *Le Temps raconté* (the title of Ricoeur's volume III) are no coincidence. For what Proust repeatedly shows us is the failure of temporal resolution, either in the form of a supratemporal experience, or of a determinate significance in time. Such a repeated failure is suggested by Proust at the level of life and its configuration and repeated refiguration, both on the ground (where we tell stories to ourselves) and in fiction, and in the very act of reading – 'the discrepancies between the creation and the reception of the text' – as Goldthorpe puts it. At the end of Proust's novel, the retrieval of lost time remains a project for a future book, perhaps the second reading of the book we have just finished. And Ricoeur's recognition, at the end of *his* book, that after all, time is inscrutable, is some sort of testimony to the subtlety of Proust's insights. If it is not entirely without limits, Ricoeur's account of narrative at least leaves us with the idea of narrative identity. (A concept Ricoeur develops in the final paper in this book.) But, argues Goldthorpe, what Proust describes is an ineliminable tension between any such identity and a consciousness which even in this looser sense, can never coincide with itself.

Jay Bernstein's essay 'Grand narratives' considers Ricoeur's narrativizing interpretation of Heidegger's idea of historical *repetition* in the wider context of the attack on grand narrative launched by Lyotard. Bernstein's scrutiny of the critics of grand narrative is based on the suspicion that they have neglected the basic point of such narratives: that 'it is only through history that human things can be understood'. And he finds in Adorno a path towards a sense of grand narrative which recognizes this requirement, without succumbing to the demonic development of enlightenment universal history – a sense that would, or should, escape Lyotard's censure.

Bernstein develops a critique of Lyotard's dismissal of grand narrative via a comparison with Adorno's understanding of modernism, through art. The notion of *excess* which (reworking Kant's sublime) characterizes modern art for Lyotard, need not negate grand narrative, argues Bernstein, but can precisely be used to understand it. Moreover, and despite himself, Lyotard himself supplies an alternative 'grand narrative' – of a society unified by dispersal. For Bernstein it is important to retain the critical function of grand narrative indicated by Castoriadis's analysis of the social imaginary, especially when supplemented by Ricoeur's account of narrative repetition, which precisely 'provides an account of the . . . historicizing action of grand narrative'. Drawing largely on Ricoeur's essay 'Narrative time' (1980), Bernstein elucidates the role of configuration and refiguration in Ricoeur's reworking of Heidegger's sense of fateful repetition. He quotes Ricoeur: 'Fate is articulated in narrative. Fate is recounted.'[12] And as Vanhoozer and Kearney also bring out, Ricoeur seeks to displace the priority Heidegger gives to Being-towards-death over communal destiny. Bernstein reserves his critical assessment of Ricoeur to the end, concluding that for all its virtues, Ricoeur's narrative theory is a response to a reading of Hegel that underestimates the dialectic of self-consciousness, within which it should properly be located.

In his essay 'Text and the new hermeneutics' Don Ihde offers us first an overview of Ricoeur's importance in combating what he describes as neo-Renaissancism, or post-structuralist textualism. Ricoeur had first entered the fray with a critique of structuralism, and the hermeneutics of *Time and Narrative* continues to link texts to the human life-world both through time and through referentiality. But if this corrective is welcome, Ihde nonetheless detects an omission – a phenomenology of reading and writing – for which he proceeds to supply an exemplary instance: the role of perception and bodily perception in reading navigational charts. This draws Ihde into transcultural considerations, fuelled by an account of the double perspectives presented in Egyptian bas-reliefs. Echoing Merleau-Ponty's insistence on the primacy of perception, Ihde reminds us of the dependence of reading and writing on perception and on the world of active engagement.

Hayden White's 'The metaphysics of narrativity: time and symbol in Ricoeur's philosophy of history' was written before the appearance of the final volume of *Time and Narrative*, ('the most important synthesis of literary and historical theory produced this century') but brings to the collection the invaluable eye of the historian. He positions Ricoeur in the debate among historians about the adequacy of the narrative form to the representation of the real. The *Annalistes* saw it as a threat to the scientific status of history, while Anglo-American defenders of narrative historiography saw a natural fit between historical events and traditional story forms. Each view, argues White, rested on too narrow a grasp of the narrative possibilities available in literature and myth. And what fell to Ricoeur was 'a reconceptualization of the possible relations existing between . . . mythic, historical, and fictional [narrative discourse] – and the real world to which they undeniably referred'. White offers a most lucid exposition of Ricoeur's overall argument for the mutual imbrication of temporality and narrativity, of the value and limitation of Braudel's *Annales* approach, and of the differences between history and fiction. But despite these differences, history and literature share a common referent: the human experience of time, the structures of temporality. This is possible because of the phenomenon of double reference. A chronicle both records events in serial order *and* expresses the experience of 'within-timeness'. To first-order symbolization of temporality is correlated a first-order experience of temporality. Historical narrative on the other hand asserts that certain events actually happened, and what it 'figuratively suggests is that the whole sequence of events . . . has the order and significance of well-made stories'. But this relationship between the narrative and the real world is not merely one of correspondence; narrative discourse fashions events into a whole *just as* do the agents of history.

Hayden White then proceeds, in a rather different way to the reflexive turn offered by Jonathan Rée, to apply this double level analysis to Ricoeur's own work. If Ricoeur has taught us to read at another level than the literal, what *more* is Ricoeur saying than might appear? The parallels between history and narrative fiction are rooted in a common metaphysical interest in the mystery of temporality, 'the relation of "eternity" to "death", which is the content of the form of temporality itself'. And if, then, historical narratives are allegories of temporality, it is clear that for Ricoeur the symbolic content of narrative history is the tragic vision of a quest for meaning ravaged by time. White reads Ricoeur, finally, offering us a work of redemption from the temptation of irony. 'In Ricoeur's view every historical discourse . . . is not only a literal account of the past and a figuration of temporality but, beyond that, a literal representation of the content of a timeless drama, that of humanity at grips with the "experience of temporality".'

The Round Table discussion originally featured contributions from David Carr, Charles Taylor, Hayden White and Paul Ricoeur. We have omitted Hayden White's original contribution in favour of the extended treatment we have just dealt with. David Carr takes as his stalking horse the widely held view that narrative offers an aesthetic illusion, that it distorts reality or life. He argues phenomenologically that even the most elementary temporal experience involves more than mere succession (e.g. with Husserl a blend of retention and protention). If narrative suggests, further, that experiences have a beginning, middle and end, is that really contentious? It seems to be true both of actions and sets of actions? 'The structure of action . . . is common to art and to life.' If it is argued that narrative selects whereas life is messy, this is true, but selection does not begin in narrative, but in life itself, with attention and planned activity. Here too there are analogies with narrative voice. Carr concludes that the distortion view of narrative itself fails to grasp the inherent tendencies – albeit incomplete – towards coherence in life itself. What he is not sure of is where Ricoeur stands on this matter. But the implication of Ricoeur's claim that narrative emplotment synthesizes the heterogeneous is that without art life would be incoherent. Carr seeks always to bring out the narrating activity within life. Where does Ricoeur stand on this issue?

Charles Taylor's contribution is to isolate and reformulate what he takes to be one of the central claims of volume I of *Time and Narrative*, that history cannot be what he calls nomologically hermetic. In the natural sciences it is plausible (though in fact just as false) to think that 'the phenomenon to be explained is completely absorbed by the law or structure which constitutes its explanation'. Positivists and structuralists alike have held this subsumption model. But human acts are not subordinated to rules; rather they aim at their realization, and may fail. Or they deliberately flout them. Structures of human action exist by events that continuously renew them. Renewal and subsumption are incompatible explanatory modes. What a nomological approach to history lacks is the understanding of the importance of structures of renewal. Is this not where narrative comes in?

Ricoeur's response to these questions, briefly, is that he hopes to have answered David Carr's question about the relation between art and life by his account of three levels of *Mimesis*. At the first level, life *prefigures* narrative. Ricoeur argues for a relation of dynamic circularity between life and narrative, and claims that in the widest sense, literature *does* feed into the world of narratives into which we are born, and that art, *poiesis*, reveals and transforms life. A fuller response to Carr's question is in effect provided by the first of Ricoeur's essays in this volume: 'Life in quest of narrative'. With Charles Taylor's account, he completely agrees – though it is important to stress that the two models, however distinct, go hand in hand – but takes the opportunity to develop a related issue: that of singular causal imputation. Hayden White's reading he finds more challenging. White, he believes, pursues the problem of reference long after it is suspended in *Time and Narrative*. And Ricoeur is worried that the tropological approach, which converts mimesis into allegory, will blur the distinction between history and fiction which is so important, not least politically. Ricoeur does, obliquely, accept the wider horizons of significance of his work, under the sign of debt and indebtedness, with which he turns to think of the victims of history, and drawing on the imagination, to what might have been.

In his concluding essay, 'Narrative identity', Ricoeur both draws out one of the consequences of his approach in *Time and Narrative* for one of the most pressing philosophical questions – that of personal identity, and also tries out the idea that it is in narrative identity that historical and fictional narrative, which so often seem to require a separate treatment, converge. Ricoeur distinguishes two different kinds of identity – sameness and selfhood – and argues that 'most of the contemporary discussions bearing on personal identity result from the confusion between two interpretations of permanence in time'. Narrative identity offers a solution. Ricoeur's remarkable catholicity of philosophical taste is now revealed, for he takes as his stalking horse Derek Parfit's *Reasons and Persons*, something of a milestone in the analytic philosophy of personal identity. Parfit offers an avowedly reductionistic method which, dealing only with impersonal facts, can only locate personal identity as a 'supplementary fact'. This, for Ricoeur, would at best repeat the Cartesian position. Ricoeur's response is first to suggest that the impersonal facts Parfit deals with are the product of a *depersonalization*, which makes the supplementarity of personal identity into a mere theoretical artefact. He then argues that even Parfit's use of science fictions rests on a grasp of narrative which is interwoven with our everyday life, where a quite different basis for identity is available (= narrative identity). Finally, he insists that we subject Parfit's claim that 'identity is not what matters' to the obvious question: 'to whom does it (not) matter?', to show that the question of identity is both presupposed, and not solved by Parfit's approach. Instead we have to take the long route through narrative. This essay is a brilliant demonstration of Ricoeur's ability to penetrate alternative positions at various levels and to give hermeneutic reframing a critical edge.

NOTES

1 Kirk and Raven, *The Presocratic Philosophers*, Cambridge, Cambridge University Press, 1957, p. 117.
2 Most obviously, for Plato, truth. I have a Nietzschean perspective in mind here.
3 See Habermas, 'Concerning the public use of history', *New German Critique*, Spring/Summer 1988, vol. 44 pp. 40–50.

4 Herman Rapaport, *Heidegger and Derrida: Reflections on Time and Language*, Lincoln, University of Nebraska Press, 1989.
5 ibid., p. 1.
6 J. J. Kockelmans, 'Heidegger's language', in J. J. Kockelmans (ed.) *On Heidegger and Language*, Evanston, Northwestern University Press, 1973. Translated by J. J. Kockelmans from E. Schöfer, *Die Sprache Heideggers*, Pfullingen, Neske, 1962.
7 Rapaport, *Heidegger and Derrida*, p. 121.
8 Translated by John P. Leavey, *Semeia* 23, 1982.
9 Cf. Derrida's discussion of Blanchot's *La Folie du Jour* in his 'The law of genre: Madness is the law, the law is madness' (translated by Avital Ronell, *Critical Inquiry*, vol. 7, no. 1, Autumn 1980, p. 77). Rapaport's book concludes with a short defence of Derrida against Habermas, arguing in effect that the latter is being undialectical in refusing to grasp or even consider the value of Derrida's slow, patient working through of the consequences of Heidegger's thought, a criticism one could make of many of those who reduce Derrida to some pre-Hegelian philosophy of difference.
10 See my *The Deconstruction of Time*, Atlantic Highlands, Humanities Press, 1988, in which I argue from a somewhat different direction for a convergence of these two limbs of time. I claim that the complexity of the temporal structures that arise from the ashes of the thesis of unity takes us a long way towards convergence.
11 Husserl, *Ideas*, London, George Allen & Unwin, 1913 (first English translation 1931) section 49. See Levinas's discussion of these brief comments in 'Simulacra: the end of the world', in David Wood (ed.), *Writing the Future*, London, Routledge, 1990.
12 'Narrative Time', *Critical Inquiry*, vol. 7, no. 1, Autumn 1980, p. 188.

2

LIFE IN QUEST OF NARRATIVE

Paul Ricoeur

It has always been known and often repeated that life has something to do with narrative; we speak of a life story to characterize the interval between birth and death. And yet assimilating life to a story in this way is not really obvious; it is a commonplace that must first be submitted to critical doubt. This doubt is the work of all the knowledge acquired in the past few decades concerning narrative, a knowledge which appears to distance narrative from lived experience and to confine it to the region of fiction. We are going, first, to pass through this critical zone in an effort to rethink in some other way this oversimplified and too direct relation between history and life, in such a way that fiction contributes to making life, in the biological sense of the word, a human life. I want to apply to the relation between narrative and life Socrates' maxim that an unexamined life is not worth living.

I shall take as my starting-point, as I cross this zone of criticism, the remark of a commentator: stories are recounted and not lived; life is lived and not recounted. To clarify this relation between living and narrating, I suggest that we first examine the act of narrating itself.

The narrative theory I shall now be discussing is at once very recent, since in its developed form it dates from the Russian and Czech formalists in the twenties and thirties and from the French structuralists of the sixties and seventies. But it is also quite ancient, in that it can be seen to be prefigured in Aristotle's *Poetics*. It is true that Aristotle recognized only three literary genres: epic, tragedy and comedy. But his analysis was already sufficiently general and formal to allow room for modern transpositions. For my part, I have retained from Aristotle's *Poetics* the central concept of emplotment, which in Greek is *muthos* and which signifies both fable (in the sense of an imaginary story) and plot (in the sense of a well constructed story). It is this second aspect of Aristotle's *muthos* that I am taking as my guide; and it is out of this concept of plot that I hope to draw all of the elements capable of helping me later to reformulate the relation between life and narrative.

What Aristotle calls plot is not a static structure but an operation, an integrating process, which, as I shall try to show later, is completed only in the reader or in the spectator, that is to say, in the *living* receiver of the narrated story. By integrating process I mean the work of composition which gives a dynamic identity to the story recounted: what is recounted is a particular story, one and complete in itself. It is this structuring process of emplotment that I shall put to the test in the first part of my presentation.

EMPLOTMENT

I shall broadly define the operation of emplotment as a synthesis of heterogeneous elements. Synthesis between what elements? *First of all*, a synthesis between the events or incidents which are multiple and the story which is unified and complete; from this first point of view, the plot serves to make *one* story out of the multiple incidents or, if you prefer, transforms the many incidents *into one* story. In this respect, an event is more than an occurrence, I mean more than something that just happens; it is what contributes to the progress of the narrative as well as to its beginning and to its end. Correlatively, the recounted story is always more than the enumeration, in an order that would be merely serial or successive, of the incidents or events that it organizes into an intelligible whole. The plot, however, is also a synthesis from a *second* point of view: it organizes together components that are as heterogeneous as unintended circumstances, discoveries, those who perform actions and those who suffer them, chance or planned encounters, interactions between actors ranging from conflict to collaboration, means that are well or poorly adjusted to ends, and finally unintended results; gathering all these factors into a single story makes the plot a totality which can be said to be at once concordant and discordant (this is why I shall speak of discordant concordance or of concordant discordance). We obtain an understanding of this composition by means of the act of *following* a story; following a story is a very complex operation, guided by our expectations concerning the outcome of the story, expectations that we readjust as the story moves along, until it coincides with the conclusion. I might note in passing that retelling a story best reveals this synthetic activity at work in composition, to the extent that we are less captivated by the unexpected aspects of the story and more attentive to the way in which it leads to its conclusion. *Finally,* emplotment is a synthesis of the heterogeneous in an even more profound sense, one that we shall later use to characterize the temporality specific to all narrative compositions. We could say that there are two sorts of *time* in every story told: on the one hand, a discrete succession that is open and theoretically indefinite, a series of incidents (for we can always pose the question: and then? and then?); on the other hand, the story told presents another temporal aspect characterized by the integration, culmination and closure owing to which the story receives a particular configuration. In this sense, composing a story is, from the temporal point of view, drawing a configuration out of a succession. We can already guess the importance of this manner of characterizing the story from the temporal point of view inasmuch as, for us, time is both what passes and flows away and, on the other hand, what endures and remains. We shall return to this point later. Let us confine ourselves for the moment to characterizing the narrated story as a temporal totality and the poetic act as the creation of a mediation between time as passage and time as duration. If we may speak of the temporal identity of a story, it must be characterized as something that endures and remains across that which passes and flows away.

From this analysis of the story as the synthesis of the heterogeneous, we can retain three features: the mediation performed by the plot between the multiple incidents and unified story; the primacy of concordance over discordance; and, finally, the competition between succession and configuration.

I should like to supply an epistemological corollary to this thesis concerning emplotment considered as the synthesis of the heterogeneous. This corollary concerns the kind of *intelligibility* that should be ascribed to the configuring act. Aristotle did not hesitate to say that every well-told story *teaches* something; moreover, he said that the story reveals universal aspects of the human condition and that, in this respect, poetry was more philosophical than history, which is too dependent on the anecdotal aspects of life. Whatever may be said about this relation between poetry and history, it is certain that tragedy, epic and comedy, to cite only those genres known to Aristotle, develop a sort of understanding that can be termed narrative understanding and which is much closer to the practical wisdom of moral judgment than to science, or, more generally, to the theoretical use of reason. This can be shown in a very simple way. Ethics as Aristotle conceived it and as it can still be conceived today, speaks abstractly of the relation between virtue and the pursuit of happiness. It is the function of poetry in its narrative and dramatic form, to propose to the imagination and to its mediation various figures that constitute so many *thought experiments* by which we learn to link together the ethical aspects of human conduct and happiness and misfortune. By means of poetry we learn how reversals of fortune result from this or that conduct, as this is constructed by the plot in the narrative. It is due to the familiarity we have with the types of plot received from our culture that we learn to relate virtues, or rather forms of excellence, with happiness or unhappiness. These 'lessons' of poetry constitute the 'universals' of which Aristotle spoke; but these are universals that are of a lower degree than those of logic and theoretical thought. We must nonetheless speak of understanding but in the sense that Aristotle gave to *phronesis* (which the latins translated by *prudentia*). In this sense I am prepared to speak of phronetic understanding in order to contrast it with theoretical understanding. Narrative belongs to the former and not to the latter.

This epistemological corollary to our analysis of plot has, in its turn, numerous implications for the efforts of contemporary narratology to construct a genuine science of narrative. In my opinion, these enterprises, which are, of course, perfectly legitimate, are themselves justified only to the extent that they *simulate* a narrative understanding that is always prior to them; by this simulation, they bring to light *deep structures* unknown to those who recount or follow stories, but which place narratology on the same level of rationality as linguistics and the other sciences of language. To characterize the rationality of contemporary narratology by its power of simulating at a second order of discourse something that we already understood as children, as being a story, is by no means to discredit these modern undertakings, it is simply to situate them precisely in the hierarchy of degrees of knowledge.

I could instead have sought somewhere else than in Aristotle for a more modern model of thought, like that of Kant, for instance, and the relation he establishes in The *Critique of Pure*

Reason between the schematism and the categories. Just a. in Kant the schematism designates the creative center of the categories, and in the categories the principle of the order of the understanding, in the same way emplotment constitutes the creative centre of the narrative and narratology constitutes the rational reconstruction of the rules underlying poetical activity.

In this sense it is a science that includes its own requirements: what it seeks to reconstruct are the logical and semiotic constraints, along with the rules of transformation, which preside over the workings of the narrative. My thesis, therefore, expresses no hostility with respect to narratology; it is limited to saying that narratology is a second-order discourse which is always preceded by a narrative understanding stemming from the creative imagination.

My entire analysis will henceforth be located on the level of this first-order narrative understanding.

Before turning to the question of the relation between the story and life, I should like to consider a second corollary which will set me on the path, precisely, of a reinterpretation of the relation between narrative and life.

There is, I should say, a *life* of narrative activity which is inscribed in the notion of traditionality characteristic of the narrative schema.

To say that the narrative schema itself has its own history and that this history has all the features of a tradition, is by no means to make an apology for tradition considered as the inert transmission of a lifeless residue. It is, on the contrary, to designate tradition as the living transmission of an innovation which can always be reactivated by a return to the most creative moments of poetic composition. This phenomenon of traditionality is the key to the functioning of narrative models and, consequently, of their identification. The constituting of a tradition indeed depends on the interaction between two factors, innovation and sedimentation. It is to sedimentation that we ascribe the models that constitute, after the fact, the typology of emplotment which allows us to order the history of literary genres; but we must not lose sight of the fact that these models do not constitute eternal essences but proceed from a sedimented history whose genesis has been obliterated. If sedimentation, however, allows us to identify a work as being, for instance, a tragedy, a novel of education, a social drama or whatever, the identification of a work is never exhausted

24

by that of the models that are sedimented there. It also takes into account the opposite phenomenon of innovation. Why? Because the models, themselves stemming from an earlier innovation, provide a guide for a later experimentation in the narrative domain. The rules change under the pressure of innovation, but they change slowly and even resist change by reason of this process of sedimentation. Innovation thus remains the pole opposite to that of tradition. There is always room for innovation to the extent that what has been produced, and in the ultimate sense in the *poiesis* of poetry, is always a singular work, *this particular* work. The rules that constitute a sort of grammar govern the composition of new works, new, that is, before they, in turn, become typical. Each work is an original production, a new being in the realm of discourse. But the opposite is no less true: innovation remains a rule-governed behaviour; the work of imagination does not come out of nowhere. It is tied in one way or another to the models handed down by tradition. But it can enter into a variable relation to these models. The range of solutions is broad indeed between the poles of servile repetition and calculated deviance, passing by way of all the degrees of ordered distortion. Popular tales, myths and traditional narratives in general stick closer to the pole of repetition. This is why they constitute the preferred kingdom for structuralism. But as soon as we go beyond the field of these traditional narratives, deviance wins out over the rule. The contemporary novel, for example, can to a large extent be defined as an anti-novel, for it is the very rules themselves that become the object of new experimentation. Whatever could be said about this or that work, the possibility of deviance is included in the relation between sedimentation and innovation which constitutes tradition. The variations between these poles gives the productive imagination its own historicity and keeps the narrative tradition a living one.

FROM NARRATIVE TO LIFE

We can now attack the paradox we are considering here: stories are recounted, life is lived. An unbridgeable gap seems to separate fiction and life.

To cross this gap, the terms of the paradox must, to my mind, be thoroughly revised.

Let us remain for the moment on the side of the narrative,

hence on that of fiction, and see in what way it leads us back to life. My thesis is here that the process of composition, of configur- ation, is not completed in the text but in the reader and, under this condition, makes possible the reconfiguration of life by narrative. I should say, more precisely: the sense or the significance of a narra- tive stems from the *intersection of the world of the text and the world of the reader*. The act of reading thus becomes the critical moment of the entire analysis. On it rests the narrative's capacity to transfig- ure the experience of the reader.

Allow me to stress the terms I have used here: the *world of the reader* and the *world of the text*. To speak of a world of the text is to stress the feature belonging to every literary work of opening before it a horizon of possible experience, a world in which it would be possible to live. A text is not something closed in upon itself, it is the projection of a new universe distinct from that in which we live. To appropriate a work through reading is to unfold the world horizon implicit in it which includes the actions, the characters and the events of the story told. As a result, the reader belongs at once to the work's horizon of experience in imagination and to that of his or her own real action. The horizon of expec- tation and the horizon of experience continually confront one another and fuse together. Gadamer speaks in this regard of the 'fusion of horizons' essential to the art of understanding a text.

I am well aware that literary criticism is careful to maintain the distinction between the inside of the text and its outside. It considers any exploration of the linguistical universe as outside its range. The analysis of the text extends, then, to the frontiers of the text and forbids any attempt to step outside the text. Here, it seems to me, the distinction between the inside and the outside is a product of the very method of the analysis of texts and does not correspond to the reader's experience. This opposition results from extending to literature the properties characteristic of the sort of units with which linguistics works: phonemes, lexemes, words; for linguistics, the real world is extra-linguistic. Reality is contained neither in the dictionary nor in grammar. It is precisely this extrapolation from linguistics to poetics that appears to me to invite criticism: the methodological decision, proper to structural analysis, of treating literature in linguistic categories which impose the distinction between inside and outside. From a hermeneutical point of view, that is to say from the point of view of the interpre- tation of literary experience, a text has an entirely different meaning than the one recognized by structural analysis in its borrowings from linguistics. It is a mediation between man and the world, between man and man, between man and himself; the mediation between man and the world is what we call *referentiality*; the mediation between men, *communicability*; the mediation between man and himself, *self-understanding*. A literary work contains these three dimensions: referentiality, communicability and self-understanding. The hermeneutical problem begins, then, where linguistics leaves off. It attempts to discover new features of referentiality which are not descriptive, features of communicability which are not utilitarian, and features of reflexivity which are not narcissistic, as these are engendered by the literary work. In a word, hermeneutics is placed at the point of intersection of the (internal) configuration of the work and the (external) refiguration of life. In my opinion, all that was stated above concerning the dynamics of configuration proper to literary creation is but a long preparation for understanding the true problem, that of the dynamics of transfiguration proper to the work. In this respect, emplotment is the common work of the text and the reader. We must follow, accompany configuration and actualize its capacity for being followed if the work is to have, even within the boundaries that are its own, a configuration. Following a narrative is reactualizing the configuring act which gives it its form. It is also the act of reading that accompanies the play between innovation and sedimentation, the play with narrative constraints, with the possibilities of deviation, even the struggle between the novel and the anti-novel. Finally, it is the *act of reading* which completes the work, transforming it into a *guide* for reading, with its zones of indeterminacy, its latent wealth of interpretation, its power of being reinterpreted in new ways in new historical contexts.

At this stage of the analysis, we are already able to glimpse how narrative and life can be reconciled with one another, for reading is itself already a way of living in the fictive universe of the work; in this sense, we can already say that stories are recounted but they are also *lived in the mode of the imaginary*.

We must now readjust the other term of this opposition, what we call *life*. We must question the erroneous self-evidence according to which life is lived not told.

To this end, I should like to stress the pre-narrative capacity of what we call life. What has to be questioned is the overly simple equation made between life and experience. A life is no more than a biological phenomenon as long as it has not been interpreted. And in interpretation, fiction plays a mediating role. To open the way for this new phase of the analysis, we must underscore the mixture of acting and suffering which constitutes the very fabric of a life. It is this mixture which the narrative attempts to imitate in a creative way. In speaking of Aristotle, we indeed omitted the very definition he gives of the narrative; it is, he says, 'the imitation of an action' *mimesis praxeos*. We therefore have to look for the points of support that the narrative can find in the living experience of acting and suffering; and that which, in this experience, demands the assistance of narrative and expresses the need for it.

The first point of anchorage that we find for narrative understanding in living experience consists in the very structure of human acting and suffering. In this respect, human life differs widely from animal life, and, with all the more reason, from mineral existence. We understand what action and passion are through our competence to use in a meaningful way the entire network of expressions and concepts that are offered to us by natural languages in order to distinguish between *action* and mere physical *movement* and psychophysiological *behaviour*. In this way, we understand what is signified by project, aim, means, circumstances, and so on. All of these notions taken together constitute the network of what we could term the *semantics of action*. In this network we find all the components of the synthesis of the heterogeneous. In this respect, our familiarity with the conceptual network of human acting is of the same order as the familiarity we have with the plots of stories that are known to us; it is the same phronetic understanding which presides over the understanding of action (and of passion) and over that of narrative.

The second point of anchorage that the narrative finds in practical understanding lies in the symbolic resources of the practical field. This feature will decide which aspects of doing, of being-able to do, and of knowing-how-to-do belong to poetic transposition.

If indeed action can be recounted, this is because it is already articulated in signs, rules and norms; it is always symbolically mediated. This feature of action has been heavily underscored by cultural anthropology.

If I speak more specifically of symbolic mediation, this is in order to distinguish among the symbols of a cultural nature those which underlie action to the point of constituting its primary meaning, before the autonomous ensembles belonging to speech and writing are separated off from the level of practice. We find these when we discuss the question of ideology and utopia. Today, I shall confine my remarks to what could be termed the *implicit* or *immanent* symbolism in opposition to that explicit or autonomous symbolism.

What, for an anthropologist in fact, characterizes the symbolism implicit in action is that it constitutes a *context of description* for particular actions. In other words, it is in relation to . . . a given symbolic convention that we can interpret a particular gesture as signifying this or that: the same gesture of raising one's arm can, depending on the context, be understood as a way of saying hello, of hailing a taxi, or of voting. Before they are submitted to interpretation, symbols are the internal interpreters of action. In this way symbolism gives an initial *readability* to action. It makes action a quasi-text for which symbols provide the rules of signification in terms of which a given conduct can be interpreted.

The third point of anchorage of the narrative in life consists in what could be called the *pre-narrative quality of human experience*. It is due to this that we are justified in speaking of life as a story in its nascent state, and so of life as an *activity and a passion in search of a narrative*. The comprehension of action is not restricted to a familiarity with the conceptual network of action, and with its symbolic mediations, it even extends as far as recognizing in the action temporal features which call for narration. It is not by chance or by mistake that we commonly speak of stories that happen to us or of stories in which we are caught up, or simply of the story of a life.

It may well be objected here that our analysis rests on a vicious circle. If all human experience is already mediated by all sorts of symbolic systems, it is also mediated by all sorts of stories that we have heard. How can we then speak of the narrative quality of experience and of a human life as a story in the nascent state, since we have no access to the temporal drama of existence outside of stories recounted about this by people other than ourselves?

To this objection I shall reply with a series of situations, which, in my opinion, compel us to grant to experience as such a virtual narrativity which stems, not from the projection of literature onto life, but which constitutes a genuine demand for narrative. The expression introduced above of pre-narrative structure of experience will serve to characterize these situations.

PAUL RICOEUR

Without leaving the sphere of everyday experience, are we not inclined to see in a given chain of episodes in our own life something like *stories that have not yet been told*, stories that demand to be told, stories that offer points of anchorage for the narrative? Once again, are not stories recounted by definition? This is indisputable when we are speaking of actual stories. But is the notion of a potential story unacceptable?

I shall stop to consider two less common situations in which the expression 'a story not yet told' forces itself upon us with surprising strength. The patient who addresses the psychoanalyst brings him the scattered fragments of lived stories, dreams, 'primal scenes', conflictual episodes. One can legitimately say with respect to analytical sessions that their aim and their effect is to allow the analysand to draw out of these story-fragments a narrative which would be at once more bearable and more intelligible. This narrative interpretation of psychoanalytic theory implies that the story of a life grows out of stories that have not been recounted and that have been repressed in the direction of actual stories which the subject could take charge of and consider to be constitutive of his *personal identity*. It is the quest of personal identity which assures the continuity between the potential or virtual story and the explicit story for which we assume responsibility.

There is another situation for which the notion of an untold story seems to be well suited. This is the case of a judge who attempts to understand a defendant by unravelling the skein of plots in which the suspect is entangled. The individual can be said to be 'tangled up in stories' which happen to him before any story is recounted. This entanglement then appears as the pre-history of the story told, the beginning of which is chosen by the narrator. The pre-history of the story is what connects it up to a vaster whole and gives it a background. This background is made up of the living imbrication of all lived stories. The stories that are told must then be made to emerge out of this background. And as they emerge, the implied subject also emerges. We can then say: the story answers to the man. The main consequence of this existential analysis of man as being entangled in stories is that narrating is a secondary process grafted on our 'being-entangled in stories'. Recounting, following, understanding stories is then simply the continuation of these unspoken stories.

From this double analysis, it follows that fiction, in particular narrative fiction, is an irreducible dimension of *self-understanding*. If it is true that fiction is only completed in life and that life can be understood only through the stories that we tell about it, then an *examined* life, in the sense of the word as we have borrowed it from Socrates, is a life *recounted*.

What is life recounted? It is a life in which we find all the basic structures of the narrative mentioned in the first part, and in particular the play between concordance and discordance, which appeared to us to characterize the narrative. This conclusion is in no way paradoxical or surprising. If we open St Augustine's *Confessions* to Book XI, we discover a description of human time which corresponds entirely to the structure of discordant concordance which Aristotle had discerned several centuries before in poetic composition. Augustine, in this famous treatise on time, sees time as born out of the incessant dissociation between the three aspects of the present – expectation, which he calls the present of the future, memory which he calls the present of the past, and attention which is the present of the present. From this comes the instability of time; and, even more so, its continual dissociation. In this way, Augustine defines time as a distention of the soul, *distantio animi*. It consists in the permanent contrast between the unstable nature of the human present and the stability of the divine present which includes past, present and future in the unity of a gaze and a creative action.

In this way we are led to place side-by-side and to confront with each other Aristotle's definition of plot and Augustine's definition of time. One could say that in Augustine discordance wins out over concordance: whence the misery of the human condition. And that in Aristotle, concordance wins out over discordance, whence the inestimable value of narrative for putting our temporal experience into order. This opposition, however, should not be pushed too far, since, for Augustine himself, there would be no discordance if we were not stretching, tending towards a *unity of intention*, as is shown in the simple example he gives of reciting a poem: when I am about to recite the poem, it is wholly present in my mind, then, as I recite it, its parts pass one after the other from the future to the past, transiting by way of the present until, the future having been exhausted, the poet has moved entirely into the past. A totalizing intention must, therefore, preside over the investigation if we are to feel the cruel bite of time, which never ceases to disperse the soul by placing in discordance expectation, memory and attention. So, if in the living experience of time discordance wins out over concordance, the latter still remains the permanent object of our desire. The opposite can be said about Aristotle. We stated that the narrative is a synthesis of the heterogeneous. But concordance is never found without discordance. Tragedy is a good example in this respect. There is no tragedy without *peripeteia*, strokes of fate, terrifying and pitiful events, a profound error, *hamartia*, made up of ignorance and of disdain rather than of meanness. If concordance wins out, then, over discordance, what constitutes narrative is indeed the struggle between them.

Let us apply to ourselves this analysis of the discordant concordance of narrative and the concordant discordance of time. Our life, when then embraced in a single glance, appears to us as the field of a constructive activity, borrowed from narrative understanding, by which we attempt to discover and not simply to impose from outside the *narrative identity which constitutes us*. I am stressing the expression 'narrative identity' for what we call subjectivity is neither an incoherent series of events nor an immutable substantiality, impervious to evolution. This is precisely the sort of identity which narrative composition alone can create through its dynamism.

This definition of subjectivity in terms of narrative identity has numerous implications. To begin with, it is possible to apply to our self-understanding the play of sedimentation and innovation which we saw at work in every tradition. In the same way, we never cease to reinterpret the narrative identity that constitutes us, in the light of the narratives proposed to us by our culture. In this sense, our self-understanding presents the same features of traditionality as the understanding of a literary work. It is in this way that we learn to become the *narrator* and the hero *of our own story*, without actually becoming the *author of our own life*. We can apply to ourselves the concept of *narrative voices* which constitute the symphony of great works such as epics, tragedies, dramas and novels. The difference is that, in all these works, it is the author who is disguised as the narrator and who wears the mask of the various characters and, among all of these, the mask of the dominant narrative voice that tells the story we read. We can become our own narrator, in imitation of these narrative voices, without being able to become the author. This is the great difference between life and fiction. In this sense, it is true that life is lived and that stories are told. An unbridgeable difference does remain, but this difference is partially abolished by our power of applying to ourselves the plots that we have received from our culture and of trying on the different roles assumed by the favourite characters of the stories most dear to us. It is therefore by means of the imaginative variations of our own ego that we attempt to obtain a narrative understanding of ourselves, the only kind that escapes the apparent choice between sheer change and absolute identity. Between the two lies narrative identity.

In conclusion, allow me to say that what we call the *subject* is never given at the start. Or, if it is, it is in danger of being reduced to the narcissistic, egoistic and stingy ego, from which literature, precisely, can free us.

So, what we lose on the side of narcissism, we win back on the side of narrative.

In place of an *ego* enamoured of itself arises a *self* instructed by cultural symbols, the first among which are the narratives handed down in our literary tradition. And these narratives give us a unity which is not substantial but narrative.

3

PHILOSOPHICAL ANTECEDENTS TO RICOEUR'S *TIME AND NARRATIVE*

Kevin J. Vanhoozer

Fully to appreciate the philosophical antecedents to Paul Ricoeur's theory of narrative involves setting *Time and Narrative* in a lengthy narrative of its own: the story or history of philosophy. The characters featured in this narrative are diverse: from Aristotle and Augustine to Wittgenstein and Virginia Woolf. It is my belief, however, that Ricoeur's recent work is most fruitfully seen as a continuation of the 'unfinished' projects of two of these protagonists in particular: Immanuel Kant and Martin Heidegger. While neither Kant nor Heidegger is particularly interested in narrative as such, their works are nevertheless concerned with what we may call the *ingredients* of narrative, namely *imagination, time* and *possibility*.

In the first section of this paper I discuss Ricoeur's approach to Kant's problem of the 'productive' or creative imagination. In the second section I focus on Ricoeur's appropriation of Heidegger's notion of the temporality of human being. I wish to argue that Ricoeur's narrative theory is an attempt to think these two problems, imagination and time, *together*. The final section considers Ricoeur's recent work in light of his larger philosophical project, the *Philosophy of the Will*, and his attempt to answer the question: What is Man? by discovering what is humanly possible. Ricoeur, represented by his earlier work in philosophical anthropology, is himself an important philosophical antecedent to *Time and Narrative*.

KANT AND THE CREATIVE IMAGINATION

Significant parallels exist between the thought of Ricoeur and Kant which have remained for the most part unnoticed. Commentators on Ricoeur often confine their remarks to his use of the Kantian limits to speculative thought. Even more relevant to Ricoeur's narrative theory, however, are Kant's seminal thoughts on time and the creative imagination, thoughts that converge in the first *Critique* in Kant's difficult but central notion of 'schematism'. Ricoeur's narrative theory may be construed as *an attempt to give linguistic and literary substance to Kant's notion of schematism.* Ricoeur looks back to Kant in his attempt to formulate a theory of the *literary* imagination, as evidenced in the following quote:

> The only way to approach the problem of imagination from the perspective of a semantic theory, that is to say on a verbal plane, is to begin with productive imagination in the Kantian sense, and to put off reproductive imagination or imagery as long as possible.[1]

My case for viewing Ricoeur's work as the continuation of Kant's unfinished project begins by noting the striking general similarity between Kant's three *Critiques* and Ricoeur's three-part *Philosophy of the Will*. The first volume of each concerns pure speculation and its limits: description of the understanding in Kant, description of human volition in Ricoeur. The middle volumes in both trilogies turn towards the practical: reason and morality in Kant, fallibility and fault in Ricoeur. Kant's third *Critique* mediates the concepts of nature and freedom with a critique of aesthetic feeling and reflective judgment; Ricoeur's as yet unwritten *Poetics* has been variously construed, but also centres on the ultimate reconciliation of freedom and nature portrayed in symbols and narratives. Ricoeur's early hints concerning his *Poetics* indicate that he intended to give the imagination a verbal orientation, thus mediating Freedom and Nature with a specifically *literary* art. I suggest that narrative is for Ricoeur the pre-eminent form of this 'poetic' language. The similarities between Ricoeur and Kant, therefore, are both substantive and methodological.

Ricoeur is most inclined to follow Kant in assigning a *mediating* function to the imagination.[2] First, the imagination as presented in the *Critique of Pure Reason* is responsible for mediating concepts and intuitions – a mediation which is the cornerstone of Kantian

35

epistemology. This is its 'schematizing' function, which I shall discuss shortly. Second, the imagination, under the heading Art, functions in the third *Critique* as the means of mediating the opposing realms of Freedom and Nature, thus bringing Kant's critical philosophy to a systematic and happy conclusion. This is the imagination's 'symbolizing' function. Ricoeur's narrative theory draws upon both the first and third *Critiques* to advance both schematism and symbolism in the history of ideas.

Kant's concepts of the productive imagination and its schematizing function are first found in the *Critique of Pure Reason* and then undergo an important modification in the third *Critique*. Though Kant formulates the notion of the productive imagination, it falls to Ricoeur to write a *philosophy* of this creative imagination and to render schematism intelligible by displaying it at work in narrative. Ricoeur's narrative theory therefore renders Kant's theory of the imagination and schematism more intelligible by giving it a *verbal*, or more precisely, a *literary* twist.

According to Kant, the imagination has two fundamental tasks which make objective knowledge possible. The first function, that of the 'reproductive' imagination, consists in reproducing *images* of absent objects. Ricoeur observes that this popular conception of imagination 'suffers from the disrepute in which the term "image" is held following its misuse in the empiricist theory of knowledge'.[3] As early as his *Symbolism of Evil*, Ricoeur decried the facile identification of imagination and image, where the latter is understood as the 'absence of the real'.

But in Kant there is a second form of imagination. The central problem of the 'Transcendental Analytic' in the *Critique of Pure Reason* deals with how concepts not derived from experience, namely, the categories, can be applied to experience. How, asks Kant, is such an application possible? 'Obviously there must be some third thing, which is homogeneous on the one hand with the category, and on the other hand with the appearance, and which thus makes the application of the former to the latter possible.'[4] This mediation between understanding and sensibility is the role of what Kant terms the 'schema' and the schema in turn is a 'product' of the imagination – hence the term 'productive imagination'.

Kant defines 'schema' in the following, not altogether helpful, manner: 'This representation of a universal procedure of imagination in providing an image for a concept, I entitle the schema of this concept.'[5] How does the schema actually enable concepts to be applied to experience? According to Kant the only feature which is common to every object of experience is its being in time. The schema therefore shows what the concept means when applied to the phenomenal realm only by placing it under a particular 'determination' or 'figure' of time. In Kant's words, 'We thus find that the schema of each category contains and makes capable of representation only a determination of time [*Zeitinbegriff*]' (*CPR*, A145 / B184). To the category 'reality', for example, corresponds the figure 'being in time'. 'Substance' has as its schema 'permanence through time', and the schema for 'necessity' is 'existence at all times'. 'Temporalizing' the concept in this manner renders it fit to be applied to the phenomenal world. We may therefore define schematism as the imaginative procedure for creating figures of time for the various categories.

Ricoeur notes that Kant, with his doctrine of schematism, is the first thinker to link the problematic of time with that of the imagination.[6] But if the schematizing operation of the imagination, the common root which unites sensibility and understanding, is an 'art hidden in the depths of the human soul' (*CPR*, A141 / B180), so too is time. Ricoeur writes:

> Are we not touching here on the intimate and unified structure of human reality? This transcendental marvel, Time, dispersed and ordered, is ultimately even more enigmatic than the transcendental imagination of which it is the hidden soul. . . . The notion of a radical genesis of the rules of intellect and intuition starting from the 'common root' of imagination and Time remains a pious promise.[7]

What Ricoeur earlier termed a 'pious promise' seems in fact to be the goal of his narrative theory, insofar as he considers narrative a form of schematism which figures and configures *human* time in stories and histories. While narrative may not be the 'common root' of imagination and time, it is at least the place where the schematizing operation is best seen at work. Ricoeur's unique contribution is to give a verbal or literary orientation to Kant's notion of schematism. For Ricoeur contends that only *narrative* discourse can create figures of *human* time. Just as painting is a *visual* representation of reality which shapes or configures *space*, so narrative is a *verbal* representation of reality which shapes or configures *time*.

I now turn to consider the fate of the creative imagination in Kant's third *Critique*, the *Critique of Judgment*, where symbolism rather than schematism comes to the fore, and where the notion of the 'reflective judgment' contains in germinal form the seeds for Ricoeur's understanding of the role of the plot in narrative. Imagination, under the guise of Art and the reflective judgment, functions in the third Critique as the means of mediating the opposed realms of Freedom and Nature. Here the imagination produces symbols rather than schemas. The imagination also appears as the power of synoptic judgment, capable of creating a unity out of a diversity of elements. I will treat this latter aspect of imagination, which Kant in the third Critique labels the reflective judgment, first.

Kant defines judgment as 'the faculty of thinking the particular as contained under the universal'[8] or alternatively the 'faculty of subsuming under rules' (*CPR*, A132 / B171). If the universal (i.e. a law or concept) is given in advance, the judgment which subsumes the particular under it is 'determinant'. Such are the judgments of the understanding, which subsume appearances under a priori concepts. But if, on the other hand, only the particular is given for which the universal must be *found*, the judgment is 'reflective'. The third *Critique* deals with this latter kind of judgment.

Kant in section 49 of the third *Critique* presents his theory of genius. By 'genius', Kant is referring to a mental faculty which I shall call the 'creative imagination'. Kant opposes genius to the 'spirit of imitation' (viz. the reproductive imagination). Far from copying a pre-existing rule or pattern, genius as defined by Kant is 'the talent which *gives* the rule to art' (*CJ*, p. 150). Art gives pleasure according to Kant because it manifests a rule governedness. However, the creative imagination does not begin with but rather *contributes* the rule to a work of art in the very process of creating it. Kant's suggestion that artistic genius includes a rule-giving aspect is thus congruent with Ricoeur's wish to render texts susceptible to explanation. For Ricoeur, the text is a structured *work* produced by an imagination which creates its own rules. Indeed, Ricoeur defines imagination in his later works as a 'rule-governed form of invention' and a 'norm-governed productivity'.[9] This 'ruled creativity' is best seen, in Ricoeur's opinion, in the phenomenon of story-telling, where the same theme, for example the quest, gives rise to countless variations.[10]

Similarly, Ricoeur's great discovery about narrative, its configurative dimension, was made standing on the shoulders of Kant. Narrative is not only an episodic sequence, but a configurational unity. Ricoeur maintains that it is 'by means of the plot [that] goals, causes and chance are brought together within the temporal unity of a whole and complete action'.[11] In other words, Ricoeur views the plot as a form of reflective judgment which enacts a *synthesis of the heterogeneous* and makes a whole out of a beginning, a middle and an end. That Kant's reflective judgment' is a first-cousin to Ricoeur's 'plot' may be seen in this citation from Ricoeur: 'A text is a whole, a totality. The relation between whole and parts – as in a work of art or in an animal – requires a specific kind of "judgment" for which Kant gives the theory in the third *Critique*.'[12]

Ricoeur faults the third *Critique* in one important respect. Ricoeur claims that Kant neglects the social and historical dimensions of the creative imagination. In his narrative theory, Ricoeur speaks of *traditions* of narrative imagination and schematism. Tradition provides a context which accounts for both the innovation and sedimentation of artistic and literary genres (i.e. forms of rule-governedness). The artist's creative imagination could not communicate with others if it did not share something of a community tradition.

While the idea of 'limits' may be the 'soul' of the Kantian philosophy, the third *Critique* provides a basis which permits *thinking* to continue where theoretical knowledge is thwarted. The ideas of reason are presented not directly, as are concepts by schematism, but rather indirectly or *symbolically*. Symbolism supplies what Kant calls a 'schematism of analogy'. In symbolism we think about an idea (to which no sensible intuition corresponds) *as* we think of something else to which an intuition does correspond.

Though Kant values symbols as a means of thinking the supersensible, he takes only a few tentative steps towards a thoroughgoing *theory* of symbolism. Kant admits that the matter has not been 'sufficiently analysed hitherto' and deserves a 'deeper investigation', but he does not himself undertake such a study.[13] Kant's project is 'unfinished' to the extent that his theory of symbols and the creative imagination is incomplete.

As a student of the symbol, Ricoeur claims that the Kantian limits to speculative thought need not exercise a purely negative function. The supersensible, beyond the reach of theoretical concepts, may find a certain fulfilment in an indirect, non-descriptive language. To paraphrase Kant, *Ricoeur has found it necessary to deny knowledge in order to make room for symbols, metaphors and narratives:* 'It is because Kant had no idea of a language which would not be *empirical* that he had to replace metaphysics by *empty* concepts.'[14] Figurative language provides the means to *speak* the supersensible, that transcendental basis for the reconciliation of Freedom and Nature which is beyond the reach of theoretical thought.

Strictly speaking, Kant restricts 'schema' to that procedure which gives images to concepts. But in speaking of the 'schematism' of the narrative function, Ricoeur metaphorically extends Kant's original notion by giving it a literary application. For Ricoeur, *words* as well as figures of time may serve as schemas. Narratives, of course, are unique in that they combine both aspects: narratives are *verbal figures of time.* Though Kant does not attempt anything so grandiose as a theory of language or literature, there are a few significant references in the third *Critique* to poetry. The poet, says Kant, ventures to make aesthetic and rational ideas, such as eternity or creation, 'sensible'. And even when the poet presents things of which there are examples in experience – e.g. death, love – he strives 'to go beyond the limits of experience and to present them to sense with a completeness of which there is no example in nature'.[15] There is therefore Kantian precedent for extending schematism into language. It is most significant that in the third *Critique* Kant deems poetry supreme among the arts:

> It expands the mind by setting the imagination at liberty and by offering, within the limits of a given concept . . . that which unites the presentment of this concept with a wealth of thought to which no verbal expression is completely adequate, and so rising aesthetically to ideas.
>
> (*CJ*, p. 171)

Kant even calls poetry 'a sort of schema for the supersensible' (*CJ*, p. 171). This phrase contains in seminal form the essential ingredients of Ricoeur's more thoroughgoing literary orientation of the productive imagination. In sum, Ricoeur's narrative theory links the idea of schematism, with its connotations of time-determination, to symbolism, the presentation of aesthetic ideas.

The rule-governed nature of the creative imagination permits the literary imagination to be placed under the rubric of understanding *and* explanation. Insofar as what is said or presented in narrative form is subject to rules (i.e. genre or plot-structure), the products of the creative imagination may be 'explained'. Though narrative aesthetically presents what is beyond the grasp of concepts, the narrative schema is not beyond the means of investigation and explanation.

In classifying narrative as a form of the creative imagination, Ricoeur is able to give not only literary substance but a more thorough analytical basis to the hitherto obscure Kantian notion of the creative imagination. Ricoeur makes both the operation of the productive imagination and time itself more intelligible by giving linguistic and literary flesh and blood to the bare skeletal schemata of Kant. In other words, Ricoeur renders the imaginative determination of time more intelligible by showing it *at work*, as it were, in narrative. The narrative act is a demonstration of that mysterious art, schematism, in operation. The plot, the central component of narrative, is nothing less than a creative synthesis of time, which makes a temporal whole out of an otherwise chaotic manifold of experience. Far from being an art hidden in the depths of the soul, then, the time-figuring power of the imagination, at work in the configurative operation of the narrative plot, is subject to exegetical analysis. It is in this manner that Ricoeur takes up Kant's notion of the creative imagination by giving it a verbal orientation and literary application.

HEIDEGGER AND THE TEMPORALITY OF HUMAN BEING

The problem of time is of course a central theme in the work of Martin Heidegger. My transition from Kant to Heidegger is made easier by Heidegger himself, who wrote a book entitled *Kant and the Problem of Metaphysics*. After considering this work, I will examine the major work of Heidegger's which has influenced Ricoeur and his narrative theory, *Being and Time*, in which *human* time comes to the fore. I will end my discussion of Heidegger by referring to Ricoeur's 'narrative correction' of Heidegger's project. This narrative 'correction' constitutes in effect Ricoeur's 'long route' to an ontology of human being.

In taking up Kant's notion of schematism, Ricoeur follows not only Kant but Heidegger. Heidegger's *Kant and the Problem of Metaphysics*, published in 1929, just two years after his *Being and Time*, is a study of Kant's first *Critique*. According to Heidegger's distinctive reading of Kant,[16] the theme of the first *Critique* is the finitude of man, a finitude rooted in a conception of the human mind as both temporal and creative. It is also Heidegger's thesis that Kant, in the second edition of the first *Critique*, 'recoiled from the ground which he himself had established'[17] and fell back onto a more logical framework. In short, Kant rediscovered temporality but then abandoned his insight. In his Kant book, Heidegger sets out to 'retrieve' Kant's abandoned project.[18]

Heidegger concludes that the Kantian foundation for meta-physics is *anthropology*. Kant sought the conditions for the very possibility of experience, and he located these conditions in the sentient, intellectual and imaginative capacities of human beings. In bringing intuition and concepts together, the imagination and its schematizing function are the conditions of the very possibility of experience itself. Heidegger therefore assigns a significance to Kant's chapter on schematism which far surpasses its modest size: 'these eleven pages of the *Critique of Pure Reason* form the heart of the whole work'.[19] Heidegger extracts from Kant the lesson that time is the condition for our cognition of objects as well as the condition of the being of the objects we cognize. Heidegger calls Kant's productive imagination the 'ontological' imagination 'because it sets out in advance the to-be characteristics which we are able to discern in the things that appear to us'.[20] It is interesting to note that the narrative imagination in Ricoeur's thought exercises a similarly 'ontological' function: it is only by virtue of narrativity that human temporality comes to expression.

In his article 'Existence and hermeneutics', Ricoeur distinguishes two types of hermeneutic phenomenology: Heidegger's (the 'short route' to ontology) and his own (the 'long route'). Whereas Heidegger attempts to inspect human being 'directly', as it were, Ricoeur believes that human existence is attained only by taking a detour through the interpretation of texts which attest to this existence. Heidegger turns hermeneutics from an analysis of texts to an analysis of this being who understands – Dasein. The consequences of this shift in problematic are far-reaching: an ontology of understanding replaces an epistemology of interpretation. Ricoeur comments: '*Verstehen* for Heidegger has an ontological signification. It is the response of a being thrown into the world who finds his way about by projecting onto it his ownmost possibilities.'[21]

To a large extent, Ricoeur is in agreement with Heidegger's interpretation of human temporality. Of course other things exist in time, but only humans possess the capacity to perceive the connectedness of life and to seek its coherence. Moreover, only humans reckon with their past and future as well as their present. This inevitable reckoning with time is at the heart of what Heidegger states is the being of Dasein: *Care*. My suggestion is that Ricoeur's narrative theory is a continuation of Heidegger's unfinished project of understanding human existence as essentially temporal. In Ricoeur's work, *telling* mediates being and time. Unfortunately, the rich connection with Heidegger's programme is lost in the translation of *Temps et récit* in the English title: *Time and Narrative*. Translating Ricoeur's book as *Time and Telling* would have had the advantage of alluding to Heidegger's magnum opus, thus suggesting the significant sequence which I shall explore more fully: Being and Time and Telling.

A brief survey of Heidegger's analysis of 'understanding' will suffice to show the large areas of compatibility between his philosophical anthropology and Ricoeur's narrative theory. Section 31 of *Being and Time* is entitled 'Being-there as understanding', and Heidegger there asserts that Dasein *is* understanding: '*Understanding is the existential Being of Dasein's own potentiality-for-Being; and it is so in such a way that this Being discloses in itself what its Being is capable of.*'[22] Dasein 'understands' a situation when it grasps the possibilities available to it, when it 'knows' what it is capable of in a given situation. The means by which understanding grasps its possibilities, and thus its own being, is 'projection' (*Entwurf*). Interpretation, according to Heidegger, is the 'working-out of possibilities projected in understanding'.[23] Because Dasein is the kind of being that is constituted by projecting itself ahead in possibilities, Heidegger can say that 'Dasein is constantly "more" than it factually is'.[24] John Macquarrie's paraphrase of this thought is worth citing: 'Man is possibility. He is always more than he is, his being is never complete at any given moment. He therefore has no essence as an object has.'[25]

Macquarrie correlates Dasein's finding himself in the world (*Befindlichkeit*) with the mode of the actual on the one hand, and *Dasein's* understanding of its situation (*Verstehen*) with the mode of the possible. 'Ontic' statements 'tell us about some entity in its actual relations with other entities' while 'ontological' statements 'tell us about the being of something and its range of possibilities'.[26] Similarly, Michael Gelven devotes a whole section in his commentary on *Being and Time* to the 'priority of the possible' in

Heidegger.[27] This 'possible' which is ontologically prior to actuality is not the 'merely possible' of things in general, but refers to possibility as an *existentiale* of Dasein.[28] In the second part of *Being and Time*, Heidegger reworks each *existentiale* in terms of temporality and claims that 'Understanding, as existing in the potentiality for Being, however it may have been projected, is *primarily* futural'.[29] The future makes ontologically possible a being whose being consists in projecting possibilities.

What is of interest to us is Heidegger's explanation of selfhood in terms of care, and his explanation of care in terms of possibility and temporality. The future is meaningful because it is a way of existing for Dasein (i.e., by projecting possibilities and advancing towards its 'ownmost' possibility – death – with anticipatory resoluteness). As Gelven rightly notes, Heidegger is explaining Dasein's being as care by showing what it *means to be in time*.[30]

In this brief survey of Heidegger's philosophical anthropology, we have seen the predominance of the notion of temporality, and the related notion of possibility. Gelven notes, however, that philosophy has traditionally lacked the resources to describe (and we might add, articulate) the realm of the possible. But with regard to Heidegger, 'the principle that possibility is prior to actuality becomes almost a guiding theme.'[31] Heidegger's hermeneutical phenomenology is a strategy for describing the possible.

While Ricoeur expresses admiration for Heidegger's analysis of temporality and possibility, his narrative theory provides a philosophy of language and an analytic rigour of method that Heidegger's 'short route' to an ontology of Dasein lacks. It is Ricoeur's belief that Heidegger lacked the linguistic and literary methodology for dealing with the notions of time and possibility. George Steiner observes that Heidegger was in his later years worried that his language had 'fallen' into traditional metaphysical categories, so that he increasingly turned to poetry as an alternative language.[32] While Heidegger's instincts might have been correct in prompting his transition to the language of poetry, his philosophy of language and interpretation theory are at best embryonic.

Ricoeur rejects Heidegger's 'short route' to ontology because the latter's phenomenology attempts ambitiously to give a direct description of Dasein's fundamental structures. But human being is not open to such direct inspection. Ricoeur's alternative – the 'long route' – reaches ontology by degrees, by way of a semantic mediation (i.e., by way of signs, symbols, texts, narratives).

Heidegger, objects Ricoeur, moves to the description of existence too quickly, without the benefit of mediation and without adequate methodological preparation. Moreover, in proceeding immediately to existential questions, Heidegger leaves himself without the means to arbitrate between conflicting interpretations. For these reasons, Ricoeur proposes to reach an ontology of human being by way of a 'detour' through language. In this manner, Ricoeur claims that he 'will resist the temptation to separate *truth*, characteristic of understanding, from the *method* put into operation by disciplines which have sprung from exegesis'.[33] In making full use of exegetical methods and explanations, Ricoeur hopes to give an analytical precision to Heidegger's ontology which is otherwise absent.

Ricoeur's *Time and Narrative* not only continues Heidegger's project, but also provides a corrective to some of the central themes in Heidegger's *Being and Time*. Ricoeur's narrative correction of the description of Dasein's temporality gives to Heidegger's analysis a literary application, an analytic rigour and a social dimension.

In setting forth in narrative form the various ways in which time may be 'reckoned' with, Ricoeur gives a literary application, and therefore analytic rigour, to Heidegger's analysis of temporality. Whereas Heidegger proceeds to describe temporality directly with the aid of phenomenology, Ricoeur prefers to approach the problems of time and temporality with the resources of a narrative theory. Narratives are literary schemas which create figures for human time. And with the narrative theory come all the exegetical and explanatory methods which give to Ricoeur's analysis of human being the means, lacking in Heidegger, to sort out the conflict of interpretations.

The power of Ricoeur's narrative theory to provide a social dimension to Heidegger's analysis of human being is most strikingly manifested in Ricoeur's confrontation with Heidegger's treatment of historicality. Heidegger asks whence, in general, can Dasein draw those possibilities upon which it projects itself. The answer is that, as 'thrown', Dasein finds itself with a heritage: 'In one's coming back resolutely to one's thrownness, there is hidden a *handing down* to oneself of the possibilities that have come down to one' (*BT*, p. 435). Ricoeur sees stories and histories as the major *form* of this heritage. Stories and histories are handed down in a narrative tradition, a tradition which is of necessity *social*. But Heidegger's preceding analysis of temporality centres on the

45

authentic, non-transferrable possibility of being-towards-death. Heidegger errs according to Ricoeur in viewing Dasein's historical heritage as 'radically monadic' rather than inherently *social*. According to Heidegger, Dasein's historicality is individualistic and future-oriented, towards potentialities-for-being and particularly being-towards-death: '*Authentic Being-towards-death – that is to say, the finitude of temporality – is the hidden basis of Dasein's historicality*'. (*BT*, p. 438).

But Ricoeur argues that narrative time is 'public' time in two senses: firstly, it is the time of interaction of various characters and circumstances; secondly, it is the time of a story's public – its audience. The possibilities it opens up are handed down in a *community tradition*. In short, narrative time, both in the text and outside it, is the time of *being-with-others*. But this, Ricoeur observes, calls the whole Heideggerian analysis of historicality into question, insofar as it depends on the primacy of individual fate and being-towards-death:

> Does not narrativity, by breaking away from the obsession of a struggle in the face of death, open any meditation on time to another horizon than that of death, to the problem of communication not just between living beings but between contemporaries, predecessors, and successors?[34]

Stories and histories continue beyond the fate of individuals. But narrative time as being-with-others also affects Heidegger's analysis of the heritage of potentialities handed down. Against Heidegger, Ricoeur states that a heritage is something transmitted from *another* to the self. Heritages are transmitted by *traditions*. In sum, narrative theory permits Ricoeur to append not only a *literary application* and an *analytic rigour*, but a *social dimension* to Heidegger's analysis of human temporality.

IMAGINATION, TIME AND POSSIBILITY: RICOEUR'S PROJECT

'Philosophy is reflection upon existence and upon all those means by which that existence is to be understood.'[35] Among these means for understanding existence, Ricoeur considers stories and histories to be pre-eminent. In his earlier work, narrative stands on the periphery. However, much of this early work deals with what we may call the *ingredients* of Ricoeur's later narrative theory:

imagination, time and *possibility*. These notions first figure in Ricoeur's philosophical anthropology, and they enter his interpretation theory by gradually acquiring a verbal or literary orientation. In other words, *imagination, time* and *possibility* are constituents both in Ricoeur's philosophical anthropology (his thinking about human being) and in his hermeneutics (his thinking about texts). In this last section I would like to show how narratives function in Ricoeur's thought to make the notion of possible ways of being-in-time more intelligible. I will then go on to claim that Ricoeur's narrative theory stands at the crossroads of his philosophical anthropology and his textual hermeneutics.

The one theme in Ricoeur's doctoral dissertation, *Freedom and Nature*, which deserves more detailed consideration in light of our overall concerns is that of possibility. *Freedom and Nature* is a description of man's fundamental possibilities. Working from a phenomenological perspective which describes consciousness and its intentional objects, Ricoeur claims that the 'object' which corresponds to willing is the *project*. It is in projects that the human effort to exist and its desire to be is most clearly witnessed.

Ricoeur comments that 'the most important trait of a project is undoubtedly its reference to the future'.[36] The project is a practical determination of a future state of affairs which depends on me. Ricoeur writes:

> This 'possible' designates the capacity for the realization of the project inasmuch as it is within my power; it is the correlate of my power over things themselves. . . . It is by virtue of an unjustifiable reduction that we decide to equate 'world' with the whole of observable facts; I inhabit a world in which there is something 'to be done by me'; the 'to be done by me' belongs to the structure which is the 'world'.[37]

That humans intend certain projects means for Ricoeur that the possible precedes the actual: 'a part of the actual is a voluntary realization of possibilities anticipated by a project.'[38] Ricoeur is thus able to refine his understanding of ethics:

> I will call ethics therefore this movement [*parcours*] of actualization, this odyssey of freedom across the world of works, this proof-texting of the being-able-to-do-something [*pouvoir-faire*] in effective actions which bear witness to it. Ethics is this movement between naked and blind belief in a

primordial 'I can', and the real history where I attest to this 'I can'.[39]

According to Ricoeur, in determining to do something, I likewise determine myself. I find and affirm myself in my acts. In Ricoeur's words: 'In the same way that a project opens up possibilities in the world, it opens up new possibilities in myself and reveals me to myself as a possibility of acting. My power-to-be manifests itself in my power-to-do'.[40] The 'possible' is thus an essential component in self-understanding. What is important to note is the central place which Ricoeur accords to the notion of possibility and its projection in his project of determining and understanding human existence.

Existence must be mediated by semantics. It is Ricoeur's thesis that we only come to understand human being and human possibilities through an analysis of symbols and texts which attest to that existence. What aspect of human existence is mediated by narratives in particular? Ricoeur believes that narratives are unique in displaying *existential possibilities*, possibilities for human action and ways of being in or orienting onself to time. Ricoeur sides with Heidegger in assigning priority to the possible. But contrary to Heidegger, Ricoeur claims that these possibilities are projected only by narratives. Only through stories and histories do we gain a catalogue of the humanly possible. The human condition, determined by and preoccupied with time, is made more intelligible by narrative. What is time? What is human time? Augustine's query receives no adequate theoretical answer. However, narrative offers a 'poetic' solution: intelligibility. Narrative theory thus stands at the crossroads of philosophical anthropology, which deals with the meaning of human being, and hermeneutics, which deals with the meaning of texts. Ricoeur answers Kant's query: What is Man? by reading stories and histories which display the whole gamut of human possibilities.

Instead of viewing imaginative literature as a product of mere fancy, Ricoeur insists that fictions not only refer to reality, but actually 'remake' it. Ricoeur argues that works of fiction are not less real but more real than the things they represent, for in the work of fiction a whole world is displayed which 'condenses' reality and gathers its essential traits into a concentrated structure or work. Fictions 'remake' human reality by projecting a possible world which can intersect and transform the world of the reader:

Fiction has the power to 'remake' reality and, within the framework of narrative fiction in particular, to remake real praxis to the extent that the text intentionally aims at a horizon of new reality which we may call a world. It is this world of the text which intervenes in the world of action in order to give it a new configuration or, as we might say, in order to transfigure it.[41]

Ricoeur claims that the task of hermeneutics is to explicate the 'world' *in front of* the text. The world of the text is the reference of fiction, and corresponds to the imagination not as norm-governed productivity, but as power of redescription. The world of the text is the keystone which supports Ricoeur's 'hermeneutical arch' (i.e., the point which mediates explanation and understanding), and furthermore it is in the notion of the world of the text that Ricoeur's hermeneutics and philosophical anthropology *intersect*.

Ricoeur defines the task of hermeneutics in terms of the world of the text:

Hermeneutics can be defined no longer as an inquiry into the psychological intentions which are hidden beneath the text, but rather as the explication of the being-in-the-world displayed by the text. What is to be interpreted in the text is a proposed world which I could inhabit and in which I could project my ownmost possibilities.[42]

The world projected by the work allows one to explore possibilities of action and so have 'fictive experiences.' By 'fictive experience' Ricoeur understands a virtual manner of inhabiting the proposed world. According to Ricoeur, *the distinctive intentionality of fictional narrative is this offering a new world*, a new way of perceiving things or possibilities.

Whereas the intentionality of history is its inquiry into the real as *actual* (things that have happened), the intentionality of fictional literature is its redescription of the real as *possible* (things that might happen or have happened). And because the world of the text proposes new possibilities for being-in-the-world, it is implicated in Ricoeur's philosophical anthropology.

Just what is the nature of the world of the text? We may straightaway assert that for Ricoeur the world of the text is not the 'actual' or empirical world of 'everyday' reality. Reality, argues Ricoeur, is larger than the positivists' conception of it. Ricoeur states unequivocally: 'My whole aim is to do away with this restriction of reference to scientific statements.'[43] Indeed, Ricoeur writes:

> The more imagination deviates from that which is called reality in ordinary language and vision, the more it approaches the heart of the reality which is no longer the world of manipulable objects, but the world into which we have been thrown by birth and within which we try to orient ourselves by projecting our innermost possibilities upon it, in order that we *dwell* there.[44]

There is more than one nod towards Heidegger in this paragraph: thrownness, projecting innermost possibilities, dwelling.

We have already noted the parallel between Ricoeur's project and that of Heidegger, the parallel between *Being and Time* on the one hand, and Ricoeur's mediation of Being and Time by *Telling*. If the object of narrative mimesis is human action, we can already begin to see how Ricoeur develops Heidegger's seminal analysis of Dasein in his theory of narrative. For human action is nothing less than 'being in time', not merely in the sense of within-timeness, but rather in the sense of reckoning with past, present and future. One of the most important roles of literature according to Ricoeur is its ability to project 'fictive' experiences of time – an important element in the analysis of human temporality. Works of literature allow us to try out various ways of being-in-the-world and of orienting ourselves to time.

With Heidegger, Ricoeur understands 'being-in-the-world' as that always-already present horizon of possibilities in which Dasein finds himself. Heidegger, says Ricoeur, was right: what we first understand in a discourse is a project – a new possibility for being-in-the-world. The world of the text, because it displays a possible way of being-in-the-world, proposes a possible understanding that the reader can appropriate for himself. In section 32 of *Being and Time*, entitled 'Understanding and interpretation', Heidegger defines interpretation as the 'working out of possibilities projected in understanding'. Ricoeur's threefold *Mimesis* bears a striking resemblance to this Heideggerian notion: *Mimesis I* corresponds to Heidegger's pre-understanding, *Mimesis II* to the projection of possibilities, and *Mimesis III* to the appropriation of these possibilities 'understandingly'. According to Ricoeur, the three 'moments' of *Mimesis* mediate Time and Telling: '*We are following therefore the destiny of a prefigured time that becomes a refigured time through the mediation of a configured time'.*[45] Ricoeur has thus recreated on the narrative level the whole process of Heideggerian interpretation.

The world of the text is a way of being-in-the-world which fictionally works out various possibilities projected in a fictional situation. Stories, then, far from being unreal and illusory, are actually the means of an ontological exploration of our relationship to beings and to Being. Ricoeur had insisted on this role of ontological exploration for the imagination even in his earliest phenomenological phase, when he used the technique of 'imaginative variation' to uncover the essence of phenomena. With his narrative theory, Ricoeur has simply refined his method while keeping the same goal. The goal, that is, remains describing human possibilities, but the means are no longer simply phenomenological, but narrative.

CONCLUSION

In conclusion, we may say that Ricoeur's narrative theory takes up the unfinished projects of Kant and Heidegger in the following ways: (1) Ricoeur gives a verbal orientation and literary application to Kant's notion of the creative imagination and Heidegger's notion of human temporality. (2) This literary application enables Ricoeur to take advantage of explanatory techniques appropriate to texts. The road to an understanding of human being must take the long detour through questions of method. (3) Narrative theory adds a social dimension to the notions of the creative imagination and human temporality which was lacking in both Kant and Heidegger.

In thus permitting Ricoeur to think time and imagination together, narrative provides Ricoeur with a strategy of describing the possible. That human possibilities are displayed in stories and histories means that Ricoeur's narrative theory stands at the crossroads of his philosophical anthropology and his textual hermeneutics. Ricoeur is a philosopher of human possibility, and in this philosophical project literature holds pride of place, for it is by reading stories and histories that we learn what is humanly possible. In making time, imagination and possibility more intelligible, Ricoeur, with his narrative theory, has written a fascinating new chapter in the history of these ideas. And in so doing, Ricoeur's narrative theory is assured of a significant place in that larger narrative, the story or history of philosophy.

NOTES

1 Paul Ricoeur, *The Rule of Metaphor*, London, Routledge & Kegan Paul, 1978, p. 199.

2 See Mary Schaldenbrand, 'Metaphoric imagination: kinship through conflict', in Charles R. Reagan (ed.) *Studies in the Philosophy of Paul Ricoeur*, Athens, Ohio, Ohio University Press, 1979, pp. 57–81, on the importance of the mediating imagination in Ricoeur's thought. Schaldenbrand claims that the mediating imagination is the central feature of Ricoeur's method, observing that his major works 'exhibit a remarkable development of imagination theory. Common to all of them is this theme: imagining mediates opposition' (p. 60).

3 Paul Ricoeur, 'Imagination in discourse and action,' in A.-T. Tymieniecka (ed.) *The Human Being in Action*, London, D. Reidel, 1978, p. 4.

4 Immanuel Kant, *Critique of Pure Reason* (hereafter *CPR*), translated by Norman Kemp Smith, London, Macmillan, 1933, A138 / B177.

5 Ibid., A140 / B179–80. We will see below that Kant analogically extends his notion of schema in the third *Critique* so that it becomes a form of artistic genius which presents not concepts but Ideas of Reason.

6 Paul Ricoeur, 'Pour une théorie du discours narratif', in *La Narrativité*, Paris, CNRS, 1980, p. 61.

7 Paul Ricoeur, *The Philosophy of Paul Ricoeur: An Anthology of his Work*, edited by Charles E. Reagan and David Stewart, Boston, Beacon Press, 1978, pp. 26–7.

8 Immanuel Kant, *Critique of Judgment* (hereafter *CJ*), translated by J. H. Bernard, London, Collier Macmillan, 1951, p. 15.

9 Cf. Ricoeur's comment 'This is how Kant conceived imagination in his *Critique of Judgment* by coordinating the free play of the imagination and the form of understanding in a teleology that had no goal beyond itself,' 'The Bible and the imagination', in Hans Deiter Betz (ed.) *The Bible as a Document of the University*, Chico, California, Scholars Press, 1981, pp. 49–50.

10 Ricoeur similarly appeals to Chomsky's work on 'generative grammar' as an example of 'ruled creativity'.

11 Paul Ricoeur, *Time and Narrative*, vol. I, Chicago, University of Chicago Press, 1984, p. 11.

12 Paul Ricoeur, *Hermeneutics and the Human Sciences*, edited by John B. Thompson, Cambridge, Cambridge University Press, 1981, p. 211.

13 See Kant, *CJ*, p. 198.

14 Paul Ricoeur, 'Biblical hermeneutics', *Semeia*, vol. 4, 1975, p. 143.

15 Kant, *CJ*, p. 158. Kant adds that 'the poet promises little and announces a mere play with ideas; but he supplies something which is worth occupying ourselves with, because he provides in this play food for the understanding and, by the aid of imagination, gives life to his concepts' (pp. 165–6).

16 Marjorie Grene, for instance, claims that Heidegger's commentary is a classic instance of *eisegesis*, of reading his own ideas back into Kant's work, in her *Martin Heidegger*, London, Bowes & Bowes, 1957, p. 66.

17 Martin Heidegger, *Kant and the Problem of Metaphysics*, London, Indiana University Press, 1962, p. 221.
18 We cannot hope adequately to deal with the full scope of Heidegger's 'retrieval' of Kant. For a more extended treatment, see Charles M. Sherover, *Heidegger, Kant and Time*, Bloomington, Indiana University Press, 1971. The present analysis is indebted to Sherover's account, with the exception that Sherover makes no attempt to relate imagination, time or schematism to narrative.
19 Heidegger, *Kant and the Problem of Metaphysics*, p. 94.
20 Sherover, *Heidegger, Kant and Time*, p. 135.
21 Paul Ricoeur, 'On interpretation', in Alan Montefiore (ed.) *Philosophy in France Today*, Cambridge, Cambridge University Press, 1983, p. 190.
22 Heidegger, *Being and Time* (hereafter *BT*), translated by John Macquarrie and Edward Robinson, Oxford, Blackwell, 1962, p. 184.
23 ibid., p. 189. Interpretation makes explicit what is primordially grasped in human awareness. The possibilities of a situation are grasped *as* concrete possibilities and interpretation exposits this *as*.
24 ibid., p. 185. Grene comments: 'It is this aspect of human being which Heidegger later calls transcendence (*Transzendenz*): a better name for it, since it carries with it the meaning of anticipation, of going beyond the given' (*Martin Heidegger*, p. 23).
25 Macquarrie, *An Existentialist Theology: A Comparison of Heidegger and Bultmann*, London, Pelican, 1973, p. 32.
26 ibid., p. 30.
27 Michael Gelven, *A Commentary on Heidegger's 'Being and Time'*, New York, Harper & Row, 1970.
28 Heidegger, *BT*, p. 183. Heidegger states that what is central in the phenomenological method in general is possibility: 'Higher than actuality stands possibility' (pp. 62–3).
29 ibid., p. 387.
30 While it is evident that the future is significant as possibility, it is less obvious to see how the past can be so. The subject matter of history is the *possible*. According to Heidegger the theme of a science of history 'is neither that which has happened just once for all nor something universal that floats above it, but the possibility which has been factically existent.' What is 'historical' or 'past' about a museum piece is the world, *Dasein's* world, to which it once belonged. A museum piece is historical to the extent that it was once meaningful in Dasein's existence. It is therefore not items in the world as such which are historical, but rather Dasein's worlds or ways of being-in-the-world which are historical. History is therefore not about 'brute facts' but past worlds. As we have seen, Heidegger analyses what it means to be in a world in terms of the possibilities Dasein finds and projects. History's interest in the past is in those 'historic' possibilities which Dasein may 'repeat' in the present. Through repetition, the 'monumental' possibilities of the existence that has-been-there may be made one's own, as possibilities for the future.
31 Gelven, *Commentary on 'Being and Time'*, p. 76.
32 George Steiner, *Heidegger*, London, Fontana, 1978, p. 78.

33 Ricoeur, *The Conflict of Interpretations*, edited by Don Ihde, Evanston, Northwestern University Press, 1974, p. 11. Ricoeur expresses a similar worry about the tendency of Gadamer's hermeneutics to present interpretation as if it were a matter of truth *or* method.
34 Ricoeur, 'Narrative time', *Critical Inquiry*, vol. 7, 1980, p. 188.
35 Don Ihde, *Hermeneutic Phenomenology: The Philosophy of Paul Ricoeur*, Evanston, Northwestern University Press, 1971, p. 11.
36 Paul Ricoeur, *Freedom and Nature: The Voluntary and the Involuntary*, Evanston, Northwestern University Press, 1966, p. 48.
37 Ricoeur, *The Philosophy of Paul Ricoeur*, p. 68.
38 Ricoeur, *Freedom and Nature*, p. 54.
39 Paul Ricoeur, 'The problem of the foundation of moral philosophy', *Philosophy Today*, vol. 22, 1978, p. 177.
40 Ricoeur, *The Philosophy of Paul Ricoeur*, p. 69.
41 Ricoeur, 'On interpretation' p. 185.
42 Ricoeur, *Hermeneutics and the Human Sciences*, p. 112.
43 Ricoeur, *Rule of Metaphor*, p. 221.
44 Paul Ricoeur, 'The function of fiction in shaping reality', *Man and World*, vol. 12, 1979, p. 139.
45 Ricoeur, *Time and Narrative*, vol. I, p. 54.

4

BETWEEN TRADITION AND UTOPIA

The hermeneutical problem of myth

Richard Kearney

In an interview given shortly after the French publication of *Time and Narrative*, Paul Ricoeur stated that one of the pressing tasks facing contemporary culture is to ensure a creative relationship between tradition and utopia.[1] In what follows, I propose to examine (1) what exactly Ricoeur means by tradition; and (2) how tradition may be positively related to utopia through a critical hermeneutics of myth.

A HERMENEUTICS OF TRADITION

In volume III of *Time and Narrative*, entitled *Le Temps raconté*, Ricoeur offers a comprehensive account of various key concepts of 'traditions'. The analysis in question is concentrated in chapter 7 of this volume – 'Vers une herméneutique de la conscience historique'. Having renounced the Hegelian claim to a 'totalizing mediation' of history in the form of Absolute Knowledge, Ricoeur proposes this alternative:

> an open-ended mediation, incomplete and imperfect, made up of a network of perspectives split between the expectancy of the future, the reception of the past, and the living experience of the present – but without the *aufhebung* into a totality where the reason of history and its effectiveness would coincide.
>
> (*TN* vol. III, p. 300)

Only by acknowledging this *split* character of history may we surmise the possibility of a 'plural unity' emerging from these divergent perspectives. This open play of perspectives, extending between past and future, requires in turn that we revise the accepted view of tradition as a *fait accompli*. Tradition is now to be understood as an ongoing dialectic between our being-effected by the past and our projection of a history yet-to-be-made (*la visée de l'histoire à faire*).

The futural project of history runs into trouble, warns Ricoeur, as soon as it slips its anchorage in past experience. History loses direction when it is cut off from all that preceded it. Paul Rimbaud was no doubt announcing the modernist manifesto when he proclaimed in his famous *Lettre du Voyant*, written in the revolutionary year of the Paris Commune 1871: '*Libre aux nouveaux d'exécrer les ancêtres.*' But if such a manifesto is applied literally to the realm of history and pushed to extremes, it runs the risk of schismatic negation. 'If it is true', writes Ricoeur,

> that the belief in *des temps nouveaux* contributed to the shrinking of our experiential space, even to the point of banishing the past to the shades of oblivion – the obscurantism of the Middle Ages! – whereas our horizon of expectancy tended to withdraw into a future ever more vague and indistinct, we may ask ourselves if the tension between expectancy and experience was not already beginning to be threatened the very day it was acknowledged.[2]

Ricoeur recommends that we resist the contemporary slide towards the extreme of schismatic utopianism. But what form should such resistance take? First, we should realize that the utopian project cancels itself out as soon as it loses its foothold in the experience of past and present; for it thereby finds itself incapable of formulating a practical path towards its ideals. Ricoeur counsels accordingly that our utopian expectancies must remain *determinate* (and therefore *finite*) if they are to become historically realizable. Otherwise they forfeit their capacity to solicit responsible commitment. In order to prevent the utopian project from dissolving into an empty dream-world, Ricoeur recommends that we bring it closer to the present by means of intermediary projects which are within the scope of social action. Invoking what he terms a 'post-Hegelian Kantian' model, Ricoeur advances three conditions which the utopian horizon of expectancy must observe: (1) it must project a hope for all of humanity and not just one privileged community or nation; (2) this humanity is only worthy of the name to the extent that it possesses a history; and (3) in order to possess a history, humanity must be the subject of history in the sense of a 'collective singular' (*un singulier collectif*).[3]

Warning against the contemporary diminution of the experiential space of tradition, Ricoeur refuses the tendency to dismiss tradition as something complete in itself and impervious to change. On the contrary, he urges us to reopen the past so as to reanimate its still unaccomplished potentialities. 'Against the adage which claims that the future is in all respects open and contingent and the past univocally closed and necessary', writes Ricoeur, 'we must make our expectancies more determinate and our experience more indeterminate' (*TN* vol. III, p. 228). It is only when our utopian project has been rendered determinate in this way that we can retroactively reveal the past as a 'living tradition'.

The critical reflection on the futural project of 'making history' thus calls for an equally critical examination of our relation to tradition – broadly understood as our 'being effected by history'. At this decisive point in his argument Ricoeur calls for a 'step back from the future towards the past'. In keeping with Marx's dictum that man makes history according to circumstances which he has inherited, Ricoeur declares that we are only the agents of history to the degree that we are also its patients. To exist in history means that 'to act is to suffer and to suffer is to act'. The countless victims of history who are acted upon by forces beyond their control epitomize this condition of suffering – in both senses of the term. But this is only the extreme case. Even those who are considered the active initiators of history also suffer history to the extent that their actions, however calculated, almost invariably produce certain non-intended consequences. (This was admirably demonstrated by Sartre in his descriptions of 'inverted praxis' in the first book of the *Critique of Dialectical Reason*, e.g. the counterproductive effects of imported gold from the American colonies on the Spanish economy in the seventeenth century, or of mountain deforestation on the Chinese harvests.)

However, to avoid the pitfall of fatalism, Ricoeur points to the necessity of always interpreting our 'being-effected-by-the-past' in positive dialectical tension with our utopian horizon of expectancy. Once this tension is lost sight of we easily succumb to a sterile antithesis between a reactionary apologism of the past and a naive affirmation of progress. Ricoeur posits a third way which leads beyond this either/or opposition. In order to respect the demands of historical continuity *and* discontinuity, a dialectical model is required which preserves the idea of a consciousness perduring through history while at the same time taking full stock of the 'decentering of the thinking subject' carried out by the hermeneutics of suspicion (i.e., Marx, Freud and Nietzsche). The ethical demand to remember the past does not oblige us to rehabilitate the idealist model of a sovereign mind commanding a total recapitulation of historical meaning. What does need to be retained, however, is the idea of tradition itself. But this retention is only permissible on the basis of a critical reinterpretation of this idea. Here Ricoeur distinguishes between three different categories of historical memory: (1) traditionality; (2) traditions; and (3) Tradition (with a capital T).

(1) *Traditionality.* Ricoeur describes this category in volumes I and II of *Time and Narrative* as a dialectic between 'sedimentation' and 'innovation'. While this description related to the role of traditionality in the specific realm of fictional narrative (i.e. what he calls *Mimesis II*), in volume III of *Time and Narrative* Ricoeur amplifies the range of reference. He argues that traditionality is to be understood in the more general sense of a formal style which transmits the heritages of the past. And this means extending the discussion from *Mimesis II* to *Mimesis III*: that is, to the rapport between narrative and the historical time of action and suffering. In this enlarged context, traditionality is now defined as a temporalizing of history by means of a dialectic between the effects of history upon us (which we passively suffer) and our response to history (which we actively operate). Traditionality, in other words, is the precondition for transmitting actual historical meaning. Ricoeur claims that this dialectical category enables us to obviate certain erroneous attitudes to the past. First, it refuses to accept that the past can be totally abolished in the manner of a schismatic utopianism or a Nietzschean 'active forgetting' (an attitude which dissolves history into an arbitrary multiplicity of incommensurable individual perspectives). But the dialectic of traditionality equally resists the idealist temptation to synchronize past and present, thereby reducing the diversity of history to the absolute identity of contemporaneous understanding (e.g. the error of romantic and Hegelian hermeneutics).

Avoiding both these extremes, the model of traditionality proposes a *fusion of horizons* (after Gadamer). It suggests how we may have access to history without simply imposing our present understanding onto the past. The past is thus opened up as an historical horizon which is at once detached from our present horizon and included in it. 'It is in projecting an historical horizon', notes Ricoeur,

> that we experience, in its tension with the horizon of the present, the effect of the past on us. This effect [*efficience*] of history on us is something which, as it were, takes effect without us. The fusion of horizons is that which we labour towards. And here the labour of history and the labour of the historian come to each other's aid.
>
> (*TN* vol. III, p. 221)

Traditionality means, in short, that 'the temporal distance which separates us from the past is not a dead interval but a *generative transmission of meaning*'.[4]

(2) The second category outlined by Ricoeur is that of *traditions*. Whereas traditionality is a formal concept, this second category functions as a material concept of the contents of tradition. This transition from form to content is necessitated by the activity of interpretation itself. Interpretation reveals that tradition is essentially linguistic (*langagière*) and so cannot be divorced from the transmission of actual meanings which precede us. Moreover, this identification of traditions with language is to be understood not just in the sense of natural languages (French, Greek, English, etc.), but in the sense of things already said by those who existed in history before we arrived on the scene. This takes into account the complex set of social and cultural circumstances which each one of us presupposes as a speaking and listening being.

Ricoeur insists that this linguistic character of historical meaning is central to the entire argument of *Time and Narrative*. The first relation of narrative to action, *Mimesis I*, disclosed the primordial capacity of human action to be symbolically mediated. The second, *Mimesis II*, operating in the structural emplotment of fiction and historiography, revealed how imitated action functions in terms of a text. Now the third mode, *Mimesis III*, comprising the effects that historical meaning has on our present action and suffering, is shown to coincide in large part with the transmission of meaning by the textual mediations of the past.

Moreover, this parallel between a hermeneutics of history and a hermeneutics of texts is corroborated by Ricoeur's demonstration that historiography, as a knowledge, by means of traces, depends largely on texts which give to the past the status of documentary witness. Thus our consciousness of being exposed to the effectiveness of history finds its complement in our interpretative response to the texts which communicate the past to us. All comprehension of historical tradition entails historical traditions of comprehension. Ricoeur sums up:

> As soon as one takes *traditions* to refer to those *things said* in the past and transmitted to us through a chain of interpretation and reinterpretation, we must add a material dialectic of contents to the formal dialectic of temporal distance (i.e. traditionality); the past puts us into question before *we* put it into question. In this struggle for the *recognition of meaning*, the text and the reader are each in their turn familiarized and defamiliarized.
>
> (*TN* vol. III, p. 222)

Drawing thus from the Gadamer/Collingwood model of question-response, Ricoeur relates the essence of traditions to the fact that the past interrogates and responds to us to the degree that we interrogate and respond to it. To conceive of the past in terms of traditions is to conceive of it in terms of proposals of meaning which, in turn, call for our interpretative response.

(3) Finally, Ricoeur defines the third category of the historical past as Tradition with a capital T (*La tradition*). This move from traditions to Tradition is motivated by the observation that every proposal of meaning is also a claim to truth. And at this point in the argument, Ricoeur rejoins the famous polemic between Gadamer as defender of tradition and Habermas as exponent of critical reason.[5] Gadamer's defence of Tradition, as Ricoeur reminds us, stemmed largely from the conviction that our historical consciousness of the past refers to some truth (i.e. is not purely arbitrary or subjective). Gadamer argued that this claim to historical truth is not something which derives from us alone but is a voice from the past which we seek to reappropriate. The Gadamerian defence of Tradition–Authority–Prejudgment presupposes that we are carried by the meanings of the past before we find ourselves in a position to judge them. Or to put in other terms, we are spoken to before we speak; we are posited in tradition before we posit tradition; we are situated before we are free to criticize this

situation. Whence Gadamer's conclusion that the Enlightenment claim to a critical standpoint of neutral ahistorical judgment residing above all prejudice, is itself a prejudice.

Ricoeur suggests that the opposition between Gadamer and Habermas is not insurmountable. The hermeneutics of tradition, he points out, already contains within itself the possibility of a critique of ideology. For as soon as we acknowledge that tradition is not some monolith of pre-established dogma but an ongoing dialectic of continuity and discontinuity made up of different rival traditions, internal crises, interruptions, revisions and schisms – as soon as we acknowledge this, we discover that there exists an essential dimension of distance at the very heart of tradition, a distance which actually invites critical interpretation. Critical hermeneutics differs radically from romantic hermeneutics on this issue. It refuses the idea that we can understand the past simply by reproducing in the present some original production of meaning, as if the temporal distanciation of meaning could be magically wished away. A critical hermeneutics of tradition insists on the necessity to discriminate between true and false interpretations of the past.

This raises the crucial question of legitimation. To resolve this problem, Habermas had declared it necessary to move beyond the 'interests of communication' exemplified by the hermeneutic sciences to the 'interests of emancipation' exemplified by the critical social sciences. Since the historical language of tradition is by its very nature subject to ideological distortion, Habermas appealed to an ahistorical ideal of undistorted communication. The danger here, however, is that this criterion of legitimacy may be deferred to an indefinitely utopian future without any grounds or precedents in history.

One might, at this point, have recourse to a transcendental reflection in order to provide universal norms of validation. But this move runs the risk of enclosing us in a monological transcendental as with Kant. Without a dialogical dimension rooted in history, the critical moment of transcendental self-reflection cannot provide adequate grounds for the ideal of undistorted communication. In short, the validation of universal norms must itself be founded in a historical dialectic between a determinate horizon of expectancy and a specific space of experience. Ricoeur's argument runs as follows:

It is on this return journey from the question of foundation to the question of historical effectiveness that the hermeneutics of tradition makes itself heard again. To avoid the endless flight of a perfectly ahistorical truth, we must try to discern signs of this truth in the anticipations of agreement operative in every successful communication, in every communication where we actually experience a certain reciprocity of intention and recognition. In other words, the transcendence of the idea of truth, which is a dialogical idea from the outset, must be perceived as already at work in the practice of communication. Thus reinstated in our horizon of expectancy, the dialogical idea is compelled to rejoin the buried anticipations of traditions itself. So understood, the pure transcendental may legitimately assume the negative status of a *limit-idea* with regard to both our determinate expectancies and our hypostasized traditions. But, short of being divorced from the effectiveness of history, this limit-idea must also become a *regulative idea* which directs the concrete dialectic between the horizon of expectancy and the space of experience.

(*TN* vol. III, p. 226, translation modified here and below)

Ricoeur recommends accordingly that we interpret tradition's pretension to truth in the non-absolutist sense of a presumption of truth. This means that we respect the truth-claims of tradition until such time as a better argument prevails. The 'presumption of truth' refers to our basic attitude of credit or trust in the propositions of meaning bequeathed by the past – a primary response which precedes the critical moment of distantiation and reminds us that we are not the originators of truth but already belong to a context of 'presumed truth'. Ricoeur believes that this model bridges the gap between the finitude of our historical understanding, stressed by Gadamer, and the validity of the idea of undistorted communicational truth, championed by Habermas.

Tradition, Ricoeur concludes, must be understood in the dynamic historical perspective of our being-effected-by-the-past (our space of experience), which in turn is related to our utopian horizon of expectancy. It is in this larger dialectic between tradition and utopia that we rediscover suppressed potentialities of past meaning which may give flesh and blood to the ideal of undistorted communication. Indeed, it is only in terms of such an interplay between memory and expectancy, that 'the utopia of reconciled humanity can be invested with an effective history' (*TN* vol. III p. 228). But Ricoeur rounds off his analysis with a warning signal. This indispensable interplay between past and future is becoming increasingly threatened in our time. As our utopian project becomes ever more distant, our common space of experience becomes more restricted. The growing discrepancy between utopia and tradition lies at the root of the crisis of modernity. 'The entire present is in crisis', notes Ricoeur, 'when expectancy takes refuge in utopia and tradition congeals into a dead residue' (*TN* vol. III, p. 235). Our contemporary task is to confront this crisis and prevent the tension betweeen utopia and tradition from further degenerating into an absolute schism. This task – which Ricoeur does not hesitate to describe as an 'ethical duty' (*TN* vol. III, p. 258) – is twofold. On the one hand, we must bring the utopian expectancies closer to the present by a strategic praxis sensitive to the concrete steps that need to be taken towards realizing what is 'desirable and reasonable'. And on the other hand, we must try to halt the shrinking of our experiential space by liberating the still untapped potentialities of inherited meaning. 'All initiative on the historical plane', Ricoeur concludes, 'consists in the perpetual transaction between these two tasks' (*TN* vol. III, p. 235).

I would add just one critical comment to Ricoeur's perceptive analysis of tradition. Is there not a sense in which the crisis of modernity also has a positive value in so far as the very gap between past and future which it opens up serves to heighten our consciousness of the problem of historical meaning? Would Ricoeur himself have devoted so much attention to the question of narrative continuity and transmission if the crucial link between tradition and utopia was unproblematically assured? Just as the cultural crisis of modernity has given rise to a proliferation of new literary forms from Joyce and Virginia Woolf to Beckett and Borges, has this same crisis not given rise to a new urgency of philosophical questioning about the very nature of historical truth – of which *Time and Narrative* is itself an exemplary witness? I am reminded here of Hannah Arendt's observation in her preface to *Between Past and Future;*

> the call to thought makes itself heard in that strange in-
> between period which sometimes inserts itself into historical

time when not only the later historians but actors and witnesses, the living themselves, become conscious of an interval in time which is entirely determined by things which are *no longer* and are *not yet*. History has often shown that it is such intervals which may contain the moment of truth.[6]

Ricoeur's hermeneutic analysis of tradition and utopia is written from just such an interval.

TOWARDS A CRITICAL HERMENEUTICS OF MYTH

In the second part of this paper I propose to examine how the critical relationship between tradition and utopia has often found expression in the mediational role of myth. The function of myth was analysed by Ricoeur in his first hermeneutical work, *The Symbolism of Evil* (1960), and is understood here in the general sense of a foundational narrative whereby a community relates itself to itself and to others. By means of a backward reference to the origins of its history, the mythic narrative seeks to account for how a particular culture or community came to be. Most civilizations have their own cosmogeny or creation myths. These, as Ricoeur points out in *The Symbolism of Evil*, are usually supplemented by anthropological myths (e.g. the myths of Adam or Prometheus) which tell the story of the genesis of human meaning and value. In this respect, myth is closely bound up with tradition as a recollection, transmission and reinterpretation of the past.

But myth also contains another crucial dimension: a utopian anticipation of the future. Here the 'social imaginary' – to borrow Ricoeur's term from *Lectures in Ideology and Utopia* (1986) – takes the form of a forward projection whereby a community expresses its unfulfilled aspirations for a better world. Without the backward look of myth, a culture is deprived of its memory. Without the forward look, it is deprived of its dreams. At its best myth may function as a creative interplay between the claims of tradition and utopia. Ricoeur spells out the implications of this interplay as follows:

> Every society possesses . . . a socio-political *imaginaire* – that is, an ensemble of symbolic discourses that can function as a rupture or a reaffirmation. As reaffirmation, the *imaginaire* operates as an 'ideology' which can positively repeat the founding discourse of a society – what I call its 'foundational

symbols' – thus preserving its sense of identity. After all, cultures create themselves by telling stories of their past. The danger is, of course, that this reaffirmation can be perverted, usually by monopolistic elites, into a mystificatory discourse which serves to uncritically vindicate the established political powers. In such instances, the symbols of a community become fixed and fetishized; they serve as lies. Over against this, there exists the *imaginaire* of rupture, a discourse of 'utopia' which remains critical of the powers that be out of fidelity to an 'elsewhere', to a society that is not-yet. But this utopian discourse is not always positive either. For besides the authentic utopia of critical rupture there can also exist a dangerously schizophrenic utopian discourse which projects a static future without ever producing the conditions of its realisation . . . here utopia becomes a future cut off from the present and the past, a mere alibi for the consolidation of the repressive powers that be. . . . In short, ideology as a symbolic confirmation of the past, and utopia as a symbolic opening towards the future, are complementary; if cut off from each other, they can lead to forms of political pathology.[7]

Myth also has its dangers. As an essentially 'imaginary' or 'symbolic' mode of expression, myth may distort a community's self-understanding by eclipsing reality behind some idealized chimera. In such instances, the nostalgia for a golden age of the past or the zealous pursuit of a messianic future may blind us to the complexities and exigencies of our present reality. Here myth serves as an ideological agency of distortion and dissimulation. Whence the colloquial use of the term myth as a synonym for illusion.

In order to discriminate between the positive and negative functions of myth a *critical hermeneutics* is required. Only in this way may myth be salvaged as a constructive mediation between tradition and utopia, maintaining both in a relationship of creative tension, a mutual dialogue which allows for tradition to be reactivated and utopia to be brought closer. Thus salvaged, myth may legitimately fulfil its dual potential of creation and critique: the disclosure of possible worlds which are suppressed in our present reality and whose very otherness provides us with alternatives to the established order. By projecting other modes of understanding, albeit on an imaginary plane, myth can function as a salutary indictment of the existing *status quo*.

The project of modernity has frequently been predicated upon a radical break with the past. In the contemporary movements of philosophy, theology, literary theory and political critique we find repeated calls for a demythologization of tradition. This critical demand to demystify is, of course, an indispensable corrective to the conservative apotheosis of tradition as a monolith of Truth; though it too can be pushed to extremes.

The need to continually re-evaluate one's cultural heritage raises the central question of myth as narrative. Narrative, understood as the human endeavour to make sense of history by telling a story, relates to tradition in two ways. By creatively reinterpreting the myths of the past, narrative can release new and hitherto concealed possibilities of understanding one's history. And by critically scrutinizing the past it can wrest tradition away from the conformism that is always threatening to overpower it.[8] To properly attend to this dual capacity of narrative is, therefore, to resist the facile habit of establishing a dogmatic opposition between the 'eternal verities' of tradition, on the one hand, and the free inventiveness of critical imagination, on the other. Every narrative interpretation, as Alasdair MacIntyre reminds us, whether it involves a literary or political reading of history, 'takes place within the context of some traditional mode of thought, transcending through criticism and invention the limitations of what had hitherto been reasoned in that tradition. . . . Traditions when vital embody continuities of conflict.'[9] This implies that the contemporary act of rereading and retelling tradition can actually disclose uncompleted and disrupted narratives which open up unprecedented possibilities of understanding. No text exists in a vacuum, in splendid isolation from its social and historical contexts. And tradition itself is not some seamless monument existing beyond time and space. It is, as Paul Ricoeur has established, a narrative construct requiring an open-ended process of reinterpretation. To examine one's tradition, consequently, is also to examine one's conscience – in the sense of critically discriminating between rival interpretations.

Most contemporary critics of myth have focused on its ideological function as a mystifying consciousness. This approach has been termed a 'hermeneutics of suspicion' by Paul Ricoeur. It interprets myth as a masked discourse which conceals a real meaning behind an imaginary one.[10] And the task it sets itself is to unmask this illusion, to uncover the hidden truth.

The modern project of unmasking myth frequently takes its cue from the investigative methods developed by Marx, Nietzsche and Freud – the 'three masters of suspicion' as Ricoeur calls them. Nietzsche advanced a genealogical hermeneutic which aimed to trace myths back to an underlying will to power (or in the case of the Platonic and Christian myths of otherworldy transcendence, to a negation of this will to power). Freud developed a psychoanalytic hermeneutic which saw myths as ways of disguising unconscious desires. Thus, in *Totem and Taboo*, for example, Freud identified myth as a substitution for lost primitive objects which provide symbolic compensation for prohibited pleasures. As such, religious myths are said to represent a sort of collective 'obsessional neurosis' whereby libidinal drives are concealed through a highly sophisticated mechanism of sublimation. And thirdly, there is Marx who proposed a critical hermeneutic of 'false consciousness' aimed at exposing the covert connection between ideological myths (or superstructures) and the underlying realities of class domination exemplified in the struggle for the ownership of the means of production (or infrastructures). Thus for Marx, the myth of a timeless and transcendental fulfilment – whether it be projected by religion, art or philosophy – is in fact an ideological masking of the historical reality of socio-economic exploitation.

While confirming the necessity for such a 'demythologizing' strategy, we must ask if this critique is not itself subject to critique. In this way, we may be able to recognize another more liberating dimension of myth – the genuinely *utopian* – behind its negative *ideological* dimension. Only by supplementing the hermeneutics of suspicion with what Ricoeur calls a 'hermeneutics of affirmation', do we begin to discern the potentiality of myth for a positive symbolizing project which surpasses its falsifying content.[11]

Myth is an ideological function. But it is also more than that. Once a hermeneutics of suspicion has unmasked the alienating role of myth as an agency of ideological conformism, there remains the task of a positive interpretation. Hermeneutics, as Ricoeur insists, has a double duty: to 'suspect' and to 'listen'. Having demythologized the ideologies of false consciousness it labours to disclose the utopian symbols of liberating consciousness. This involves discriminating between the falsifying and emancipating dimensions of myth.

Symbolizations of utopia pertain to the 'futural' horizon of myth. The hermeneutics of affirmation focuses not on the origin (*arche*) *behind* myths but on the end (*eschaton*) opened up in *front* of them. It thereby seeks to rescue mythic symbols from reactionary domination and show that once the mystifying function has been dispelled we may discover genuinely utopian anticipations of 'possible worlds' of liberty and justice. A positive hermeneutics offers an opportunity to rescue myths from the ideological abuses of doctrinal prejudice, nationalism, class oppression or totalitarian conformism; and it does so in the name of a universal project of freedom – a project from which no creed, nation, class or individual is excluded. The utopian content of myth differs from the ideological in that it is *inclusive*. It opens up human consciousness to a common goal of liberation instead of closing it off in inherited securities.

Where the hermeneutics of suspicion construed myth as an effacement of some original reality (e.g. will to power, unconscious desire, the material conditions of production or domination), the hermeneutics of affirmation operates on the hypothesis that myth may not only conceal some pre-existing meaning but also reveal new horizons of meaning. Thus instead of interpreting myths solely in terms of first-order reference to a predetermining cause hidden behind myth, it discloses a second-order reference to a 'possible world' projected by myth. It suggests, in other words, that there may be an *ulterior* meaning to myths in addition to their *anterior* meaning – an eschatological horizon which looks forward as well as an archeological horizon which looks back. Myth is not just nostalgia for some forgotten world. It can also constitute, in Ricoeur's words, 'a disclosure of unprecedented worlds, an opening onto other possible worlds which transcend the established limits of our actual world' and function as a 'recreation of language'.[12]

This epistemological distinction between the two horizons of myth (i.e. archeological and eschatological) also implies an *ethical* one. Myths are not neutral as romantic ethnology would have us believe. They become authentic or inauthentic according to the 'interests' which they serve. These interests, as Habermas recognized in *Knowledge and Human Interests*, can be those of critical emancipation or ideological domination. Thus we could say, for example, that the religious myths of a Kingdom may be interpreted either as an opiate of the oppressed (as Marx noted) or an antidote to such oppression (as the theology of liberation reminds us).

Similarly, it could be argued that national myths can be used to liberate a community or to incarcerate that community in tribal bigotry.

The critical role of hermeneutics is, therefore, indispensable. But this does not mean that we simply reduce mythic symbols to literal facts. It requires us rather to unravel the hidden intentions and interests of myth so as to distinguish between their role of ideological 'explanation' (which seeks to justify the *status quo* in a dogmatic or irrational manner) and their role of utopian 'exploration' (which challenges the *status quo* by disclosing alternative ways of understanding our world). *Demythologizing*, as an urgent task of critical thought, must not be confused here with *demythizing* which, as Ricoeur defines it, would simply lead to a positivistic impoverishment of culture.[13]

The crisis of modernity is characterized, in part at least, by the separation of myth and history: a divorce which is exemplified in the desacralization (*Entzauberung*) of tradition. But this offers us a certain critical distance. It means that we are no longer subject to the ideological illusion that myth explains reality. We are far less likely now to commit the error of believing that myth provides a true scientific account of history. Indeed it is arguable that it is the very demythologization of myth's ideological function which permits us to rediscover its genuine utopian function. Or to put it in another way: having eliminated the ideological abuse of myth as a false explanation of how things are, we are now free to appreciate the properly symbolic role of myth as an exploration of how things might be. We thus begin to recognize that the virtue of myth resides in its ability to contain more meaning than a history which is, objectively speaking, true. This is what Ricoeur calls 'saving myth' – by demythologizing its ideological perversions and misuses. To save myth from ideology is to safeguard it as a *poetics of the possible*.[14]

What is needed, finally, is a hermeneutic dialectic between a critical *logos* and a symbolic *muthos*. Without the constant vigilance of reason, myth remains susceptible to all kinds of perversion. For myth is not authentic or inauthentic by virtue of some internal essence; its legitimacy depends upon the particular interpretation which each generation of each historical community provides. In short, myth is neither good nor bad but interpretation makes it so.

Every   mythology   implies   an   on-going   confliction   of interpretations. And this conflict entails a central ethical component. It is our ethical duty to ensure that *muthos* is always conjoined with *logos* so that the narratives of tradition may serve as an agency of universal liberation rather than as the glorification of one particular community to the exclusion of all others. 'Liberation cannot be exclusive', as Ricoeur rightly observes. 'In genuine reason (*logos*) as well as in genuine myth (*muthos*) we find a concern for the universal emancipation of man.'[15]

It would seem that this universalist potential of myth is best served by ensuring that the utopian forward look of myth critically reinterprets its ideological backward look so that the horizon of history is kept open. A critical hermeneutics of myth is, therefore, one which acknowledges our need to 'belong' to the symbolic narratives of historical tradition while simultaneously respecting the need to 'distance' ourselves from them. If we ignore the claims of 'belonging' to a traditional pre-understanding, we run the risk of elevating reason to the rank of an absolutely neutral knowledge. Here one succumbs to the Hegelian or positivist temptation to ignore the historical finitude of human consciousness. The danger of reason dispensing thus with all mythic narratives of tradition is that it degenerates into a self-serving rationalism: scientific reason, as an absolute end in itself, becomes a new ideology in its own right. This is why Ricoeur insists that the rational critique of myth is 'a task which must always be begun, but which in principle can never be completed'.[16] It is equally incumbent upon us, of course, to heed the demand for a critical distance from the myths of tradition. Because without such a distance our understanding remains a slave to the blind prejudices of history. For myth to remain faithful to its utopian promise it must pass through the purgatorial detour of critique.

NOTES

1 'Entretien avec Paul Ricoeur', *Le Monde*, Paris, 7 February, 1987. See also Ricoeur's discussion of this subject in *Time and Narrative* vol. III, translated by Kathleen McLaughlin and David Pellauer, Chicago, University of Chicago Press, 1988, chapter 7; 'L'Idéologie et l'Utopie in *Du texte à l'action*, Editions du Seuil, Paris, 1986, pp. 379–93; 'The creativity of language: an interview' in Richard Kearney, *Dialogues with Contemporary Continental Thinkers*, Manchester, Manchester University Press, 1984, pp. 29–31.
2 *TN* vol. III, p. 215. This paradox is explained by Ricoeur as follows:

If the newness of the *Neuzeit* is only perceived in the light of the growing difference between (past) experience and (future) expectancy, in other words, if the belief in modernity rests on the expectancies which become removed from all anterior experiences, then the tension between experience and expectancy could only be recognized when its point of rupture was already in view. The idea of progress which still related a better future to the past, rendered even closer by the acceleration of history, tends to give way to the idea of utopia, as soon as humanity's hopes lose all reference to acquired experience and are projected into a future completely without precedent. With such utopia, the tension becomes schism.

(*TN* vol. III, p. 215)

3 Kant identified this common project with the constitution of 'a civil society administering universal rights'. Ricoeur grants this as a necessary condition of the historical rapprochement between utopia and tradition. Without the 'right to difference', the claim of universal history may be monopolized by one particular society, or grouping of dominant societies, thereby degenerating into hegemonic oppression. And on the other hand, the many examples of torture and tyranny still to be found in modern society remind us that social rights and the right to difference are not in themselves a sufficient condition for the realization of universal justice. One also requires the existence of a constitutional state (*un État de droit*) where both individuals and collectivities (*non-étatiques*) remain the ultimate subjects of right. And in this respect, Ricoeur observes, it is important to recall that the Kantian project of a 'civil society administering universal rights' has not yet been achieved. This project remains for us a fitting guide in our efforts to give *practical* shape to our utopian expectancies.

4 ibid. Before it is allowed to congeal into an inert deposit, tradition 'is an activity which can only be comprehended dialectically in the exchange between the past which is interpreted and the present which interprets' (*TN* vol. III, p. 228).

5 See Paul Ricoeur, 'Hermeneutics and the critique of ideology' in *Hermeneutics and the Human Sciences*, edited by John B. Thompson, Cambridge, Cambridge University Press, 1981, pp. 222–46.

6 Hannah Arendt, Preface to *Between Past and Future*, London, Faber, 1961, p. 9.

7 Paul Ricoeur, 'The creativity of language: an interview' in Richard Kearney, *Dialogues with Contemporary Continental Thinkers*, Manchester, Manchester University Press, 1984, pp. 29–30.

8 Walter Benjamin, 'Theses on the philosophy of history' in Hannah Arendt (ed.) *Illuminations*, London, Fontana, 1973, p. 57. Paul Ricoeur makes a similar point in *Time and Narrative* vol. I, translated by K. McLaughlin and D. Pellauer, Chicago, University of Chicago Press, 1984, pp. 68–70:

Let us understand by the term tradition not the inert transmission of some already dead deposit of material but the living transmission of an innovation always capable of being reactivated by a return to

71

the most creative moments of poetic activity . . . a tradition is constituted by the interplay of innovation and sedimentation. . . . Innovation remains a form of behaviour governed by rules. The labour of imagination is not born from nothing. It is bound in one way or another to tradition's paradigms. But the range of solutions is vast. It is deployed between the two poles of servile application and calculated deviation, passing through every degree of 'rule-governed deformation'. The folklore, the myth and in general the traditional narrative stand closest to the first pole. But to the extent that we distance ourselves from traditional narrative, deviation becomes the rule. . . . It remains, however, that the possibility of deviation is inscribed in the relation between sedimented paradigms and actual works. Short of the extreme case of schism, it is just the opposite of servile application. Rule-governed deformation constitutes the axis around which the various changes of paradigm through application are arranged. It is this variety of applications that confers a history on the productive imagination and that, in counterpoint to sedimentation, makes a narrative tradition possible.

9 Alasdair MacIntyre, *After Virtue*, London, Duckworth Press, 1981, p. 206.
10 Paul Ricoeur, 'The critique of religion' in *The Philosophy of Paul Ricoeur: An Anthology of his work*, edited by Charles E. Reagan and David Stewart, Boston, Beacon Press, 1978, p. 215.
11 For further discussion of this relationship between ideology and utopia see Paul Ricoeur, 'Science and ideology' in John B. Thompson (ed.) *Hermeneutics and the Human Sciences*, Cambridge, Cambridge University Press, 1981, pp. 222–47 as well as the Ricoeur texts cited in note 1. See also Karl Mannheim, *Ideology and Utopia*, London, Routledge & Kegan Paul, 1936; and Frederic Jameson, 'The dialectic of utopia and ideology' in *The Political Unconscious*, London, Methuen, 1981.
12 Paul Ricoeur, 'Myth as the bearer of possible worlds: an interview' in Richard Kearney, *Dialogues with Contemporary Continental Thinkers*, pp. 36–45.
13 On this distinction between the 'explanatory' and 'exploratory' functions of myth and the critical procedures of demythologization and demythization see Paul Ricoeur, *The Symbolism of Evil*, New York, Harper & Row, 1967; and 'The language of faith', *Union Seminary Quarterly Review*, no. 28, 1973, pp. 213–24. See also Rudolf Bultmann, *The Theology of the New Testament*, London, SCM, 1952, pp. 295ff. See also Rudolf Bultmann and Karl Jaspers, *Myth and Christianity*, New York, Noonday Press, 1957; and René Girard, 'Qu'est-ce qu'un Mythe' in *Le Bouc Emissaire*, Paris, Grasset, 1982. I have outlined a critique of Girard's position in 'René Girard et le Mythe comme Bouc Emissaire' in Dumouchel (ed.) *Violence et vérité*, Grasset, Paris, 1985, pp. 35–49. For an application of the demythologizing project to the national myths of Irish culture and politics see my 'Myth and motherland' in *Ireland's Field Day*, London, Hutchinson, 1985 and my *Transitions: Narratives in Contemporary Irish Culture*, in particular Part 4 on

'Ideological narratives', Manchester, Manchester University Press, 1987.

14 See our discussion of this theme in Kearney's *Poétique du possible*, Paris, Beauchesne, 1984, pp. 190–9.

15 Paul Ricoeur, 'Myth as the bearer of possible worlds', pp. 39–42.

16 Paul Ricoeur, 'Science and ideology', p. 245. See also Ricoeur's discussion of the Habermas/Gadamer hermeneutic debate on this rapport between belonging and critical distance in 'Hermeneutics and the critique of ideology', in *Hermeneutics and the Human Sciences*, pp. 63–100. Also his more recent analyses in *Lectures on Ideology and Utopia*, New York, Columbia University Press, 1986 and *Du Texte à l'action: essais d'herméneutique*, II, Paris, Editions du Seuil, 1990, especially Part III, entitled *Idéologie, utopie et politique*, pp. 281–406.

5

NARRATIVE AND PHILOSOPHICAL EXPERIENCE

Jonathan Rée

All great storytellers have in common the freedom with which they move up and down the rungs of their experience as on a ladder. A ladder extending downward to the interior of the earth and disappearing into the clouds is the image for a collective experience to which even the deepest shock of every individual experience, death, constitutes no impediment or barrier.

Walter Benjamin[1]

I am so convinced by Paul Ricoeur's view that narrative is the fundamental structure of the experience of time that I really have nothing to say about it. However, there does seem to me to be an empty space in Ricoeur's argument, at a place where one might have expected an interesting reflexive development. For whilst Ricoeur's interpretations of Proust, Woolf, Mann and Braudel will probably persuade us that novels and history books call upon a phenomenologically fundamental capacity for narrative, in readers and writers alike, they may also leave us wondering whether or not the same applies to theoretical works, and particularly to philosophy – even, perhaps to Ricoeur's own book.[2]

It is in fact quite startling, given its topic and its doctrine, that *Time and Narrative* is written with exemplary austerity: its structure and style are those of a universal encyclopedia, rather than an ingratiating story. But then, perhaps the idea of an encyclopedia itself encodes an essentially narrative theme: 'the circuit of an education' is what 'encyclopedia' ought to mean, according to its etymology; and the concept of education seems to be structured round an archetypal plot, which leads individuals from infancy through a series of ordeals which bring them closer and closer to the condition of a wise old man. This suggests that a theorist dedicated to metaphysical truth and a storyteller in thrall to human interest may have more in common than either of them suppose; indeed, they might turn out to be the same person, and writing exactly the same book.

The suggestion that philosophy resembles narrative, and might even be a form of it, is liable to seem a banal tautology: in some people's lexicons, the word 'narrative' has become so versatile that there is hardly anything to which it cannot be applied, from lyrical poems to logical proofs. My argument will not rely on any such terminological latitude however. In fact I shall use the word 'narrative' rather more specifically than Ricoeur and his excellent translators do. In *Time and Narrative*, it covers the same ground as 'story', and this is appropriate because Ricoeur's main purpose is to consider narrative in relation to temporality. But, as Ricoeur also emphasizes, narrative can also be connected with questions of personality, particularly through the ideas of 'narrative point of view' and 'narrative voice'. But point of view and (especially) voice are absent from most ways of presenting stories, or at least undeveloped: I am referring to epic, romance and especially drama. They come into their own in a specific way of presenting stories, and (like many theorists) I prefer to confine the term 'narrative' to this particular form. The essence of narrative, in this sense, is that it is narrated; that is to say, the audience is called upon to imagine, by a kind of projection, a definite person or personality telling the story. Oral storytellers employ narrative in this sense, especially in the genres of 'monologues' and children's stories. And narrative is also a speciality of the novel. Simone de Beauvoir bore witness to its power when she recollected her first encounter with *The Mill on the Floss*. Naturally enough she sympathized with Maggie Tulliver; but also, far more fatefully, she fell in love with the narrator: 'I identified with the author', she wrote; and 'one day other adolescents would bathe with their tears a novel in which I would tell my own sad story.'[3] Authors choose a narrative form when they want to give nuanced, perhaps ironical depictions of the inner lives of their characters, because narrative will make their audience weigh the words it hears not only as descriptions of a fictional world, but also as expressions of a narrator's personality. It will add a dimension of personal intimacy to the pleasure of following the story.

NARRATIVE AND THE IDEA OF MODERNITY

The suggestion that philosophy is narrative, or narrative-like, is in danger of getting itself entangled with two points commonly associated with modernity. Modernity (or the Enlightenment project) is said to be characterized by a naive faith in the possibility of representation, especially in epistemological senses of that word. It construes representation in an essentially geometrical way: that is to say, it takes itself to live in a spatial world which is completely amenable to visual inspection and mathematical calculation. Thereby, it violently suppresses all other worlds, and does so with a clear conscience because it is incapable of noticing their existence. It prides itself on its rationality and its science, and turns its back on feeling and virtue. In Richard Rorty's formulation, modernity makes a fetish of a fiction called 'the mind' which is supposed to reflect the world like a mirror; in Alasdair MacIntyre's version, it refuses to acknowledge the need for some conception of the goal of life, and consequently excludes itself from the personal fulfilment which it restlessly seeks; in Walter Ong's, it substitutes the cold impersonality and instantaneousness of the visual world (especially the printed page) for the warm togetherness of voice and temporality. Foucault discovers modernity in the displacement of analogy by analysis in 'the classical age'; Heidegger, in the rise of the representative 'world picture' in place of pre-modern 'expression'; and Dilthey in the defeat of the 'plastic thought' of the Renaissance by the sharp, unfeeling abstractions of Galileo and Descartes. Modernity, in other words, can be seen as a flight from temporality and personality – in short, from narrative.

At the hub of modernity, it seems, there is a certain theory of knowledge and of philosophy. Knowledge is a mirror, and the philosopher's business is to help you look into it, and see . . . not yourself, surprisingly enough, but the objective world. If the metaphor breaks down, this is only a symptom of the self-destruction of the project; so it seems a safe bet that the much-anticipated advent of post-modernity will involve a return to the unpretending ways of narrative, and a restoration of its rightful dominion over upstart science.

The most influential description of the deceptions in which modernity and philosophy are supposed to collude is in Hegel's *Lectures on the History of Philosophy*. The 'culture of modern times', Hegel said, began with Descartes, who 'made it his starting-point that philosophic propositions must be mathematically handled and proved' – which was a deep mistake, since 'the mathematical method . . . is ill-adapted for speculative content.' Thus in order to understand Descartes properly, according to Hegel, we must extricate the content of his work, which alone has 'universal interest', from the inappropriate mathematical form in which Descartes expressed it.

I am not sure it has been sufficiently noticed how paradoxical it is that Hegel should advise us to forget about the deductive, mathematical 'form' of Descartes's philosophy. It is not just that Hegel prided himself on studying philosophers in their own words; nor is it only that, as a matter of rather obvious fact, Descartes's principal writings (the *Discourse on Method* and the *Meditations*) show no trace of the irksome form from which Hegel promises to liberate them (they are very conspicuously cast as narratives, one as an autobiography and the other as a diary). The chief paradox is that Hegel should not have hailed the alleged (if imaginary) contradiction between the speculative kernel of Descartes's philosophy and its mathematical shell as the very essence of modernity: a narrative content (he could have said) masquerading as the antithesis of narrative.

This leads me to the second of the two well-known points about modernity which I mentioned. This too can be expressed in terms of philosophy and narrativity. But on this view – which is associated particularly with post-structuralism – the vice of modern philosophy is not its repression of narrativity, but its exorbitant, indeed Procrustean imposition of it – both in its temporal aspect (historicism) and in its personal one (humanism): hence modernity, in short, is bewitched by a single 'grand' narrative, telling of man's great journey of self-discovery.

It seems then that modern philosophy is criticized first for neglecting narrative and then for being obsessed with it. Of course, there is no need to blame this inconsistency on the theorists of modernity. It may be, for example, that early modernity (up to 1800, let us say) was anti-narrative, whilst modern modernity is the opposite. But it would be more plausible to say that the two conflicting impulses are both present in the modern world, and that this is exactly the neurosis of modernity and modern philosophy: they pretend to be the negation of narrative, which is in fact their very element: they are subject to a narrative compulsion which they can neither control nor acknowledge. The discontents

of civilization, therefore, are due to the tormentingly repeated
return of the narrativity which its philosophy tries, in vain, to
repress.

THEORY AND PRACTICE

Attractive as such diagnoses of the philosophical ailments of
modernity may be, there is something about them that puts me
off – the manner of a wily investigator, sleuthing out the relationship between philosophy and narrative, and triumphantly
brandishing the findings as if they proved a guilty secret: the
very philosophers who had been self-righteously promoting the
claims of perspectiveless epistemology and timeless metaphysics
are shown to be, in practice, mixed up with narrative, in other
words with time and personal point of view. But even if it is true
that philosophers typically tell stories, and that these stories are,
paradoxically enough, evocations of the possibility of transcending story-telling, this could be a proof of their sophistication,
rather than a demonstration that they have wasted their time and
ours in an enterprise whose self-stultifying fraudulence has only
now been exposed. Actually, the diagnosticians of modernity's
discontents might perhaps be advised to attend to their own contra-
dictions before prescribing remedies for those of others. (They
might consider, for example, whether their own notions of modernity
and philosophy are not infected with the same chauvinism of the
present moment, and the same essentialism about intellectual
genres and historical epochs, which they see as the plague of the
modern world.)

The anti-narrativism which is supposed to be essential to philosophy has two aspects: literalism, or the belief that true knowledge
can and must be transmitted directly and impersonally, in no
particular voice and from no particular point of view; and simultaneism, or the belief that proper knowledge must be apprehended
all at once, so that it can elude the pitfalls of fallible memory.
And in some cases at least, it seems to be true that philosophers
have deluded themselves that the field of knowledge lies spread
out before their mind's eye, and that they have found a frictionless
and absolutely faithful way of transcribing it. John Stuart Mill,
notorious as the Gradgrind of Victorian philosophy, is an obvious
case in point. For did he not denounce 'narrative' on the grounds
that it was preoccupied with external incident at the expense of

spiritual truth? And did he not imagine that he could provide a completely neutral record of the truths of science and logic?

Perhaps. On the other hand, though, he was famously persuaded of the indispensability of poetry (though only, it must be admitted, if the poems were sufficiently short to avoid lapsing into narrative). And he even argued that illusions could in some ways be 'better than the truth'. In his diary, he wrote that

> those who think themselves called upon, in the name of truth, to make war against illusions, do not perceive the distinction between an illusion and a delusion. A delusion is an erroneous opinion – it is a believing a thing which is not. An illusion, on the contrary, is an affair solely of feeling, and may exist completely severed from delusion. It consists in extracting from a conception known not to be true, but which is better than the truth, the same benefit to the feelings which would be derived from it if it were a reality.[5]

And if you turn from Mill's programmatic statements to his actual literary and theoretical practice, you will find that, far from shunning narrative, Mill exploits it to the full. This obviously applies to the *Autobiography* which – though intended as his last philosophical testament – is not a compilation of timeless truths, but a time-obsessed tale about the sequence, date and duration of the various delusions that had enthralled the evidently idiosyncratic narrator. But it also applies to the *System of Logic*, which is written with the same attention to expository sequence as one would expect from a novelist;[6] and which, again like a novel, fascinates (and perhaps repels) its reader by the constant presence of the narrator's sometimes unctuous personality, as revealed, for instance, in warnings against 'the shallow conceptions and incautious proceedings of mere logicians'; and in the painstaking way Mill introduces and assesses the large cast of characters who populate his pages: not just 'quasi-characters' (in Ricoeur's useful phrase) such as Mysticism, but actual people: Hobbes, Whewell, Whately, d'Alembert, Coleridge, Leibniz and even, very coyly, James Mill ('an authority I am less likely than any other person to undervalue').

The *System of Logic* is, then, drenched in temporality and animated by a strongly characterized narrator. Of course, Mill believed in the existence of 'great moral truths', and this old-fashioned conviction may raise a sarcastic smile from most critics of modernity. But he also believed that the meaning of 'the more serious convictions of mankind' was 'always in a process either of being lost or of being recovered' – a belief which evidently justified him in writing books which in some ways resemble novels about a character – the narrator – who is always in search of the highest truths, but who never quite gets to them. Their interest and their power to move or instruct their readers, therefore, depend hardly at all on the acceptability, in the last analysis, of the belief that there are such truths. They would be unimpaired, for example, if the belief had to be demoted to the status of an unrealizable principle of hope: and then there would be no trace of the comic mismatch of philosophical belief and literary practice for which post-philosophical commentators are on the lookout.

Of course, the fact that Mill's philosophy is narrativistic does not mean that anyone else's is. Indeed, his leanings towards German thought, his love of 'heroism', and his revulsion from eighteenth-century utilitarianism may make him a wholly untypical figure. On the other hand, it is striking that almost the same pattern can be found in his loved and hated mentor, Jeremy Bentham, whose excesses in the pursuit of literalism and simultaneism are probably more extreme than the most savage caricatures of philosophical folly. He believed that all knowledge ought to be presented in 'synoptic tables' – tree diagrams which would display all facts simultaneously as 'so many parts of one and the same picture', and he believed that, especially for philosophical, legal and political purposes, language ought to be purged of all terms whose meaning could not be presented in such diagrams.

But his repeated failure to get his synoptic method into working order led him to the eventual conviction that it was a hopeless task to try to eliminate 'fictionality' and 'figurativeness' from language, desirable as it might be; and so he began to revel in this messy residue of (as he saw it) unreason. This not only made his writings veer wildly between laughable solemnity and oppressive flippancy; it also opens them, like Mill's, to a narrative interpretation, so that they can be read as a picaresque account of his own perverse adoration for the admittedly impracticable idea of escaping narrativity altogether. The most anti-narrativist of philosophers thus turns out to be a waggish raconteur.

PHILOSOPHICAL EXPERIENCE

The cases of Bentham and Mill are, of course, only infinitesimal evidence of a general affinity between narrative (which deals with personality and fleeting experience) and the traditional aims of philosophy, to which it is so widely assumed to be totally opposed. So I shall conclude by trying to make the case on general grounds.

If the works which are called philosophical have anything in common apart from a contingent identity conferred by academic institutions and library catalogues, it is their concern with argument, with dialectic. Another way of expressing this commonplace, is that philosophers are normally on peculiarly intimate terms with the doctrines which they want to rebut: they cultivate error, try to show it to its best advantage, and then, rather than abruptly discarding it, they criticize it repeatedly, offering diagnoses rather than denunciations, and showing no desire to move on to something else.

One natural way of presenting this sort of procedure is Plato's dramatic dialogue, where different characters speak their own words without the interference of a narrator. But problems arise when writers try to achieve the same effects without resort to drama. In *The Principles of Human Knowledge*, Berkeley laid the following trap for his readers: 'We see only the appearances, and not the real qualities of things. What may be the extension, figure or motion of any thing really or absolutely, or in itself, it is impossible for us to know.'[7] The problem with these sentences, of course, is that they say the opposite of what Berkeley is usually presumed to really mean; but there is no explicit warning (such as quotation marks, or a frame sentence like 'Some people may argue that . . .') to alert readers to the fact. You just have to approach them carefully by way of the preceding sentences:

Colour, figure, motion, extension, and the like, considered only as so many *sensations* in the mind, are perfectly known, there being nothing in them which is not perceived. But if they are looked on as notes or images, referred to *things* or *archetypes* existing without the mind, then are we involved all in scepticism. We see only the appearances.

But an author's problems in presenting such a journey-through-error without baffling the readers can be solved, to a large extent, by exploiting the principal resources of narrative, namely time,

81

and narrative personality. The simplest use of the first is when a doctrine which is to be examined is assigned to a specific time in the past. Histories of philosophy can be seen as deployments of this technique, but there are many other examples: Descartes's *Discourse* and *Meditations* have already been mentioned; or there is the opening of Spinoza's *On the Improvement of the Understanding*:

> After experience had taught me that all the usual surround-ings of social life are vain and futile . . . I finally resolved to inquire whether . . . there might be anything the discovery and attainment of which would enable me to enjoy continu-ous, supreme, and unending happiness. . . . I therefore debated whether it would not be possible to arrive at the new principle . . . without changing the conduct and usual plan of my life; with this end in view I made many efforts, but in vain.[8]

The second device – narrative personality – incites the philos-opher's readers to project a definite image of the mind from which the philosophy is supposed to be issuing, and of the relations it has with other characters (and quasi-characters). Great philosophical writers (Wittgenstein and Heidegger, for example) may owe much of their power to the ways in which their readers are left with a deep impression of a personal style, a narrative voice no less vivid than those of, say, Charles Dickens or George Eliot.

A less formal way of putting this point is that philosophy is a branch of writing concerned with a particular kind of experience. Just as elegies are concerned with the loss of people you love, so works of philosophy deal with events when you find meaning slipping away from you, and you recognize the vacuity or friability of convictions which you used to think were as solid as a rock.

This suggests that the question of the actual attainability of absolute knowledge or complete understanding, whilst it may be central to philosophy, is perhaps its least important part. For as Kierkegaard wrote in his dairy:

> It is quite true what philosophy says: that Life must be understood backwards. But that makes one forget the other saying: that it must be lived – forwards. The more one ponders this, the more it comes to mean that life in temporal existence never becomes quite intelligible, precisely because

at no moment can I find complete quiet to take the back-ward-looking position.[9]

The endless postponement of the moment of truth is perhaps also, finally, the reason why the idea of a ladder stretching from far below us, through our own finite vantage-point, and stretching on until it disappears from sight, is a natural metaphor not only for story-telling but for philosophy too; the image, as Benjamin saw, 'for a collective experience to which even the deepest shock of every individual experience, death, constitutes no impediment or barrier'.[10]

The insistently personal and temporal devices of narrative, mar-vellously described by Ricoeur, are, if I am right, peculiarly suit-able for treating experiences of this kind. This opens out the prospect of giving his work a reflexive turn, which might enable us to understand the variety of philosophical classics not just in terms of worn-out doctrinal categories (like realism or idealism) but in terms of the kinds of emplotment they use in response to the elusive difficulties of philosophical experience.

NOTES

1 Walter Benjamin, 'The Storyteller' (1936), in Hannah-Arendt (ed.) *Illuminations*, translated by Harry Zohn, London, Jonathan Cape, 1970, p. 102.
2 Paul Ricoeur, *Time and Narrative*, translated by Kathleen McLaughlin and David Pellauer, Chicago, University of Chicago Press, 1984–8.
3 Simone de Beauvoir, *Memoirs of a Dutiful Daughter*, translated by James Kirkup, Harmondsworth, Penguin, 1963, p. 140.
4 G. W. F. Hegel, *Lectures on the History of Philosophy*, translated by E. S. Haldane and E. F. Simson, London, Kegan Paul, 1892–6, vol. III, pp. 282, 224.
5 Diary entry for 11 January 1854; see J. B. Schneedwind (ed.), *Mill's Essays on Literature and Society*, New York, Collier Books, 1965, p. 348.
6 John Stuart Mill, *A System of Logic* in J. M. Robson (ed.) *Collected Works*, vols VII and VIII, Toronto, University of Toronto Press, 1973–4, pp. 683, 40, 682, 684.
7 *The Principles of Human Knowledge*, London, Fontana, 1962, I, p. 87.
8 *On the Improvement of the Understanding*, translated by R. H. M. Elwes, New York, Dover, 1955, p. 1.
9 Søren Kierkegaard, *The Diary of Søren Kierkegaard*, edited by Peter Rohde, New York, Philosophical Library, 1960, section 136 (1843), p. 111.
10 Benjamin, 'The Storyteller', p. 102.

6

RICOEUR, PROUST AND THE APORIAS OF TIME

Rhiannon Goldthorpe

Ricoeur's monumental meditation upon time and narrative ends where Proust's even more monumental novel begins: with the word 'recherche'.[1] It is the keyword of Proust's title, *A la recherche du temps perdu*, and the keyword of Ricoeur's penultimate sentence in *Temps et récit*. There it opens up new perspectives at the very moment when – given the title of the last of Ricoeur's three volumes, *Le Temps raconté* – we had expected completion. The title of Proust's last volume, *Le Temps retrouvé*, suggests, too, the conclusion of his hero's search. But both titles have in common a deceptive simplicity and a deceptive conclusiveness. Their simplicity is deceptive because both are ambiguous (and therefore untranslatable). Is *Le Temps raconté* time narrated (whether fictionally or historically), time recounted, or time told? Does the noun designate a single, specific time or the plurality implicit in a collective singular? Is *Le Temps retrouvé* to be understood as time, once lost or wasted, now recovered, or does it imply the loss of the intuition of eternity with the reinstatement of time? Each title is deceptively conclusive because both volumes imply the absence of any transcendent vantage-point from which time could be definitively told. Ricoeur's search implies, but does not yet take, a step beyond the limits of narrative; Proust's novel ends, when his hero Marcel has reached the limits of his provisional narrative, with the tentative promise, in the conditional tense, of a future work.[2] Further, Ricoeur's inconclusiveness depends in large measure on his having taken Proust's as a test-case: Proust the novelist falsifies the philosopher's hypothesis, stimulating a new search and new hypotheses. But Proust, whether knowingly or not, falsifies his own. He does so not simply and explicitly in the linear movement of the narrative, in which reinstated time follows the hero's intuitions of the extra-temporal. He does so (or time – 'l'Artiste, le temps' – does so) at the very moment when those intuitions seem to confirm the hypothesis that time can be transcended. I propose to consider those moments of self-subverting confirmation in relation to the hypotheses both of Proust (or of his hero-narrator), and of Ricoeur.

Ricoeur's relevant hypothesis is that fiction may be capable of resolving the aporias of time which, he thinks, have effectively resisted the solutions offered by philosophical speculation – aporias which our urge to narrate confronts. Ricoeur suggests that they are, first, the impossibility of reconciling the phenomenological perspective of lived time with the perspective of cosmological time; second, the problem of reconciling our experience of the dispersal of time in the three *ekstases* of past, present and future with the notion of time as a unified whole – a notion which would imply both the possibility of our thinking about time from a point outside time, and the possibility of exploring the relationship between time and its 'other' – eternity. These major aporias bring with them numerous secondary but none the less crucial ones (for instance, the alterity of the past set against its persistence in the present, the present conceived as a 'punctual' instant or as duration); they are explicit throughout Ricoeur's analysis, and he is concerned to show that philosophical reflection, from Aristotle to Heidegger, has failed to resolve them. Rather, he argues, our most fundamental mode of resolving them is through the poetic, rather than theoretical, mediation of narrative.

Further, the mediation betweeen time and its aporias on the one hand, and narrative itself on the other hand, is effected, he suggests, through the three stages of a process of mimesis. The first, *Mimesis I*, or 'figuration', refers us to the pre-comprehension or implicit understanding which we have of human action and its temporality – that is to say, of the way in which everyday activity orders past, present and future in relation to each other. Such an understanding recognizes in action itself temporal structures which prefigure narration. *Mimesis II* involves the operation of 'configuration' or emplotment in narrative: the term 'emplotment', or 'mise en intrigue', rather than simply 'plot' or 'intrigue', stresses the dynamic quality of the operation. It acts as the crucial pivot between our pre-comprehension of the temporality of practical action and the transfigured understanding of a re-ordered temporality which we achieve in our reading of the literary work. The pivotal function of emplotment operates in three ways: it mediates between individual events and the story taken as a whole; it integrates heterogeneous elements such as agents, ends, means, interactions and circumstances; and it mediates by both reflecting and resolving, in its own temporal structures, the paradox of temporality. It does so by combining the linear chronology of its purely episodic elements with a new dimension deriving from a sense of closure and totality, whereby the so-called 'natural' order of time is reversed, and, in retrospect, events and episodes are seen not as having occurred in simple succession, but as having been ordered in relation to that end. In his discussion of *Mimesis III*, or the process of 'refiguration', Ricoeur develops Wolfgang Iser's phenomenology of the act of reading in order to suggest that the text offers, in its configuration, a set of instructions which the reader actualizes or performs, whether passively or creatively. This activity will enable the reader, particularly in the process of rereading, to achieve a new evaluation of time and reality which will itself open out onto the world of action. The power of fiction to effect a poetic resolution of the aporias of time, and the limits of that power, are illustrated in Ricoeur's analysis of three works, chosen not only because they exemplify the temporal implications of the process of emplotment outlined above, but because they themselves thematize time, as Ricoeur puts it. That is to say, the lived experiences of the characters themselves create a number of imaginative variations on the aporias of time which transcend the everyday, which attempt to resolve the lived experience of 'discordance' within a 'concordant' verbal structure, and which are offered to the reader with a view to his refiguration of his ordinary temporal experience. These works are *Mrs Dalloway*, *Der Zauberberg*, and *A la recherche du temps perdu*, and it is to Proust that Ricoeur gives the last word.

Ricoeur takes as the focus of his argument those episodes of involuntary memory which the ageing Marcel experiences at the Guermantes party in *Le Temps retrouvé* – episodes which are associated with an intuition of the extra-temporal and the eternal. Ricoeur's contention is that these intuitions are not themselves the experience of 'time regained'. They are simply a transition between the experience of time lost – whether interpreted as time past, as time wasted, or as time dispersed – and the retrieval of lost time through the composition of the work of art. He argues, moreover, that this retrieval is itself threatened by the inevitability of old age and death, and accompanied by the knowledge that the work of art must be composed within the same unstable temporal dimension as that of lost time. The emplotment of the novel thus sets the intuition of eternity achieved through involuntary memory against the disillusion which precedes that intuition and the awareness of mortality which follows it, thereby exploring the aporia of time as dispersal and as unity (Ricoeur vol. II, pp. 212–18; pp. 143–8). But during the earlier period of lost time – and this is a particularly stimulating section of Ricoeur's argument – the thematic configuration of the text is shown to anticipate a number of other solutions: the stylistic solution of the metaphor (which I shall discuss more fully later), the optical solution, as Ricoeur calls it, of recognition, and the spiritual solution of the retrieved impression (Ricoeur vol. II, pp. 218–23; pp. 148–51). This spiritual solution in itself involves a triple process: Marcel's deciphering of the signs of lost time in the experience of love or of social life, his intuition of the relationship between the traces of his impressions and the creation of the work of art which explores their meaning, and, finally, the discovery of the reversible equation between life and literature which that relationship effects. Now Ricoeur's analysis of Proust is all the more stimulating in that it precedes his consideration of the role of the reader in the refiguration of experience which fiction brings about. Ricoeur does not subsequently return to his discussion of Proust. But if we pursue his earlier analysis of *A la recherche du temps perdu* in the light of the process of reading, which involves its own transactions between present attention, memory and anticipation, we in fact find a greatly heightened, though by no means entirely negative, tension between the linear and non-linear aspects of emplotment and configuration and their attendant aporias – a tension more acute than Ricoeur himself suggests. Furthermore, the 'concordant' moment of Marcel's discovery – the intuition of eternity and of the extra-temporal – is undermined, we discover, not only in the forward movement of emplotment and the renewed realization of 'discordance' analysed by Ricoeur. As we shall see, it is more crucially undermined at the very moment of its enunciation, or of our reading of its enunciation, although – and this is one of the major paradoxes of the reading process – that undermining is not, itself, enunciated. It occurs at one of the points when the reader confronts the 'said' with the 'unsaid': one of those places of indeterminacy, as they are termed by Ingarden, Iser and, in turn, Ricoeur: one of those blanks which, according to Iser, 'arise out of contingency and inexperience-ability', but which underlie all processes of interaction – including the interaction of reader and text.[3] As Iser suggests, when the 'unsaid' comes to life in the reader's imagination, so the 'said' expands to take on greater significance than might have been supposed. And since, as Ricoeur maintains, our experience of time (as distinct from temporality) is mute, it might seem to be particularly appropriate to consider its articulation in the 'unsaid' of the text. This is what I now propose to do.

But first, what happens at the 'said' level of the text at that crucial moment when Marcel – who is both the protagonist and the narrator of events – experiences the revelation of the extra-temporal and perceives the relationship between involuntary memory, the discovery of the identity of the self, and the creation of the work of art? (And we may notice that at this point in the narrative there is no irony-generating gap between protagonist and narrator: the gap is located elsewhere.) Marcel, stumbling on a paving stone in the Guermantes courtyard, as he had, years before, stumbled on the uneven stones of St Mark's Square, is invaded by a long-forgotten vision of Venice. Then the chink of a spoon on a plate revives the train journey of the previous day, when he had been convinced of his lack of creativity. A moment later the touch of a starched napkin brings back the sight of the sea – the 'blue breasts' of the sea – which he discovered from his window during his first visit, as a young boy, to Balbec (Proust vol. IV, pp. 445–8; Kilmartin, pp. 898–901). Each experience brings with it a feeling of intense joy and of the irrelevance of death. Each suggests an identity (the word is Marcel's) between the present and the hitherto forgotten past – for involuntary memory depends upon a prior forgetting. It is an identity which sets the common elements of present and past outside time, where consciousness can both passively and actively enjoy their extra-temporal essence, where the vicissitudes of the future and the threat of death itself are annulled, where man is freed of the order of time. And it now seems possible – indeed, necessary – to translate such intuitions into an 'équivalent spirituel', a work of art in which the superimposing of two terms in metaphor will seal the identity of two moments in time 'et les enfermera dans les anneaux nécessaires d'un beau style' (Proust vol. IV, p. 468).[4] An affirmation, then, of extra-temporality, of identity and of necessity – in two senses, it may be noted, of the term necessity. This, then, is what we are explicitly both shown and told. But what we are shown, both here and elsewhere in the text, at the implicit level of the untold and the unsaid, is something quite other: an undermining of the extra-temporal at the very moment when it is postulated. We are shown through a 'blank' in the narrative not what is common to two different moments, but two different and mutually self-cancelling memories of the same moment, offered without commentary. And we are shown metaphor functioning not as the abstracting and superimposing of a common element, but as metamorphosis, as constantly mobile redescription, which the reader registers not by closing the gap between the first and second term, but by reading the gap between successive second terms. These discrepancies and mobilities of memory and metaphor arise from those places of indeterminacy within the configuration of the text which are regis-tered in the act of reading: they may create a sense of temporal indeterminacy at the level of refiguration, but they will still depend upon the time of narrative and reading. This process whereby the 'said' is negated by the 'unsaid' and moves to a new significance is best exemplified by what appears to be the last episode of involuntary recall experienced at the Guermantes party. (It is not, incidentally, mentioned by Ricoeur, but it exemplifies particularly clearly if, again, implicitly, the perhaps unconscious discordance which underlies Marcel's experience of concordance.) After the paving stones, the spoon, and the napkin it brings back to life the earliest, and the most seminal, of the recollected moments. While waiting in the library and pondering on memory Marcel finds by chance a copy of George Sand's novel *François le Champi*, and he is disconcerted by the sudden pang of suffering which it releases, and which, though intense, is none the less in tune with his present joy:

> Je m'étais au premier instant demandé avec colère quel était l'étranger qui venait me faire mal. Cet étranger, c'était moi-même, c'était l'enfant que j'étais alors, que le livre venait de susciter en moi, car, de moi ne connaissant que cet enfant, c'est cet enfant que le livre avait appelé tout de suite, ne voulant être regardé que par ses yeux, aimé que par son coeur, et ne parler qu'à lui. Aussi ce livre que ma mère m'avait lu haut à Combray presque jusqu'au matin, avait-il gardé pour moi tout le charme de cette nuit-là.
>
> (Proust vol. IV, pp. 462–3)

My first reaction had been to ask myself, angrily, who this stranger was who was coming to trouble me. The stranger was none other than myself, the child I had been at that time, brought to life within me by the book, which knowing nothing of me except this child had instantly summoned him to its presence, wanting to be seen only by his eyes, to be loved only by his heart, to speak only to him. And this book which my mother had read aloud to me at Combray until the early hours of the morning had kept for me all the charm of that night.

(Kilmartin vol. III, p. 920–1)

Oblivion alone had made possible the survival of the moment now remembered. But what the reader remembers, or may remember, is that Marcel's account – much earlier in the novel, but also narrated in retrospect – of his mother's reading of *François le Champi* had never depended upon the sudden upsurge of involuntary memory. It had been part of that narrow segment in time and space of bedtime in the old house in Combray – a segment which had always remained within Marcel's recall through its association with the trauma of his mother's absence and of the withheld goodnight kiss, and through its association, too, with the unexpected comfort of her reading, in compensation, from his grandmother's new birthday present to him, specially unwrapped – *François le Champi* (Proust vol. I, p. 41–3; Kilmartin vol. I, p. 44–6). That segment did not need for its recovery the power of the madeleine dipped in tea which recreated the rest of Combray, its church, its two walks, the other rooms of the old house. It lies outside that orbit, but not outside time. It precedes the tasting of the madeleine in the order of the narrative and in the order of events, but the chronology of its recollection in relation to those other revived memories, and the point in time from which it is retrospectively narrated, are both indeterminate. Its significance is qualitative, rather than datable. What we had taken to be the availability for memory of this experience had, as we thought, created or maintained continuity, but not order, within an other-wise discontinuous experience. But now, it seems, towards the end of the novel, a new discontinuity intervenes: involuntary memory implies not simply the narrator's having forgotten, but his having forgotten that he had always ostensibly been capable of remember-ing the experience in question. Now this gap, this indeterminacy, this negation within the narration of time, this discrepancy between narrated time and read time may well lead us to reflect not only on the 'said' relationship between memory and artistic vocation, but on the 'unsaid' indeterminacies of chronology and memory in experience itself. The temporal discrepancies or apparent imperfections of textual configuration may therefore stimulate, at the thematic level, a more complex refiguration of experience. For the fragility of continuity and with it, perhaps, the vulnerability of an ageing consciousness, is dramatized anew, and more radically, at the moment of its rediscovery, generating a sense of pathetic irony which is never registered by the oblivious and euphoric narrator.

But the reader may find other ways of satisfying the urge for coherence which is, according to Iser, so fundamental to the act of reading, and which Proust's text thematically frustrates. The reader may seek to motivate consistency at the level of the requirements of narration itself, rather than at the level of what is – or, indeed, is not – narrated. For Marcel's sudden recall at the Guermantes party of the night when his mother gave way to his childish distress dramatizes the major reversal of the 'plot' of the narrative – whether we take it to be the 'plot' of Marcel's own history or the 'plot' of Proust's fiction. This reversal is the change from Marcel's conviction of his creative impotence, born that night, to an equally strong sense of his determination to fulfil his artistic vocation, born at the moment of remembering – a reversal all the more poignant given the life-span of the intervening interval and the fortuitousness of its elision. The reader recognizes in this reversal one of the most familiar of plot patterns – that of 'loser wins' – and that recognition may absorb the apparent inconsistency of what is narrated into the coherence of the narrative form: a response which itself enacts the ability of narrative to impose pattern – or enacts our need for narrative as a creator of pattern. Does experience motivate narration, or does narration motivate experience, exemplifying through a form of inverted causality that reversal of the so-called 'natural' order of time analysed by Ricoeur? It is not only involuntary memory which presupposes forgetting: for the drama of moral and aesthetic reversal to occur, what had always been remembered must also be forgotten. So we become aware of the paradoxes of time not simply through emplotment itself, but through the dramatization, implicit but none the less crucial, of the relationship, and the space, between

experience or figuration on the one hand and emplotment or configuration on the other. And even if we accept the fiction that the
narrative we are reading is not yet fiction, is not yet the work of art
which Marcel proposes to write, we find that, like any narrative,
autobiographical or historical, it is drawn within the orbit of fiction. It is subject to what Ricoeur calls the 'crossed reference' of
history and fiction – the insertion of the imaginary within our
reconstruction of the past, the imitation of historical narrative in
our fictions – an interdependence which is necessary for the production of meaning, however provisional that meaning may be
(Ricoeur vol. III, pp. 264–79; pp. 180–192). This relationship
reminds us that we need to narrate our life to ourselves, to tell
tales to ourselves about it so that we may find it legible.

However, Marcel's rediscovery of *François le Champi* does not
only enact the instability of unity and dispersal, of continuity and
discontinuity in time and narration. It reminds us, too, of the
charms and imperfections of reading itself – of those indeterminacies, and of the elusiveness of meaning which, *in* reading, we
have just been experiencing. It also reminds us of the discrepancies
between the creation and the reception of a text, whether caused
by wilful repression, by the contingencies of misunderstanding, or,
again, by the imperfections of memory. In recalling the night when
his mother stayed to read with him Marcel also remembers 'ce
qui m'avait semblé inexplicable dans le sujet de *François le Champi*
tandis que maman me lisait le livre de Georges Sand' (Proust vol.
IV, p. 462) ('what had seemed to me too deep for understanding
in the subject of *François le Champi* when my mother long ago had
read the book aloud to me' (Kilmartin vol. III, p. 919). And if
we go back ourselves to his earlier account of that night we find
that the book's persistent and enigmatic charm, whether at the
conscious or unconscious level of memory, has very little to do
with the coherence and completeness of the reading. Further, Proust's reader finds it impossible to locate the point in time at which
the older Marcel became aware of the gaps in his mother's reading,
and may therefore later call into question the dramatic and seminal
rediscovery of *François le Champi* in the Guermantes library:

> L'action s'engagea; elle me parut d'autant plus obscure que
> dans ce temps-là, quand je lisais, je rêvassais souvent à tout
> autre chose. Et aux lacunes que cette distraction laissait dans
> le récit, s'ajoutait, quand c'était maman qui me lisait à haute

voix, qu'elle passait toutes les scènes d'amour. Aussi tous
les changements bizarres qui se produisent dans l'attitude
respective de la meunière et de l'enfant et qui ne trouvent
leur explication que dans les progrès d'un amour naissant
me paraissaient empreints d'un profond mystère dont je me
figurais volontiers que la source devait être dans ce nom
inconnu et si doux de 'Champi' qui mettait sur l'enfant
qui le portait sans que je susse pourquoi, sa couleur vive,
empourprée et charmante.

(Proust vol. I, p. 41)

The plot began to unfold: to me it seemed all the more
obscure because in those days, when I read, I used often to
daydream about something quite different for page after
page. And the gaps which this habit left in my knowledge
of the story were widened by the fact that when it was
Mamma who was reading aloud she left all the love-scenes
out. And so all the odd changes which take place in the
relations between the miller's wife and the boy, changes
which only the gradual dawning of love can explain, seemed
to me steeped in a mystery the key to which (I readily
believed) lay in that strange and mellifluous name of *Champi*,
which invested the boy who bore it, I had no idea why, with
its own vivid, ruddy, charming colour.

(Kilmartin vol. I, p. 45)

Further, Marcel refuses to fill in those blanks for the reader of his
own narrative. We have to discover from our own repertoire of
knowledge that what Marcel's mother repressed was the detail
of the love and eventual marriage of a foundling child and his
third adoptive mother. We have to register for ourselves the irony
of Marcel's response to the name of Champi, which signifies for
its bearer, and for the community in which he lives, the stigma of
having been abandoned in the fields, and the burden of having to
justify his precarious existence. We may or may not perceive the
contrast between the courage of the foundling François and
the distress of the cosseted Marcel, deprived of his goodnight kiss.
We may or may not notice the 'embedding' of the motif of loss
and recovery when the older Marcel finds the book *François le
Champi* again in the Guermantes library, and, with it, rediscovers
the child he was. Our reading, we gather, like Marcel's, must

93

depend on the vagaries of performance, knowledge and memory, and may be as vulnerable as his reading of his own experience.[5]

The instability of involuntary memory seems, then, to offer a fragile basis for the extra-temporal stability of identity which Marcel seeks, and thinks he has found. Is he less deluded in his trust in metaphor? For if the mediating event, passively undergone, between past, present and future is the experience of involuntary memory, its mediating expression is the metaphor. Indeed, involuntary memory is a lived metaphor which is the fruit of chance, but which none the less, as we saw earlier, turns contingency into necessity and the transient into the eternal.

> la vérité ne commencera qu'au moment où l'écrivain prendra deux objets différents, posera leur rapport, analogue dans le monde de l'art à celui qu'est le rapport unique de la loi causale dans le monde de la science, et les enfermera dans les anneaux nécessaires d'un beau style, ainsi que la vie, quand, en rapprochant une qualité commune à deux sensations, il dégagera leur essence commune en les réunissant l'une et l'autre pour les soustraire aux contingences du temps, dans une métaphore.
>
> (Proust vol. IV, p. 468)

> truth will be attained by [the writer] only when he takes two different objects, states the connexion between them – a connexion analogous in the world of art to the unique connexion which in the world of science is provided by the law of causality – and encloses them in the necessary links [circle] of a well-wrought style; truth – and life too – can be attained . . . only when, by comparing a quality common to two sensations, [he succeeds] in extracting their common essence and in reuniting them to each other, liberated from the contingencies of time, within a metaphor.
>
> (Kilmartin vol. III, p. 924–5)

Or, as Proust puts it elsewhere, it is only through metaphor that style can achieve eternity.[6] In theory, then, as Marcel the narrator tells us, metaphor too creates that extra-temporal truth which he seeks: a superimposing of the same within the other or the different, the discovery and invention of identity not only within the self and within the external world but between both, outside time: an intuition of mystical stasis. It would appear that through his narrator Proust attempts to resolve the major aporias of time – the problem of reconciling dispersal with unity, the same with the different, or of perceiving the relationship between time and eternity – by asserting the possibility of moving outside time altogether. But the metaphors which reveal and recreate Marcel's experiences are, we discover, of a quite different order.

If we look at the narrator's commentary on involuntary memory and metaphor we find that it is on the whole less rich in metaphor than many of the preceding three thousand or so pages. But it is extremely difficult to read those metaphors which we do find in a way which bears out the narrator's theory. For as they exploit our own reading memory, we read them as expressions not of mystical stasis but of the movement of time, and as moments of reading which carry with them their own retentions and protentions, or their own potential for anticipation and retrospection. For instance, when the touch of the starched napkin at the Guermantes party evokes the first visit to Balbec, the vision of the sea 'se gonfla en mamelles bleuâtres' (Proust vol. IV, p. 447), the blue breasts of its waves – its 'blue and bosomy undulations' (Kilmartin vol. III, p. 901) – eclipsing the present hôtel de Guermantes. Now at first this metaphor might indeed reinforce the sense of superimposed identical moments which abolish the passage of time, for we remember that Marcel, contemplating the sea at Balbec years before, had described and remembered the languid waves as the lazy, gently breathing beauty of an indolent water-nymph (Proust vol. II, p. 65).[7] But that memory casts the reader's mind forward to a later memory associated with the second visit to Balbec when Marcel, looking again at the sea, remembers the 'molle palpitation' and the 'sein bleuâtre' of the sea personified in his earlier metaphor. He now consciously rejects it: 'ce voisinage fluide, inaccessible et mythologique de l'Océan éternel n'existait plus pour moi' (Proust vol. III, p. 179) ('the fluid, inaccessible, mythological proximity of the eternal Ocean, no longer existed for me' (Kilmartin vol. II, p. 811)). He now sees it as a modern landscape, earthy, solid, but dynamic; no longer an eternal ocean, but inscribed in time. However, the change does not bring a sense of discouraging discontinuity – rather, a sense of exhilaration. He had rejected his earlier vision not simply because the first term of the metaphor, the sea, had changed with the time of the seasons but because, Marcel the narrator reminded us, the young man Marcel could now *see* what he could not see before: 'surtout parce que mes yeux, instruits par Elstir à retenir précisément les éléments que j'écartais volontairement jadis, contemplaient longuement ce que, la première année, ils se savaient pas voir' (Proust vol. III, p. 179) ('above all because my eyes, taught by Elstir to retain precisely those elements that once I had deliberately rejected, would now gaze for hours at what in the former year they had been incapable of seeing' (Kilmartin vol. II, p. 11)). Elstir the painter, one of the exemplary artists of *A la recherche du temps perdu*, had taught Marcel towards the end of his first visit to Balbec that metaphor is not a matter of discovering repetition and identity, of achieving stasis, but rather of creating metamorphoses. It is not a matter of superimposing common elements, but of transposing different ones, as Elstir transposes sea and land in his picture *le port de Carquethuit*, and as Marcel, inspired by Elstir, does in describing the sea during this second visit to Balbec. It is not a matter of creating stability, but of exploring mobile and permeable limits. Metaphor is a matter of radical redescription. The redescription of sea as land in Elstir's painting, as in Marcel's second vision, makes *difference* visible, rather than identity. Identity is restored only through what is for Marcel a secondary and inferior faculty, intelligence:

> Ou plutôt on n'aurait pas dit d'autres parties de la mer. Car entre ces parties, il y avait autant de différence qu'entre l'une d'elles et l'église sortant des eaux, et les bateaux derrière la ville. L'intelligence faisait ensuite un même élément de ce qui était, ici noir dans un effet d'orage, plus loin tout d'une couleur avec le ciel et aussi verni que lui, et là si blanc de soleil, de brume et d'écume, si compact, si terrien, si circonvenu de maisons, qu'on pensait à quelque chaussée de pierres ou à un champ de neige, sur lequel on était effrayé de voir un navire s'élever en pente raide et à sec comme une voiture qui s'ébroue en sortant d'un gué, mais qu'au bout d'un moment, en y voyant sur l'étendue haute et inégale du plateau solide des bateaux titubants, on comprenait, identique en tous ces aspects divers, être encore la mer.
>
> (Proust vol II, pp. 193–4)

Or rather one would not have called them other parts of the sea. For between those parts there was as much difference as there was between one of them and the church rising from the water, or the ships behind the town. One's intelligence then set to work to make a single element of what was in

96

one place black beneath a gathering storm, a little further all of one colour with the sky and as brightly burnished, and elsewhere so bleached by sunshine, haze and foam, so compact, so terrestrial, so circumscribed with houses that one thought of some white stone causeway or of a field of snow, up the slope of which one was alarmed to see a ship come climbing steeply, high and dry, like a carriage rearing up from a ford, but which a moment later, when you saw on the raised uneven surface of the solid plain boats staggering drunkenly, you understood, identical in all these different aspects, to be still the sea.

> (Kilmartin vol I, p. 896; translation modified)

Now this process of redescription, or of what Ricoeur calls 'seeing as' in his book *La Métaphore vive* – this process of seeing-as is far from being a self-indulgent exercise in ornamental preciosity. Rather, it can be read as a crucial phase, for Marcel, in the developing, temporal interaction of consciousness and world. The inaccessible, immobile ocean, circumscribed in a mythological metaphor already outworn before Marcel uses it, and outgrown before his second visit to Balbec, is now seen as an accessible and permeable element – permeable to its 'other', and to human consciousness and activity, whether practical or aesthetic – that activity which, for Ricoeur, supplants the inertia of imitation as the essence of mimesis. The earlier metaphor of the sea-nymph, derivative and habitual, had maintained that 'mince liséré spirituel', that slender mental margin which Marcel elsewhere deplored as a barrier precluding the interaction of mind and world (Proust vol. I, p. 83; Kilmartin vol. I, p. 90). The new metaphor dramatizes a new way of intending a world in which traditional categories and traditional denominations are held in tension with their dissolution. Now it may be objected that Marcel's new 'seeing-as' on his second visit is still indirect and derivative, in that he simply sees the world through Elstir's own pictorial metaphor. But the point is that now, as Marcel exuberantly translates Elstir's image into his own 'transposition d'art', the metaphor acts not as a barrier nor as a mere substitution of one term for another, nor as an escape from time, but as a dialectical mediation which functions as a negation of past habitual categories, simultaneously maintains them in tension with a new vision, and enacts change in time. It reminds us of Ricoeur's redefinition of metaphorical truth as the preservation 'of the "is not" within the "is" '.[8] Further, Marcel's metaphoric transposition of metaphor negates not only the stasis of the world, but sees movement and time within the apparent stasis of pictorial art. In its cognitive euphoria it renews the experience of, and reflection upon, the time of the world and of consciousness, the interdependence of knowing, imagining and feeling, of language, representation and action, of the processes of figuration, configuration and refiguration. In comparison with this experience and practice of metaphor as the expression of the hero's growth through time, and of his growing awareness of that growth, Marcel's later theory of metaphor as the extra-temporal bulwark against decline through time may seem to be regressive. It is a regression unperceived by the older Marcel of *Le Temps retrouvé*, who is euphorically deceived by the *limits* of involuntary memory. But it is noted by the reader whose own memory may bridge the gaps of the text. Our suspicion of regression is reinforced by the allusive return in the hôtel de Guermantes of the image, earlier erased, which once expressed the stasis of the sea, and which may now be thought to have erased, in returning, the more dynamic function of metaphor. The erasure seems to arrest the narrative at the level of configuration in an 'emplotment' which is foreshortened by a sense of closure and totality.

But once more, the apparent loser wins - although his victory may seem precarious. We find that the seemingly short-circuited tension between stasis and progression has simply been displaced into one of the most economical metaphors of the whole work - a metaphor which plays on the ambiguity of a single word to convey the structure of metaphor metaphorically. This is an image which has been quoted already, and its ambiguity is highlighted by the discrepancy between the two English translations to which I then referred. For as we saw, Marcel's actual word, 'anneaux' - 'les anneaux nécessaires d'un beau style' - may be read either on the one hand as 'rings' or 'circles', or on the other as the links of a chain, distinct but interdependent - a forged but flexible continuity, rather than rigid circularity. The closure implicit in one sense is held in tension with the progression implicit in the other. And if it is objected that the crucial verb is 'enfermer', that the narrator aims to enclose his experiences of involuntary memory in the chains of metaphor, it can be replied that the verb is in the future tense - a future more of deferral than of command. The retrieval of lost time is still a project for the future: in the last few pages we find that the narrative we have just been reading is not yet the book which Marcel intends to write, and which, he quite tentatively suggests, would be a much more precise transcription of time and reality. And so we have to go back to the beginning of the book we already have, to read it again in the light of that new future and of that other, non-existent book – the non-existent resolution of the aporias of time. But when we do read it again, we find that it sometimes bears a strange resemblance to Marcel's brief sketch of his future work: that work is, and is not, the book we have just read.

Proust's novel ends, then, with a sting in the tail, and so, it may be said, does Ricoeur's analysis of narrative as the resolution of the aporias of time. In his postscript, written during the final revision of his text, he avers with humility that the topic, time, which his three volumes have subjected to scrutiny, is in fact inscrutable. He also asserts that time is unrepresentable, and suggests that narrative, in its effort to represent time, must also recognize its own limits. Its greatest, though not complete, success in resolving the aporias of time – in bridging phenomenological and objective time or in reconciling totality and dispersal – lies in its creation, Ricoeur maintains, of a narrative identity. And here identity should be construed not as a sameness (*idem*), but as a self-ness (*ipse*) (Ricoeur vol. III, p. 355; p. 246). Narrative identity, thus defined, would include change and mutability within the cohesion of a life. But Proust is perhaps more radical. Through Marcel he tries to explore the limits and acknowledge the limitations of the relationship between narrative and temporality without the safety net of narrative identity, for the vocation to create that identity through writing is itself too unstable to constitute or guarantee that creation: 'Ainsi toute ma vie jusqu'à ce jour aurait pu et n'aurait pas pu être résumée sous ce titre: Une vocation' (Proust vol. IV, p. 478) ('And thus my whole life up to the present day might and yet might not have been summed up under the title: A Vocation' (Kilmartin vol. III, p. 936)). Together, the book we have just read and the book which Marcel has not yet written stand as the two terms of a metaphor at once instantaneous and sustained, holding in tension, as Ricoeur says metaphors do, the 'is' and the 'is not' – or, it might be added, the past and the future, the known and the unknown. The two books perhaps also stand as a metaphor not for identity, however unstable, but for the gap in consciousness which can never be closed in self-coincidence or in self-knowledge, since consciousness, by virtue of its existence in time, and by virtue of its very efforts to know or to recognize itself, is what it is not and is not what it is, is always ahead of itself, even when it attempts to retrieve the past. Ultimately, despite his intuitions of eternity, Marcel's provisional book – the book we have read when we reach the 'end' of *A la recherche du temps perdu* – this provisional book and his final silence suggest that the aporias of time may lie even beyond configuration. It is that 'lying beyond' that the act of reading must endlessly refigure.

NOTES

1 Paul Ricoeur, *Temps et récit*, Paris, Editions du Seuil, vol. I, 1983, vol. II, 'La Configuration du temps dans le récit de fiction', 1984, vol. III, 'Le temps raconté', 1985; Marcel Proust, *A la recherche du temps perdu*, edited by Jean-Yves Tadié, Paris, Gallimard, Bibliothèque de la Pléiade, vols I-IV, 1987–9. (The novel was first published between 1913 and 1927.) Page references to *Temps et récit* (published in English as *Time and Narrative*, translated by Kathleen McLaughlin and David Pellauer, Chicago, University of Chicago Press, 1984–8) will be given in the text to the French and English editions, in that order. For Proust, references will be given to the above edition and, in most cases, to the more recent of the two available English translations: *Remembrance of Things Past*, translated by C. W. Scott Moncrieff and Terence Kilmartin, Harmondsworth, Penguin Books, 1983 (first published by Chatto & Windus in 1981). This will be abbreviated as Kilmartin. Exceptions will be indicated in the notes.
2 The revised edition of *A la recherche du temps perdu* (see note 1) provides a meticulously faithful version of Proust's novel, based on an exhaustive study of recently available manuscripts and successive drafts. It none the less suggests that there can never be a strictly definitive edition of the work, of which the later parts were published after Proust's death.
3 Wolfgang Iser, *The Act of Reading: A Theory of Aesthetic Response*, London, Routledge & Kegan Paul, 1978, p. 166. (First published as *Der Akt des Lesens: Theorie Ästhetischer Wirkung*, Munich, Wilhelm Fink, 1976.) See Ricoeur vol. I, pp. 116–17, pp. 76–7; vol. III, pp. 244–9, pp. 167–71.
4 This phrase is rendered by its first English translator as 'the necessary circle of fine style' and in the revised version as 'the necessary links of fine style'. See *Time Regained*, translated by Stephen Hudson, London, Chatto & Windus, 1931, p. 239, and Kilmartin vol. III, p. 925. The significance of this divergence will become apparent later.
5 Apart from their evidence of Proust's suppression of chronological markers, with its consequent effect of indeterminacy, his successive

drafts are significant in what they reveal about the complexities of configuration and the problems of refiguration which they in turn create for the reader, and about the interplay of repression, wish-fulfilment, recognition and afterthought in creativity. In Proust's early drafts the George Sand novel read to Marcel by his mother is the more 'innocent', *La Mare au Diable*. Proust's later reference to *François le Champi* in his typescript included details which were omitted in his more allusive final version. (The incestuous implications of George Sand's story had been noted at performances of a dramatic adaptation in 1849 and 1888.) Proust thus gives the reader clues which he refuses to make explicit. Furthermore, he suppresses before the final version the older Marcel's comparison between the emotions aroused by his relationship that night with his mother and his later experiences of unrequited love – an analogy which the reader of the published novel is left to infer. Most significantly, a late typescript variant indicates that the reference at the end of the novel to the evocative power of *François le Champi* had at first immediately followed Marcel's account of his mother's reading. However, in the earlier version the book's power to revive the past, when it is taken up again in later years, does not depend on an upsurge of involuntary memory. The postpone-ment of this episode for a little less than 3,000 pages and the inconsistency thus created suggests a greater fidelity to the aporias of time than to coherent foreclosure, while the stages of emplotment seem designed, whether consciously or unconsciously, to introduce a number of crucial 'blanks' or gaps which the reader must negotiate in the process of refiguration. For the relevant drafts and variants, see *A la recherche du temps perdu*, vol. I, pp. 676, 694, and 1117–22.

6 *Contre Sainte-Beuve*, edited by Pierre Clarac, Paris, Gallimard, Bibli-othèque de la Pléiade, 1971, p. 586.

7 The allusion in the final volume is reinforced two pages later when Marcel also remembers Vinteuil's music: 'volutes bleues de la mer matinale enveloppant des phrases musicales qui en émergent partielle-ment comme les épaules des ondines' (Proust vol. III, p. 870); 'the blue volutes of the morning sea and, enveloped in thcm, phrases of music half emerging like the shoulders of water nymphs' (Kilmartin vol. III, p. 903).

8 Paul Ricoeur, *La Métaphore vive*, Paris, Editions du Seuil, 1975, p. 313; *The Rule of Metaphor*, London, Routledge & Kegan Paul, 1978, p. 249.

7

GRAND NARRATIVES

J. M. Bernstein

Grand narratives, or meta-narratives as they are sometimes called, are second-order narratives which seek to narratively articulate and legitimate some concrete first-order practices or narratives. Typically, a grand narrative will make reference to some ultimate originating principle or ultimate *telos*; it will seek to place existing practices in a position of progress toward or regress from the originating principle or ultimate end. Because grand narratives are second-order discourses they cannot be directly empirically confirmed; this has made them objects of suspicion to empiricists, positivists, and anyone who takes empirical confirmability as the criterion of cognitive worth. Because grand narratives have traditionally sought to articulate historical experience with the ultimate terms of human understanding – truth, salvation, good-ness, peace, happiness, etc. – they have become objects of suspicion to those who wish to critique (destruct/deconstruct/overturn) metaphysics. The grandness of grand narratives has made them almost universal objects of suspicion. And yet the point, the grounding purpose of the practice of grand narration, has been overlooked, namely, grand narration's requirement that its objects be articulated historically, and that it is only through history that human things can be formed and understood. Perhaps, then, there is a story to tell about grand narratives. So, let us begin . . .

Once upon a time it was written: 'Universal history must be construed and denied.' Later, and elsewhere, we read: 'Most people have lost the nostalgia for the lost (grand) narrative.'[1] How are we to arbitrate these claims? How are we to understand the difference between Adorno and Lyotard on the question of grand narratives when they both refer us to an analogous comprehension of modernity/post-modernity in, most explicitly, their analyses of modern art, but nonetheless refer those analyses themselves to – meta-narratively place them in? – different stories about where and who we are? In asking this question, I take it as non-controversial that the necessity of denying the universal history that we must construe from here tokens a nostalgia for another history, another narrative. One could, and Adorno does, call this other history 'utopia', but that just tells us how 'other' that history will be, how different its narration will be from the one whose present fatality determines our own. In claiming that we ought to deny the universal history that is our history, Adorno is not suggesting that utopia is a social space beyond history or beyond (meta-)narration; rather, the claim is that there is another form of historical praxis and another sense of grand narrative which escapes the repressive universality of modernity. The universal history that 'must be construed' *de*-legitimates the present, hence it must be denied; but because this construal and denial contradict the normative work of legitimation which informs the practice of grand narration, then in accordance with the principle of immanent critique, where we compare a concept with the reality presumptively instantiating it, this contradiction entails a 'nostalgia' for another grand narration. Conversely, to surrender a concept because it fails to correspond to given reality is to make given reality the absolute arbiter of reason and rationality, and is hence to surrender even the rudiments of the idea of critical reason.

Anachronistically, Adorno is claiming against Lyotard that what appears as the eclipse of enlightenment universal history is in fact its demonic realization. This can entail a 'nostalgia' for another grand narrative only if a sense of grand narrative can be elaborated which avoids the necessities of enlightenment universal history which make it demonic. A sketch of such a sense of grand narrative is the goal of this paper.

Central to both Adorno's and Lyotard's understanding of modernity and the place of grand narratives in it is their remarkably similar understanding of modern art, and it is with that understanding that we need to begin (again).

I

Both Adorno and Lyotard attempt to develop an aesthetics which gives pride of place to the idea of excess or non-identity.[2] Lyotard elaborates his position in terms of a valorization of Kant's notion of sublimity over his notions of taste and beauty. Like Adorno, Lyotard regards the dominant, non-avant-gardist regimes of modern art to be governed by a logic of identity, whether we pace out that logic in terms of a political demand to produce the 'correct' images, the 'correct' narratives, the 'correct' forms (*PC*, p. 75); or in terms of an apparent ideology of 'anything goes', that is in reality governed by money and the rule of the marketplace (*PC*, p. 76). These are the modern logics of realism; in the first case, realism amounts to a correspondence between a work and a cultural policy, while in the latter case we have a realism which 'accommodates all "needs", provided that the tendencies and needs have purchasing power' (ibid.). Works accomplished in accordance with either of these logics permit a stabilization of the referent, a stabilization which admirably performs the task of 'preserving various consciousnesses from doubt' (*PC*, p. 74).

According to Lyotard the affirmation of meaning, the affirmation of identity, communication and understanding that is the end-product of such art corresponds to Kant's model of judgments of taste, judgments that such-and-such is beautiful, because such judgments are made on the basis of an adequation between a work and our *capacity* for making determinate cognitive judgments. The harmony between imagination and understanding which grounds judgments of taste marks the objects in response to which the judgment of taste is made as compatible with our capacity for bringing intuitions under concepts without, in these judgments, actually so doing. Hence judgments of taste are 'formally' cognitive while being actually, contentfully, non-cognitive. Because judgments of taste are formally cognitive, they allow for communication, agreement, consensus; they permit us to regard our existing cognitive equipment as having sufficient scope to comprehend whatever might come before it.

Beauty affirms realism; and this makes beauty and taste incompatible with modernity since 'modernity, in whatever age it appears, cannot exist without a shattering of belief and without discovery of the "lack of reality" of reality, together with the invention of other realities' (*PC*, p. 77). The Kantian conception of the sublime is a figure of a corollary principle for art of the shattering of reality and belief, the negation of determinate meaning, which Lyotard regards as the defining principle of modernity. The feeling of sublimity occurs when

the imagination *fails* to present an object (to the understanding) which might, if only in principle, come to match
a concept . . . . We can conceive the infinitely great, the
infinitely powerful, but every presentation of an object
destined to 'make visible' this absolute greatness or power
appears to us painfully inadequate. Those are ideas of which
no presentation is possible.

(PC, p. 78)

To present the idea that the unpresentable exists is the task of
properly modernist art. But to say this is not to say anything very
different from Adorno's thesis, which takes as its point of departure
Kant's aconceptual conception of judgments of taste, that properly
modernist works of art invoke a form of the unity or togetherness
of their elements which is incommensurable with all *given* models
of conceptual unity. For both, modernist works of art are not non-
cognitive, but negatively cognitive; both thus defining the principle
of modern art as the progressive negation of given meaning forms.
For Lyotard and Adorno a modern work is non-identical with
existing modes of ordering; such works resist, are acts of resistance
against whatever concepts we have available to say of any object
it is the 'same' as some other. Modern works of art for Adorno
and Lyotard are an excess with respect to understood forms of
meaning, and it is their (orderly and coherent) excessiveness which
makes them modern.

And yet there is a difficulty in this comparison or identification
of Adorno and Lyotard, for what the excessiveness of modern art
signifies for each of them is radically different. For Adorno the
quasi-cognitive character of modern works of art is a *challenge* to
the reigning enlightenment conception of order, meaning and truth
(truth as correspondence, universality, etc.), where this conception
itself is construed as a realization of rationalizing tendencies evident but non-dominant in previous epochs, which has been finally
and disastrously consummated in the logic of capital exchange
relations. Aesthetic excess signals, in its cognitive function, the
alienation of art from truth as it is dominantly conceived of, while
simultaneously pre-figuring the possibility in principle of another
mode of truth-telling, another kind of conceptual regime and
praxis, another history. In Lyotard, the shift away from judgments
of taste to judgments of sublimity as a model for our understanding
modern art marks a weakening, in comparison to Adorno, of the

cognitive claims and significance of modern art. Employing the sublime as a figure of modernity allows Lyotard to consider autonomous art, the sort of art which functions through a continual interrogation of the question 'what can be said to be art (and literature)?' (*PC*, p. 75), as an unqualified achievement of modernity, whose principle of progressively negating meaning, progressively disenchanting the world, defines modernity. Hence for Lyotard, sublime, avant-garde art heuristically confirms his view of postmodern science as 'theorizing its own evolution as discontinuous, catastrophic, non-rectifiable, and paradoxical' (*PC*, p. 60) in its concern for undecidables, conflicts characterized by incomplete information, '*fracta*', catastrophes and pragmatic paradoxes. Sublime art figures, then, the death of grand narratives as sources for legitimation by heuristically keeping the principle of modernity visible. I claim that this offers modern art a weaker status than that generated by Adorno's analysis because for Lyotard sublime art merely confirms the open conceptual horizon that postmodern science has already achieved for itself; it possesses no independent cognitive significance.

Now it is certainly striking, although not very surprising, that two such disparate philosophers should attempt to theorize the nature of modernist art by drawing on central moments from Kant's aesthetics; and in another setting it would be pertinent to attempt to interrogate the difference between Adorno's taste-based theory and Lyotard's sublime-based theory. Although it is worth stating here that Lyotard's preference for the sublime appears distinctly odd: first, because he does not show, nor is it clear how he could show, how the characteristic features of the sublime object, its infinite greatness or power, are relevant to works which although undoubtedly modernist are equally unquestionably not sublime in Kant's sense; and second, because he fails to question the aconceptuality of judgments of taste, that is, a work's inability to be brought under any known concept despite its general compatibility with our capacity for making determinate conceptual judgments. Belief can be shattered in many ways.

What is at issue here is the use Lyotard makes of the model of sublime, modernist art. Again, for Lyotard, modernist art exemplifies a project that is sustained not by a given teleology, and hence a legitimating grand narration of its unfolding history, but rather by a continual first-level interrogation into its own nature. Since that first-level interrogation progresses through the continual defeat of previous answers to the question ('what is art? painting? literature?'), the very idea of legitimation through second-level grand narration becomes otiose and redundant. And this, we are told, is the postmodern, i.e. self-consciously modernist, condition not only of art but of knowledge as well; and not only of art and knowledge, but *hopefully* of social life in general. Now unavoidably, inevitably, Lyotard's argument defeats itself, immerses itself in a pragmatic paradox of its own, for like Descartes in the *Discourse on Method*, whom Lyotard grudgingly cites in this regard (*PC*, p. 29), the defence of the suspension of narrative and historical legitimation is legitimated narratively, even if Lyotard's text, unlike Descartes's, does its best to hide its narrative dimensions.[3] How else but narratively are we to read Lyotard's 'accounts' of the evolution of modern science, philosophy and art? Does not his account reveal how postmodern science *is* theorizing its own evolution in its paralogical concerns by placing it into his story of the eclipse of grand narrative? And what is this revealing if not an act of legitimation?

Perhaps there is nothing here which Lyotard would wish to deny. Perhaps the inevitability of a recourse to grand narrative is not so inevitable; it is just, perhaps, that we are still locked into the game of legitimation. Or so Lyotard might say.

While I shall want to argue that the inevitability of our present recourse to grand narrative is not as benign or as easily dismissed as Lyotard might like, that demonstration can wait a moment for a prior consideration imposes itself on us here. If it is right to say that the difference between Adorno's and Lyotard's legitimations of the excessiveness of modern art depends on the grand narratives into which they place their accounts; and further, that our initial impulse is to say, quite unhesitatingly, that they evaluate the significance of modern art differently because they *interpret* modernity differently, then we cannot resist the conclusion that grand narratives *are* interpretations of a special sort. And if the question is now posed, 'what special sort of interpretation is at issue here?' then we might subscribe to the view of interpretation Foucault offers us in his 'Nietzsche, genealogy, history'.[4]

> If interpretation were the slow exposure of the meaning hidden in an origin, then only metaphysics could interpret the development of humanity. But if interpretation is the violent or surreptitious appropriation of a system of rules,

which in itself has no meaning, in order to impose a direction, to bend it to a new will, to force its participation in a different game, and to subject it to secondary rules, then the development of humanity is a series of interpretations.

Or, as we would prefer to say, the development of humanity is a series of grand narratives.

It seems plausible to regard Lyotard's rejection of grand narratives as a rejection of grand narratives *as* metaphysics; in promoting the Foucault/Nietzsche view of interpretation, we are acceding to this rejection of grand narratives. But Lyotard is mistaken in believing that this rejection of grand narratives is equivalent to the wholesale dismissal of the concept of grand narratives. What needs clarifying and analysing here is the concept of 'excessiveness', for it would appear that the very excessiveness which Lyotard believes characterizes modern art and entails the rejection of grand narratives is employed by Foucault to characterize the sort of interpretations which traditionally have been regarded as grand narratives. If grand narratives are not metaphysics, 'the slow exposure of the meaning hidden in an origin', but nonetheless more than systems of first-order rules, then there is, perhaps, an Other metaphysics, say, a metaphysics of excess. Grand narratives are excess; they are the series of excesses in accordance with which humanity becomes intelligible to itself, gives itself a history, and has history as a central determinant of that intelligibility.

II

There is an evident complimentarity between Lyotard's remark that 'most people have lost the nostalgia for the lost narrative' (*PC*, p. 41), and his conception of the development of an idea and practice of justice that is not linked to consensus, but conceives justice as involving a recognition of the 'heteromorphous' nature of language games. 'This orientation', he says, 'corresponds to the course that the evolution of social interaction is currently taking; the *temporary contract* is in practice supplanting permanent institutions in the professional, emotional, sexual, cultural, family, and international domains, as well as in political affairs' (*PC*, p. 66). Language games, concrete local practices, do not require legitimation; and because they are 'heteromorphous' they are incapable of receiving any general, grand narrative accounting. The idea of a temporary contract involves the recognition that each language game is an open system, and no general rules, principles or conceptualities can plausibly govern the interaction among language games. Yet I confess to finding Lyotard's list of domains increasingly under the sway of temporary contracts, and the mention of temporary contract itself uncanny. With respect to the list, the uncanniness is easy to track down, for the list corresponds to just those domains where nostalgia lingers. It is our sexual, racial, familial, national and professional identities that now appear as increasingly dissociated, and that are now often felt to be places of loss, repression, silence; as impossible positions from which we must speak and act, and yet find ourselves unable to do so. Arguably, our silence in these locales corresponds to the lack of a grand narrative that could give our estrangement voice.

The temporary contract is an anti-narrative device prohibiting us from speaking our social identities, or their loss, by insisting that the *social* space we share with others is no space at all, or, at least, there is nothing essential to our engagements with others that is intrinsically 'social'. And now we know what made the temporary contract appear uncanny: it replicates the demand for dis-sociation which Descartes had made in the *Discourse on Method* in his suggestion of a provisional, 'temporary' moral code, knowing that it is not the code itself which is to be provisional, but our moral attachments to state, church, society, others. Temporary contract is the truth of social contract theories: temporary, provisional engagements with 'society' for the sake of an asocial, ahistorical self, for the sake of an *ego cogito*. This is a self which regards as 'excess' (!) 'all the promises by which some part of one's freedom is taken away',[5] i.e., all promises which could not be revoked for a greater convenience to oneself, all promises that might privilege the good of the social whole over one's own good. To make even these provisional or temporary contracts, which, temporarily, 'limit one's desires', would be pointless if it were not the case that they provide a means to one's private ends, 'acquiring all the true goods that would ever be in [one's] power' (*PC*, p. 41).

Lyotard's defence of 'heteromorphous' language games, an irreducible plurality of language games, knowingly or unknowingly, provides a *thin* veneer of sociability and historicality, a thin veneer of respectability and legitimacy, to the anti-social, anti-historical, anti-narrative tendencies of capital. The progressive negation of meaning of aesthetic modernism mimics the restlessness of capital itself, capital's liberation of desire from all natural boundaries, the refusal of all limits, all teleologies implicit in the domination of use value by exchange value. Of course, even the deracinated social world of capital, governed, tendentially, by temporary contracts, is still a world, social and historical in its roots; and so inevitably legitimates itself through grand narratives repeatingly telling the story of the end of grand narrative, the end of ideology, the end of metaphysics, from Descartes to Lyotard.

III

Lyotard's grand narrative attempts to provide a unification of society as inevitably dispersed; the excessive signification of the temporary contract figuring the *eidos* of justice as one in which *we* (all of us – collectively) recognize our dispersed identities by recognizing that *we* (all of us – collectively) do not exist except as members, players of local, 'heteromorphous' language games. In pressing his claim that language games are 'the minimum relation required for society to exist' (*PC*, p. 15), the minimum social bond, to the point where they are implicitly taken as the complete and sufficient condition for the social bond, Lyotard dissimulates, as had the philosophical tradition before him, the question of society as an historical question. Temporary contract theory, like social contract theory before it, emptying the space where the interrogation of the meaning of the being of society intersects with the historical destiny of peoples, the space, that is, where since Plato the question(s) of metaphysics and the question(s) of politics, of the political, have been seen as one – and, of course, as not one, as different. If in Plato the interaction and intersection of the political and the metaphysical is resolved, and so silenced, by the subordination of politics to metaphysics, then with Lyotard we have the perverse fulfilment of this silence where the presumptive end of metaphysics comes to entail the end of the question of politics and the political *tout court*.

IV

I have wanted to digress into the connections between Lyotard's rejection of grand narratives and other features of his argument because even those readers of Lyotard who have found themselves out of sympathy with his overall argument have nonetheless wanted to support his rejection of grand narratives. Lyotard, correctly I believe, presents his critique of grand narratives as the linchpin for his positive argument; in order to sustain a critical distance from Lyotard it is necessary, in some way, to defend grand narratives. However, I have already suggested that the conception of grand narratives that needs defending and is capable of being defended is not the conception of grand narratives Lyotard rejects. So far as I can detect, the concept of grand narrative Lyotard dismisses is the narrative analogue of the concept of interpretation dismissed by Foucault; and the concept of grand narrative I wish to defend is the narrative analogue of the concept of interpretation Foucault defends.

Grand narratives are second-order discourses that order, criticize, align, disperse, disrupt and gather the first-order discourses and practices that make up the woof of social life. Grand narratives are the excessive interpretations which institute the institution of society, which repeat otherwise what is and has been in order that *we* might be who we are and will be, in order that we might become who we are. To put names and forms to this proposal: grand narratives are here being conceptualized as the merging of Castoriadis's analysis of the social imaginary[6] with Ricoeur's account of narrative repetition. Let me say something about each of these in turn, beginning with Castoriadis.

In the wake of the critiques of the philosophies of presence which go under the names of Nietzsche, Heidegger, Derrida, *et al.*, we can perhaps find ourselves in agreement with a thought like this: any society, epoch or period, as a distinguishable system of meaningful practices, is in need of a foundation, a ground, an origin, an ultimate source of legitimation which, however, cannot be had. There is nothing, no thing which grounds or founds a society; there exist no discriminable objects, ideas, laws of nature or articulated theoretical constructs that do work that must be done if societies are to exist. Yet, there have been and do exist societies. Castoriadis proposes that we consider the putative founding moments of different societies – God, law, justice, *technē*, personhood, free will, language games, etc. – as historically creative acts of social auto-institution, where the ultimate term of signification, the so-called transcendental signified or condition for the possibility of that society, *qua* social, is a social imaginary. Castoriadis's concept of the social imaginary is a replacement concept for the primary concepts of metaphysics, it is the concept of a metaphysical concept with a *difference*.

About the need/necessity/role of this imaginary Castoriadis says the following:

> Functionality draws its meaning from outside itself; and symbolism necessarily refers to something that is not of the symbolic – and that is not simply real-rational either. This something, the element that provides the functionality of each institutional system with its specific orientation, and over-determines the choice and connections of the symbolic networks; this creation specific to each historical period, its singular way of constituting, perceiving, and living out its existence; this primary and active structuration, this central signifier-signified; the source of meanings that are given as beyond all discussion and dispute; the support for the articulation of and distinction between what does and does not matter; and the origin of that excess of being attached to practical, affective, or intellectual objects of investment (whether individual or collective) – this element is none other than a society or period's *imaginary*.[7]

Societies require support because the plurality of practices and meanings they involve must interact, be functional and/or significant with respect to one another, but neither functionality nor signification possesses the sort of natural or ontological characteristics which would allow this requirement to be met by having the questions posed by functionality and symbolic signification remaining unanswered. There are questions, questions like: How do we make qualitatively distinct labours commensurable in order that social exchanges of goods may occur? On what social goods may a price be put? To what degree are economic transactions to be governed by non-economic considerations? What are the ends of education? What role are our sexual and/or racial identities to play in political, economic and cultural affairs? What constraints are to be placed on law-making?, etc., that cut across the 'hetero-morphous' character of language games which Lyotard regards as constituting the limit and condition for rational and intelligible interrogation. Social functionality is more than social contiguity; and social meaning is more than representation (internal or external), expression or communication. This 'more than', however, cannot be answered in terms of any *theory* of society, justice, community, God, man, history, whatever, since such a theory will, perforce, deny the radical transformations, the discontinuous *othering* that history, our history, has always been and failed to be insofar as it has remained within the boundaries of what could be theoretically ratified. Rather, it is the 'more than' that allows reason to be rational, institutions to be functional, laws to obligate, giving them a space in which to operate and a back/ground against which and through which they can draw their 'force'.

Perhaps we can summarize Castoriadis's thought so far in this way: he agrees with the critique of metaphysics, its destruction or deconstruction, that are no such transcendentals, or ideas, or categorical objects such as were presumed to exist by the tradition of metaphysics; however, the need for such objects exists, and further the role presumptively fulfilled by them has been fulfilled, albeit not by them as they were presumed to be. On the contrary, the work of grounding or founding has been accomplished by nothing, that is, by nothing having the status or characteristics of an object which could, in fact or in principle, be made present. There is, we might say, something sublime or excessive about the foundations of society, the grounds for truth. In making this claim I am attempting to suggest that Lyotard's employment of the Kantian philosophy of the sublime, taken as revealing 'the incommensurability of reality to concept' (*PC*, p. 79), underestimates the significance of what is excessive to what can be conceptually grasped. For Lyotard the technical expertise of art presents the fact that the unpresentable exists (*PC*, p. 78); which is to say, art figures the limit of conceptual understanding as surpassable, and hence as forever to be surpassed. Sublime art's relation to present understanding and reason is for Lyotard critical and negative; it reveals the limit as a limit capable of being surpassed. Castoriadis, however, regards the excess of the radical social imaginary as having a positive function, as a condition of representation. He writes:

And by pushing the analysis, we can arrive at significations that do not exist *in order to* represent something else, but appear as the ultimate articulations imposed by society on itself, its needs, and world – as the 'organizing schemas' that constitute the condition of representability for everything society gives itself. But by their very nature, these schemas do not themselves exist in the form of representations that

113

one could, with the aid of analysis, put one's finger on. One cannot speak here of 'images', however vague and indefinite the meaning one gives this term. God may be, for each believer, an 'image' – or even a 'precise' representation – but as an imaginary signification, God is not the 'sum' of these images, their 'average,' or what they have 'in common'. God is their condition of possibility; he allows these images to be images 'of God'. Nor can one consider the imaginary core of the phenomenon of reification as an 'image'.[8]

Imaginary significations are 'sublime' in Lyotard's sense of the term: they are not objects of theoretical understanding or representation. And it is the role imaginary significations play within signifying systems that makes them, by definition as it were, beyond representation. Nonetheless, that role is one of founding or grounding.

There is, to be sure, something oddly familiar about Castoriadis's conception of the social imaginary, namely, its strong family resemblance to the Hegel/Durkheim conception of religion and the primary objects of religious discourse.[9] What distinguishes Castoriadis's account, or better, gives it its specificity, is its attempt to sustain the social imaginary *as* imaginary; and further, then, to understand the excessive nature of imaginary significations as the key to explaining the connection between historicality and novelty. Now the linkage between historicality and novelty can be more directly and easily comprehended in terms of the open texture of the rules governing the terms employed in different language games; and indeed such an analysis is a good deal of the point of Lyotard's account. However, what a theory like Lyotard's cannot explain is either the kind of unity that certain societies or periods appear to possess, or the consequent kind of discontinuous temporality which pervades our sense of historical change. While too much can be made of the presumed unity of a social totality, leading us to overlook the relative autonomy and specificity of particular sorts of practices, it is none the less the case that any people's practices are more than a random collection. That 'more than', that articulation of different practices with respect to one another in various relations of domination, subordination, compatibility and exclusion is provided by the social imaginary.

The social imaginary, instituted and instituting, is neither real nor unreal (a fiction), neither true nor false, neither rational nor irrational; it is rather that through which, and in accordance with which, these necessary but ontologically anomalous characteristics of language and meaning become operative. Because the social imaginary has the features it does, because as instituted through the social imaginary the institution of society is ontologically anomalous, the problem or the question of society, the problem or question of history cannot be definitively answered. Rather, history is a discontinuous series of creative responses to the anomalous being of the socio-historical, which as a series is characterized by the consistent refusal of historical societies to recognize their essentially instituting/instituted being, the unsurpassable contestability of the meaning of being in general.[10] This last statement is, of course, meta-narrative. It is also an act of narrative repetition.

V

Grand narratives are one of the central ways in which the social imaginary of a people is instituted and becomes manifest; and grand narratives are 'grand' because what they narrate is the work of the social imaginary itself. Although Castoriadis explicates the role and work of the social imaginary as inscribing the fateful historicality of social life, he fails to detail how historicality reaches language. Grand narratives are the language game in which the historicizing work of the social imaginary reaches language; and Ricoeur's interpretation of narrative repetition can be construed as providing an account of the specifically historicizing action of grand narration.

Ricoeur's strategy in 'Narrative time' is to reflectively relate various features of narratives – plots, endings, etc. – to corresponding features of temporality; where the levels or forms of human temporal organization – within-time-ness, historicality, and temporality – of Heidegger's existential analysis of time in *Being and Time* are employed as guides to the understanding of temporality. Ricoeur's discussion of historicality and repetition occurs after he has shown how the analysis of narrativity confirms the Heideggerian existential analysis of time. In this discussion Ricoeur is attempting to demonstrate how the analysis of narrative can lead to a correction of the Heideggerian analysis of historicality on one 'decisive topic' (*NT*, p. 180).

Ricoeur begins his analysis with a rehearsal of the three criterial traits of historicality provided by Heidegger: (1) the appearance of time as extended between birth and death, hence as it is experienced as both cohesion and change, as, that is, becoming; (2) the reversal of the priority given to the past in the structure of care by the recognition that the primary direction of care is towards the future; and (3) 'As care, Dasein *is* the "between" '[11] of birth and death, a stretching-along between birth and death (*NT*, pp. 180–2). However, the finite character of this stretching-along inbetween is not provided by the experience of being between birth and death alone; rather, the future orientation of care is authentically experienced as finite, according to Heidegger, only on the condition that it is experienced as a being-toward-death. 'Only Being-free *for* death, gives Dasein its goal outright and pushes existence into its finitude.'[12] For Heidegger human beings *are* temporal beings rather than being the sorts of being who merely suffer or undergo temporal transformation; and the temporal character of human being is finite because it is bounded by birth and death. In order to properly live the finite temporality one is, one must recognize the bounded character of human temporality, and for Heidegger this means recognizing death as both a limit and a condition for one's projects.

It is at this juncture in Heidegger's account that the notions of fate and repetition make their appearance. In being-toward-death Dasein is picking up and recognizing the possibilities of its *heritage* as compromising the possibilities for authentic existing; in so doing, in handing down to itself its heritage in the anticipation of its death, Dasein recognizes the finitude of its existence as fate. *Repetition* is just the *explicit* going back into the possibilities of existence, going back to one's heritage, and grasping it, choosing it, handing it down to oneself. Heritage receives the simplicity of fate through repetition. Here Ricoeur comments:

> But what makes this extraordinary analysis problematic is the monadic character of repetition as fate. It is only thanks to a transfer of the senses of fate, governed by the theme of being toward death, to the notion of common 'destiny' that we reach the communal dimension of historicality.
>
> (*NT*, pp. 182–3)

It is the troubling monadic character of fate, and hence the priority of (individual) fate over (communal) destiny which Ricoeur hopes to evade and reverse through an understanding of narrative repetition.

Ricoeur has already in his account proposed one feature of narrative repetition in his affirmation of Louis Mink's concept of configurational understanding. In configurational understanding we read the end of a narrative back into its beginning, and its beginning into its end, and hence learn to read time backwards, 'as the recapitulation of the initial conditions of a course of action in its terminal consequences' (*NT*, p. 183). In this way narrative plot establishes human action in time and in memory; memory *repeats* a course of events 'according to an order that is the counterpart of the stretching-along of time between a beginning and an end' (*NT*, p. 183). Further, Ricoeur claims, the concept of repetition implies a retrieval 'of our most fundamental possibilities, as they are inherited from our own past, in terms of a personal fate and a common destiny' (*NT*, p. 183).

Narrative repetition hence involves a deepening of the movement of time through its explicit retrieval of past events *as* conditions, *as* potentialities which make the actual, the end of the narrative, possible (present). The end of the narrative makes the beginning of the narrative a beginning for that end; hence repetition gives to the temporal movement of the narrative that sort of necessity we call fate or destiny. Narrative repetition reads temporal passage as authentic historicality; and, at the limit, narrative repetition is the transformation of temporal passage into authentic historicality. This latter occurs when repetition is more than a form of understanding narrative; when, that is, repetition becomes integral to the work of narration itself. At this juncture, when narrative repetition is construed actively in terms of narrating, narrative repetition and authentic historicality appear as reciprocally defined concepts. Ricoeur takes this thought one step further when he questions whether we can conceive of the repetition essential to authentic historicality independently of narrative repetition. What could such non-narrative fate be? Heidegger gives us no clues, nor could he. 'Fate', Ricoeur says, 'is articulated in narrative. Fate is recounted' (*NT*, p. 188).

Once we bind fate as repetition to narrative in this way, then the essential role of being-toward-death and the priority of personal fate over communal destiny in Heidegger's account of authentic historicality must be brought into question. Binding repetition to narrative begins to reverse the priority given to personal fate over communal destiny most evidently because narrative forms depend upon communal resources for their completion. Death, salvation, happiness, or some more particular work or state of affairs can be the terminus of a narrative only through its communal comprehension of being an end, a *telos*. Moreover, in the analysis of narrative Ricoeur offers, he shows how 'the narrative of a quest, which is the paradigmatic example appropriate to this level, unfolds in a public time' (*NT*, p. 188); and public time is not the anonymous time of ordinary representation, but the time of interaction, the time whose movement is determined by the nature of our engagements with others. Personal fate, including the death of a hero, is gathered in a narrative whose sense depends upon its transcending the terms of an individual fate. The narrative terms which provide the conditions for an individual having a fate, make that fate always something more than personal.

This leads Ricoeur to question a fundamental thesis of Heidegger's, namely, his thesis that the potentialities of a heritage are transmitted from oneself (as thrown) to oneself (as thrown project). Surely a heritage is something transmitted from another to the self? But even this appears to be a limit case of what is the more usual situation where it is a 'community, a people, or a group of protagonists which tries to take up the tradition – or traditions – of its origin' (*NT*, p. 189). Ricoeur's point here is that in taking up and reactivating, reinterpreting a tradition an individual has the tradition itself as his *telos*, where by definition tradition is conceived of as what spans generations, extending beyond the lives, the births and deaths of those who participate in the tradition. Heidegger individualizes what is a collective phenomenon, and in so doing wrongly gives being-free toward death a role it cannot fulfil. It may be plausibly argued that only mortal beings can have or participate in a tradition, since traditions are precisely modes of identity in difference, of temporal cohesion through temporally disparate existences. But such a recognition does nothing for Heidegger's positioning of death, and does not explicate why the reactivation of the tradition is best conceived of in terms of narrative repetition.

Having made this point, Ricoeur continues: 'It is this communal act of repetition, which is at the same time a new founding act and a recommencement of what has already been inaugurated, that "makes history" and that finally makes it possible to write history' (*NT*, p. 189).

VI

Must we not read Ricoeur's account of collective narrative repetition as an account of grand narrative? We can hardly do otherwise. Grand narratives are second-order discourses because they are fundamentally repetitions, a repeating otherwise of what has already been; and collective narrative repetitions are grand because they reactivate lost origins – origins which only become origins which have been lost through their narrative articulation – and reassign practices to new or 'forgotten' ends. To prohibit grand narration is to prohibit narrative repetition, and to prohibit narrative repetition is to prohibit us from 'living' historically. Without repetition history is something that we might live 'within' and suffer, it can happen to us and condition our lives, but it cannot be approached as such. And this, of course, is the very point Heidegger was attempting to make in his distinction between authentic and inauthentic existence. In *Being and Time* Heidegger went astray because he reduced the question of historicality to one which could be answered from within the confines of an individual existence. Historicality is the collective appropriation of a set of historical practices *as* historical.

Looking at Lyotard from this angle, must we not say that it is narrative repetition which is left out of his model of the 'open system' (*PC*, p. 66) as exemplifying modern/postmodern historicality? At one level, the point being made here could be stated in terms of the now familiar doubt as to the worth of the claim that sets of practices are not in need of 'backing', that everything is in order as it is (if only philosophers would recognize it). Since the same move which debilitates the question of legitimation also debilitates the possibility of critique, then perhaps the critique of legitimation is neither as straightforward nor as innocent as it appears. But it is not this issue which needs to be interrogated here, although what needs interrogating is certainly related to the question of critique. What needs to be questioned here is whether the form of historicality espoused by Lyotard is not one whose very 'openness' makes the question and the problem of time/history/community invisible.

To insist on the 'heteromorphous' nature of language games, for example, is to do more than recognize the relative autonomy of one set of practices from another; it is to deny that 'we', whoever 'we' are in such a scheme, can coherently reflect upon the conceptual and causal connections that make the variety of practices we engage in more than a heap. To insist upon the 'heteromorphous' nature of language games is to deny that these games stand in relations of domination, subordination, inclusion and exclusion with respect to one another; and that we could, coherently, desire or rationally conceive things to be otherwise. For Lyotard there is no 'we' to whom the question of who 'we' are might be addressed. To insist upon the 'heteromorphous' nature of language games, then, is to insist that we become amnesiacs without the capacity for collective self-reflection. Roughly, I am suggesting, first-order discourse stands to the second-order discourse of grand narration as consciousness stands to self-consciousness. This is not to say that first-order discourses and practices are enacted without reflection or deliberation; but reflection and deliberation of this sort are not the same as self-consciousness in its full sense. Self-consciousness in its full sense, which of course can never be complete, requires the self to traverse the conditions of its present comportment in and towards its world; which is just, as Heidegger, Hegel and others have argued,[13] to recollect and appropriate the traditions and heritage to which the self in question belongs. Memory and self-consciousness are different aspects of the same. Narrative repetition, grand narration, just is the collective form of human self-consciousness.

And yet we cannot avoid asking here: how is narrative repetition possible? How can history be recommenced, be made? How does a new founding act found? Must we not admit here that narrative repetition is possible only because human beings are 'creative', free and autonomous beings who can read and interpret their past differently? And does not the idea of the radical social imaginary explicate the possibility of the kind of difference implied by the idea of making history, of history recommencing, of instituting a different history? Founding acts are grand narratives. Grand narratives, if they work, institute a new social imaginary; but then, it is not an act, a man, a people which found history; it is what can never be conceptualized, referred to, named or be brought under the rule of theory: the social imaginary itself. Founding history is something we do, and cannot do; something which is already done and yet to be achieved.

VII

To state this same thought in more traditional and contentious terms, grand narratives so construed represent the dialectic of self-consciousness. In saying this I mean to affirm that grand narratives are, indeed, the continuous self-presentation of self-consciousness to itself, which for many, including Ricoeur, is the account of narrative and reason that 'we' must reject. Ricoeur claims that the loss of credibility the Hegelian philosophy of history has undergone is an event that cannot be denied (*TN*, p. 202). Yet, Ricoeur clearly misconstrues the significance of Hegel's claim that the history of the world represents the successive stages in the development of that principle whose substantial content is the consciousness of freedom. A sympathetic and plausible reading of Hegel's philosophy of history would take his claims concerning freedom and reason to state that the categorial significance of history is revealed when the significance of historical narration as the form through which the meaning of history gets determined is itself revealed. Freedom and reason are Hegel's terms for our capacity for self-determination, but a self-determination that always occurs in concrete historical settings whose meaning is revealed through its narration. Thus, Ricoeur's sceptical doubts concerning Hegel's 'total mediation' (*TN*, pp. 202–6) ends up committing the same kind of self-contradiction that we previously saw in Lyotard. Whatever events Ricoeur points to as evidence that falsifies Hegel, above all 'Europe's claim to totalize the history of the world' (*TN*, p. 204), must be construed, if legitimate, as events that could be so narrated, and thus as confirming that the meaning of those events is determined through our self-conscious narrative practice.

Of course, it would be a complex matter to show that something like this claim is Hegel's.[14] For the present, and acknowledging all the short-cuts I've taken, the claim is that as autonomous beings we are, or have grand narratively come to regard ourselves as being (Hegel's narrative), the sorts of beings who cannot regard any given, any fact or event as having meaning except in so far as so determined by us. The terms of that determination are always historical and communal, hence the categorial parameters of meaning are the (excessive) self-determinations of historical peoples. And this is so even when we narrate the story that we no longer are so sure about who 'we' are, that the narrating subject

J. M. BERNSTEIN

has become plural and difficult in new and different ways. To say that grand narratives are interpretations is just to say that they are the product of autonomous beings; to say that those interpretations are narratives, wherein we place ourselves by demonstrating the, always contestable, crises and problems of the past can only be resolved 'this' way, is to say that we are rational beings. Because the ultimate terms of our narratives are excessive, then we must also say that as free and rational beings our freedom and rationality are always present and yet to be achieved. What 'we' cannot renounce, without renouncing ourselves, is the role of grand narrative itself.

NOTES

1 The first quote is from Theodor W. Adorno, *Negative Dialectics*, translated by E. B. Ashton, London, Routledge & Kegan Paul, 1973, p. 320. The second is from Jean-François Lyotard, *The Postmodern Condition: A Report on Knowledge*, translated by Geoff Bennington and Brian Massouri, Minneapolis, University of Minnesota Press, 1984, p. 41. Hereafter referred to as *PC*.
2 For a commendable comparison of Lyotard's and Adorno's aesthetics, whose destination differs significantly from mine, see Albrecht Wellmer, 'On the dialectic of Modernism and Postmodernism', *Praxis International*, vol. 4, no. 4, 1985, pp. 337–62.
3 For a defence of the reading of Descartes suggested here see my *The Philosophy of the Novel: Lukacs, Marxism and the Dialectics of Form*, Brighton, Harvester Press, 1984, pp. 157–79.
4 In his *Language, Counter-Memory, Practice*, translated by D. F. Bouchard and Sherry Simon, Oxford, Basil Blackwell, 1977, pp. 151–2.
5 *The Philosophical Works of Descartes*, translated by Elizabeth Haldane and G. R. T. Ross, Cambridge, Cambridge University Press, 1969, vol. 1, p. 95; and for the next quote, p. 98.
6 The work of Castoriadis is little known in the English-speaking world; hopefully, this will soon change. A translation of his major work, *L'Institution imaginaire de la societé*, Paris, Editions du Seuil, 1975, by Kathleen Blamey, was published in 1987 by Polity Press (Cambridge) under the title *The Imaginary Institution of Society*. Already available in English is a collection of essays by Castoriadis, *Crossroads in the Labyrinth*, translated by Kate Soper and Martin H. Ryle, Brighton, Harvester Press, 1984. The superb final essay in that volume on Marx and Aristotle is a good place to start one's reading of Castoriadis. The passages quoted below are from a short extract from *L'Institution* translated by Brian Singer which appears in John Fekete (ed.) *The Structural Allegory*, Manchester, Manchester University Press, 1984, pp. 6–45. For a fuller defence of Castoriadis's position see my 'Praxis and

122

aporia: Habermas' critique of Castoriadis,' *Revue Européene Des Sciences Sociales*, tome XXVII, No. 86, 1989.
7 ibid., p. 29.
8 ibid., pp. 26–7.
9 For a clear statement of this position see Merold Westphal, *History and Truth in Hegel's Phenomenology*, Atlantic Highlands, N.J., Humanities Press, 1978, ch. 7.
10 I am here suggesting that we align the Heideggerian question of the meaning of being in general with the thesis that the central concepts of political life and political theory are 'essentially contestable', i.e., value-laden because subject to positioned political contestation. I hope to elaborate this thesis in a forthcoming study on the question of the connection between the critique (destruction/deconstruction) of metaphysics and the nature of the political.
11 Martin Heidegger, *Being and Time*, translated by John Macquarrie and Edward Robinson, Oxford, Blackwell, 1962, p. 427.
12 ibid., p. 435.
13 For a splendid discussion of this issue see Ernst Tugendhat, *Self-Consciousness and Self-Determination*, translated by Paul Stern, London, M. I. T. Press, 1986.
14 For the rough beginnings of such a reading see Robert Pippin, *Hegel's Idealism*, Cambridge, Cambridge University Press, 1989.

8

TEXT AND THE NEW HERMENEUTICS

Don Ihde

INTRODUCTIONS: TEXTS

Today's world of Euro-American philosophy has seemingly immersed itself in the phenomenon of the text. It is as if the virtual totality of things has been subsumed under the paradigm metaphor of the *written*, which in turn relates to a particular activity, reading. Thus we find faddish conference titles such as 'Writing the Future', 'Writing Woman', or 'Writing the Body', abounding. I shall call this contemporary immersion Neo-Renaissancism. And my justification for this nomination comes from that marvelous French – rather than Borgesian Chinese – encyclopedia, *The Order of Things* by Michael Foucault.

Foucault rearranges the world according to *epistemes*, sort of atomic Heideggerian epochs of Being, in which discourse is ordered differently in each discontinuous era. In this scheme of things not only are such concepts as 'man', 'perception', 'biology' invented and then disappear, but certain discourses or organizations of knowledge and practice may be fulcral, such as the Renaissance which draws from the Middle Ages, but disappears into the Modern era which precedes ours.

And the organization of knowledge-discourse which characterizes this fulcral period is one which has as one of its principles, the primacy of *writing*. In short, this is pre-Derrida, Derrida. Hear what Foucault has to say: the sixteenth century is one which is marked by the great metaphor of the book

> which one opens, that one pores over and reads in order to know nature, [and] is merely the reverse and visible side of another transference, and a much deeper one, which forces

124

language to reside in the world, among the plants, the herbs, the stones, and the animals.[1]

This metaphor continues to pervade the beginning of the seventeenth century, Foucault tells us, where 'such an interweaving of language and things, in a space common to both, presupposes an absolute privilege on the part of writing.[2] For here is an age also fascinated with its new technologies, including the invention of printing, the arrival from the east of new manuscripts, and a literature not governed by voice, not to mention a *written* music.

> Henceforth, it is the primal nature of language to be written. The sounds made by voices provide no more than a transitory and precarious translation of it. What God introduced into the world was written words. Adam, when he imposed their first names upon the animals, did no more than read those visible and silent marks. . . . Vigenere and Duret both said – and almost in identical terms – that the written had always preceded the spoken, certainly in nature, and perhaps even in the knowledge of men.[3]

Here is the Neo-Renaissancism of an 'inscription', a 'trace' which calls for both a Primal Text and its adumbration into the infinity of interpretation:

> Knowledge therefore consisted in relating one form of language to another form of language; in restoring the great, unbroken plain of words and things; in making everything speak. . . . [Here] the task of commentary can never by definition, be completed. . . . [But] there can be no commentary unless below the language one is reading and deciphering, there runs the sovereignty of an original Text. . . . The language of the sixteenth century [thus]. . . . found itself caught, no doubt, between these interacting elements, in the interstice occurring between the primal Text and the infinity of interpretation.[4]

I suggest, in one sense, that the current absorption with the Text is thus a return to this fulcral period, although with a difference.

I shall not follow Foucault any further other than to remark that what follows the sixteenth- and seventeenth-century primacy of writing is the modern period which recharacterizes language under a different principle of organization, a principle which in typical semiotic fashion, inverts the previous order. Such an inversion, naturally, means that writing is replaced with speech which becomes primary in the modern era:

> Henceforth, the primary Text is effaced, and with it the entire, inexhaustive foundation of the words whose mute being was inscribed in things; all that remains is representation unfolding in the verbal signs that manifest it, and hence becomes discourse.[5]

Speech inverts writing and commentary is inverted into criticism. Here we see, placed at the seventeenth century, the pre-Derrida/ Derrida invention of speech and presence, the echo of which is then attached to Husserl. And given the retrogressive movement of Neo-Renaissancism, today we move back from the episteme of speech – and I shall say, *perception* which is also 'invented' in the modern era – to the once previous world of the text.

In this playful, but serious, introduction, I have obviously begun to situate myself. And that situation is one which seeks its position at the interstice between writing and the heard, between reading and speech, which is to say, between the text and perception. For I am uncomfortable with the paradigm metaphor of the text, and I am concerned with the almost forgotten role of perception within the lifeworld which I take to be larger than the reduction of it to a textual schema.

RICOEUR AND THE NEW HERMENEUTICS

First, I must locate Ricoeur with respect to this scheme of the text and the primacy of writing: What is today 'post-structuralism' and deconstruction, yesterday was structuralism. In that recent yesterday, Ricoeur had also entered the fray. The results of those battles are seen in *The Conflict of Interpretations* (French publication 1969, English publication 1974). Under the subtitle of *Hermeneutics and Structuralism*, Ricoeur juxtaposed a series of interpretive processes between an essentially structuralist and a *phenomenological* hermeneutics. In this juxtaposition, structuralism was shown to be a perspective which not only emphasized synchrony over diachrony, but occupied an antipodal position to hermeneutics: 'This is why structuralism as philosophy will develop a kind of intellectualism which is fundamentally antireflective, anti-idealist, and antiphenomenological.'[6] This stance falls out from 'the subordination, not the opposition, of diachrony to synchrony.'[7] In short, the problem of temporality in relation to both history and human existence motivated this earlier, but already new hermeneutics.

One of the ingenious points made in this debate was that what could count as privileged examples for such synchronic interpretations, was itself only a small range of examples. Thus Ricoeur accused structuralism of having to favour precisely those modes of thought and culture which remained caught in the world of bricolage. 'Totemic thought, it seems to me, is precisely the one that has the greatest affinity to structuralism.'[8] His counterpart was the ancient biblical, particularly Old Testament tradition which emphasized diachrony, or the series of revelatory *events* which motivated a historically minded people. Thus in the end, 'bricolage works with debris; in bricolage the structure saves the event; the debris plays the role of a preconstraint, of a message already transmitted.'[9] But within a basically temporalistic tradition such as the biblical one, 'the reuse of biblical symbols in our cultural domain rests, on the contrary, on a semantic richness, on a surplus of what is signified, which opens towards new interpretations.'[10] Here temporality linked to history is already a primary factor in the new hermeneutics.

Today, Ricoeur continues the debate within the context of today's rampant *textuality*. But his approach is again, instructive. It is reflected in the title of the recent *Time and Narrative* volumes. It is not accidental that the term, narrative, is already suggestive of a more actional, dynamic process than the term, text. For in this nuanced difference there already lies the role of a revised phenomenological hermeneutic which places itself within the current debate, and in such a way that its forgotten dimensions are again taken up.

What Ricoeur restores to the debate is the emphasis and base of all writing within the context of a human-world relationship. But an interrelation between the human and the world across *temporality* and through *reference*. Thus when he takes up the question of narrative, it is in the context of prefiguration through *configuration*, which is to say that there is a structure of narrative, through a *refiguration* which is a temporal movement which redoes in an actional way any previous configuration. Here we have the maintenance of the essentially gestalt model of a phenomenological analysis, but it occurs also in terms of that which points beyond itself in terms of *reference*. At the end of volume II, Ricoeur provides the following summary:

> The problem of the refiguration of time by narrative will, therefore be brought to its conclusion only when we shall be in a position to make the referential intentions of the historical narrative and the fictional narrative interweave.[11]

Here, just as in the earlier debates with structuralism, Ricoeur has juxtaposed himself against the implicit internalism of post-structuralism. There remains, for Ricoeur, *referential intention*. But this referential intention is not anything like a sentential one, it is rather a gestaltist one which becomes clear only through the multiple dimensions of metaphor (*La metaphor vive*) and through the interrelation of the existent human and a world:

> Our analysis of . . . time will at least have marked a decisive turning point . . . by providing something like a *world of the text* for us to think about, while awaiting its complement, the *lifeworld of the reader*, without which the signification of the literary work is incomplete.[12]

Narrative is both actional and structural. As a plot it provides structure, meaning, but in the movements from configuration through refiguration in both historical and fictional narrative, there is revealed the constitution of textual worlds in correlation with human lifeworlds.

Because the purpose of this paper is not simply Ricoeur-exposition, I shall not undertake a long excursus, but shall rather suggest several of the threads of continuity and modification which go to make up this new hermeneutic:

(1) Echoing the relation between experience and language found in the *Symbolism of Evil* in which those primitives of the experience of suffering and evil find expression in an already doubled expression (the analogues of stain, sin and guilt), narrative, which is *muthos*, also interrelates experience and now narrative expression:

> My basic hypothesis [is] that between the activity of narrating a story and the temporal character of human experience there exists a correlation that is not merely accidental but that presents a transcultural form of necessity. . . . time becomes human to the extent that it is articulated through

a narrative mode, and narrative attains its full meaning when it becomes a condition of temporal existence.[13]

(2) The task of eliciting this connection is necessarily hermeneutic rather than structural. In short, here is again the contrast between the limits of a semiotics in contrast to a lifeworld semantics:

> It is the task of hermeneutics, in return, to reconstruct the set of operations by which a work lifts itself above the opaque depths of living, acting, and suffering, to be given by an author to readers who receive it and thereby change their acting. For a semiotic theory, the only operative concept is that of the literary text. Hermeneutics, however, is concerned with reconstructing the entire arc of operations by which practical experience provides itself with works, authors and readers.[14]

(3) Often now citing the notion of the Husserlian lifeworld, and its use of a genetic, i.e. historical–ontological derivations, the movement of time and narrative is from 'the destiny of a prefigured time that becomes a refigured time through the mediation of a configured time.'[15] At the level of prefiguration is the realm of concrete human action, situated within whatever historical or fictive context is referred to. Here is the ground level of agents, with actions, having motives. 'There is no structural analysis that does not borrow from an explicit or an implicit phenomenology of "doing something".'[16]

(4) There is also a modification of the usual noematic–noetic analysis of phenomenology in the Ricoeurean approach to texts and narrative, in that any theory of writing must relate correlatively to a theory of reading. It is here that the problem of reference in its narrative context arises:

> An aesthetic of reception cannot take up the problem of communication without also taking up that of reference. What is communicated, in the final analysis, is, beyond the sense of the work, the world it projects and that constitutes its horizon.[17]

But the 'world of the text' is not, and cannot be equivalent to *the* world. Here is where Ricoeur distinctively breaks with the current penchant to reduce world to text:

Reference and horizon are correlative as are figure and ground. All experience both possesses a contour that circumscribes it and distinguishes it, and arises against a horizon of potentialities that constitutes at once an internal and external horizon for experience.[18]

But, in this interplay Ricoeur also argues that 'language does not constitute a world for itself. It is not even a world. . . . Language is for itself the order of the Same. The world is its Other.'[19]

(5) But the correlation a priori of human and world is one in which 'all reference is co-reference.'[20]

What a reader receives is not just the sense of the word, but, through its sense, its reference, that is, the experience it brings to language, and, in the last analysis, the world and the temporality it unfolds in the face of this experience.[21]

(6) Finally, because this form of referentiality is not merely literal or descriptive, particularly in fictional and historical narrative, it refers through *complexity*. One might say that the 'primitive' of narrative is precisely this complexity, the complexity of what Ricoeur previously studied as metaphor. 'I tried to demonstrate in *The Rule of Metaphor* that language's capacity for reference was not exhausted by descriptive discourse and that poetic works referred to the world in their own specific way, that of metaphorical reference.'[22]

What we arrive at through this hermeneutic process is the already mentioned correlation of the world of the text with the lifeworld of the reader. Thus in a fictional text: 'what is interpreted in a text is the proposing of a world that I might inhabit and into which I might project my own most powers. . . . Poetry (or fiction) through its *muthos* [narrative], redescribes the world.[23]

Here, then, is a brief sketch of a new hermeneutics addressed to the problem of time and narrative, within which the role of the reader in relation to the text is a relation between the lifeworld of the reader and the world of the text. Its framework is phenomenological, now modelled after, but dynamically creviced from, the Husserlian concept of an actional lifeworld situated between the historical and the imaginative within the movements of refiguration, configuration and prefiguration.

I probably need not say that I find this approach refreshing in the contemporary world of deconstruction and hermeneutics. Ricoeur seems somehow to always address that which is most contemporary, and yet at the same time retain his sense of balance. For that I am grateful, and from that I have often learned.

But if Ricoeur has been able to reformulate a phenomenological hermeneutic to address the textuality of the contemporary scene, there are also aspects of a relation between phenomenology and the phenomena of writing and reading which have *not* yet been addressed. And it is here that I shall take up my own position within this discourse.

PERCEPTION, READING AND WRITING

What has been left out, to my mind, is precisely what could be called *a phenomenology of reading and writing*. At best it has been implicit and operational behind the scenes. What I propose to do is to open precisely the field of this phenomenology of reading and writing, and to do it by way of reintroducing the role of *perception*, or better, perceptual action, into the arena.

One could, of course, recall both the Husserl of the lifeworld period here, as well as Merleau-Ponty's primacy of perception. For Husserl, in his analysis of the Galilean world, argued that it was a break with the basic lifeworld which, at bottom, must refer back to the ordinary perceptions and actions of humans, an echo of which we have found in Ricoeur's position. Similarly, although somewhat more subtly with respect to the interpretation of perception, one finds the analyses of Merleau-Ponty regarding motility, perceptual gestalts, etc., particularly in the worlds of painting and the arts.

I shall begin by taking note of that most extreme deconstructionist, Jacques Derrida, by suggesting that within the techniques of interpretation and deconstruction he so frequently employs regarding seemingly odd or distorted readings, there lurks an *implicit* phenomenology of perception. I noted in an earlier article, 'Phenomenology and deconstructive strategy', that such an implicit phenomenology lies within Derrida's treatment of texts:

> Take a text: If one views a text (perceptually) it usually appears first as writing which is centered on the page, surrounded by margins, but the focal center is clearly the bulk of what is written. Then, if one reads the text, what usually

emerges as focal is what the text is about, however complex that may be, as indeed any text usually is. What does Derrida do with a text? Posed in the way I have indicated, he immediately decenters what seems to be focal and immediate. His focus is radically shifted to titles, signatures, margins, borders, divisions, etc. In short, he draws our attention to features which are there, but usually taken at most as background, secondary or unimportant features.

In a sense this is a highly 'phenomenological' technique. For example, in an analysis of perception, phenomenologists like to point out that while what stands out (figures) are usually most obvious because they are the referenda of our usual perceptions, all figures take their position upon a background which is equally present and which constitutes the field of perceivability. In short, this move 'decenters' focal perception so as to attend to taken-for-granted but important fringe features. Similarly, to point out that all perceptions include not only manifest surfaces, but latent 'backsides,' is to 'decenter' at least the usual interpretations of perception. I am suggesting that this device – perhaps taken to Nietzschean excess – is a familiar ploy of Derrida. Inded, one can see, once the operation is known, how to follow along with such deconstructions. (Is there a Derrida text which addresses itself to the empty background of the page? If not, there ought to be.)

Once the focus is decentered, however, a second more radical step is taken. In the Derridean tactic this seems to be a kind of playfulness which then wants to read the fringe back into the center as a kind of shadow presence. This tactic appeared early in the assertion of the primacy of writing in *Of Grammatology* and *Writing and Difference* If writing 'precedes' speech (decentering the subject), its 'evidence' is the trace which must be found but since the trace is not obvious the finding calls for a kind of play. Similarly in 'late' Derrida, the margins, signatures and borders get played back into the focal text. It is in the brilliance of this playing that Derrida becomes genius-magician with his supporters noting only the genius and his enemies only the magician.[24]

132

This, however, is to *indirectly* broach the problem of a phenomenology of reading and writing. Rather, now I would like to develop a different example-set by looking at an interesting historical illustration of the role of perception and bodily position in relation to the phenomena of reading and writing.

I have deliberately chosen an example in which there is the establishment of a *reading perspective* which is then implicated in a large praxical perspective. The example relates to the reading of charts, particularly navigational charts such as are used by seamen. I shall then associate this 'micro-perception', i.e. actual bodily position and perceptual perspective, with what I shall call a 'macro-perception' or the interpretive praxis which permeates a larger set of cultural perspectives.

As early as the fourteenth century there began to appear a new set of maps or charts in Europe called *portulans*. These were basically what today would be called pilot charts, or maps which display in a visually isomorphic way, the coastal and land configurations along some sailing route.

These charts were different from the also then popular Mappae Mundi which displayed a different picture of the world. The 'world maps' of the medieval imagination displayed an essentially mythical world which had the shape of a round earth, crossed by two rivers in the shape of a 'T'. These maps located Jerusalem as the center of the earth, were land oriented, and usually filled with mythological characters and locations – they obviously could not be used for any voyaging or navigation! The portulans, in contrast, were among the first 'empirical' maps and carefully traced routes along coasts and between land masses. They were sea-oriented and routes were also laid out in terms of an imposed 'grid' – only in this early case, the grid was not yet that of today's longitude and latitude grid, but of the dominant *winds*. Thus upon the face of the earth, there were guidelines for sailing, the grid of the winds (all of which were named in those days).

Note, now, two other features concerning these maps, features which in reading seem almost too obvious: (1) First, the map was an abstract, but essentially isomorphic map regarding the shape of the coastline, land masses, etc.; but (2) the isomorphism was displayed to a reading perspective, to a position *above* the earth itself. These features we take as so obvious, so taken-for-granted, that it never occurs to us that such a representation has a certain oddness. That oddness is one which is experienced by the actual navigator – for he (or she) does not actually see the landmass or coastline in this fashion. Rather, the bodily position of the actual navigator is one of being located upon the deck or vessel. Thus from *reading* the chart to finding one's position from a *lateral* perspective on board the boat, there must be added a particular hermeneutic act, the act of transferring a perspective and position from overhead to lateral.

In short, with the portulans, we have the constitution of an 'empirical' view of the world, but constituted from the noetic position of the 'god's-eye' perspective, from above.

Now this is, in fact, a normal situation for *reading*. And this obtains with respect to reading other 'texts' than those of charts. That is, normally, we sit, with book in front of and usually below our eyes, or, as was quite normal in the Middle Ages, standing, reading from above. In that respect there was already a sedimented practice regarding the reader/text position with relation to a bodily–perceptual stance.

The isomorphism of representing an actual coastline introduces a reading 'realism' into the process which has stronger implications for both a privileged perspective and for the associated hermeneutic acts of interpretation needed to fill out the navigational praxis.

To make this feature stand out with even more distinctness, let us do a few phenomenological variations upon map-reading, first by varying the noematic or object correlates: (1) Maps need not be isomorphic nor overhead. One could, as is also done in directing someone to one's house, have given a set of written directions: 'You take Hollins Road for about a mile, until you hit the Griswold Pub; then right until you get to Wistful Cottage, my place.' Here the positionality of the reading is not so important since isomorphism is not part of the process, but there is the hermeneutics of reading which must recognize from a written description of the features of a perceived landscape; or (2) one could have as part of the navigational map (and as, fortunately is common in British circles) a representation of a lateral perspective either separately or added to the regular chart. In this case the position of the navigator on board corresponds to what is seen in the chart. 'The two towers, when lined up, serve as range markers for the entrance to Swipshold Harbour.' Here the all too frequent ambiguity suffered in trying to interpret where one is when approaching an unfamiliar landfall, is eased. In the overhead perspective, I must imagine what towers belong to what chart representations, and what they must look like to someone in a lateral position.

This simple example, so familiar, should be expanded. Take what is equally familiar to the inhabitant of a literate culture, the representation of any number of landscapes from elevated or 'bird's-eye' perspective: I have a large book on the history of gardening and from very early times one finds representations which are from elevated or overhead perspectives. These seem to be cross-cultural insofar as they occur in *literate* cultures. Thus medieval gardens, Renaissance gardens, Chinese, Japanese, Indian and Persian gardens are likely to be displayed from overhead or elevated perspective, ‑perspectives which are rarely actually occupied by the gardener.

The same, however, is not the case with respect to many *non-literate* cultures! Instead, representation will frequently be lateral, often not even in perspectival form at all. Thus in certain South American bark paintings, one finds simply a field of scattered figures (humans, animals, canoes, etc.) displayed on the painting, but ,each to be seen as from the side, laterally. Or, if organized, the laterality may take the shape of some series of laterally displayed figures, as in some Australian aboriginal bark paintings. In short, the establishment of a coherent or 'empirical' display, and the favoured 'god's' or 'bird's-eye' implied position seems to be lacking.

But is it lacking? Or is this the trace of a different seeing of the world – I am reluctant here to call it a 'reading' of the world, since reading in a non-literate culture will be somewhat metaphorical, or perhaps projected from ours.

I return briefly to navigation, this time with an example from a non-literate culture, from a culture without maps. I refer to the equally or even more ancient practices of South Pacific navigation, the principles of which have only recently been reconstructed by westerners. Note that historically, the South Pacific peoples successfully navigated and populated virtually the entirety of the Pacific in times equal to or more ancient than our Middle Ages. Thus their methods were clearly pragmatically successful.

But they did this without maps, and, as I shall show, without utilizing our praxis of overhead perspective. How? I shall call their system a *perceptual hermeneutics*. We again might be tempted to say that they 'read' nature as their 'text'. But again this is to take our own presuppositions and cross-culturally impose the habits of a

reading or literate culture into these perceptions. Let me sche-
matically indicate several features of this perceptual hermeneutics
to illustrate what is involved.

(1)   Once a pathway through the sea was known, there were
       methods of retracing those pathways. Starpaths were
       very well known to these navigators. From childhood
       the boys would canoe with their elders and the stars –
       which were interpreted as pillars of the skyhouse – were
       named and known through canoeing songs. Then, once
       identification was learned, the various formulae, not
       unlike the instructions I cited earlier in telling one how
       to reach my cottage, were given in other verses of these
       songs. 'If you wish to reach Tahiti, you follow the Great
       Eastern Bird until the ghost island, Mapu, reaches you,
       then you turn and follow the Fish, etc.' These memori-
       zed formulae have persisted to the present and David
       Lewis, the anthropologist-sailor who has studied these
       methods the most, was able to get Hawaiians to retrace
       a voyage from Hawaii to Tahiti which had not been
       made for 300 years – without instruments or charts!

(2)   Another feature is the need to be able to steer a straight
       course often in reduced visibility or even in storms.
       These navigators learned to follow direction by
       becoming kinesthetically sensitive to the dominant swell
       patterns of the Pacific. The trade winds create long
       parallel swells which persist through the sailing season,
       and which can be detected even under or in the midst
       of confused local seas. That is, they can, if the navigator
       sits down into the belly of the catamaran and feels them
       with his testicles! – so say the Polynesians.
          Moreover, these swell patterns also refract when
       approaching an island, and the refraction is one of
       the clues to finding the island. Thus, like listening to the
       bass rhythm of a musical piece, the detection of swell
       patterns provides perceptual clues to direction.

(3)   And how does one spot an island, particularly if on a
       voyage of discovery? The answer is again perceptual:
       islands with mountains and jungles (a) cast a greenish
       glow upon the sky for many miles away, (b) closer, the
       clouds which collect over an island landmass do not

move – even though higher clouds are moving – and may be spotted from great distances. (c) Birds at dusk return to their roosts, with some species beginning the return from fifty miles out, others from thirty miles out, etc. The navigator knows all the birds and notes their dusktime direction.

And so it goes, a subtle, perceptual hermeneutics, utilizing neither map nor overhead perspective. Indeed, range marking, even the abstraction of 'ghost islands' are all described from lateral perspective. But there is one more, and especially striking, feature which helps sediment this system of navigation as an *embodied position* system. On board, as with many seagoing terms and languages, the language of spatial orientation and position changes. It becomes one in which the fixed variable needed for this relativistic system becomes one's actual bodily position. Thus one does not speak of 'going to' Tahiti, rather, one speaks of Tahiti 'approaching us' or 'coming to us'. For the boat also does not 'go through the sea', rather the 'sea passes by us'. Here is a primitive 'Einsteinean' world in which whatever is measured must take into account the position of the actual observer.

If such a perceptual system might seem strange to us, it is when we begin to compare the two systems that even more interesting factors emerge. For example, if I am able to sympathetically enter the perceptual world of the Pacific Navigator (did I ever leave it? since I do live my body and am positioned with respect to the world, even if I overlook the dominance of laterality in ordinary action), then when I ask 'from what position could I have established that my canoe is "going" to Tahiti?' the answer would be, 'from the fixed "god's-eye" view which is above me, but which I do not actually occupy.' For at sea, when the horizons are in motion, when the bow wave passes the bow, it is perceptually relative to say that the sea is passing by my craft, or I am passing through the sea. But both statements reflexively imply a position from which the statement is 'true'. Thus in this now cross-cultural example of a variation, I begin to discern the primacy, in my own culture, of an imagined or quasi-perspective as the privileged one.

Yet it is a perspective which today we take for granted, which is familiar and sedimented. Nor do we note its strangeness or oddity. Could it be that it in any way implies a relation between our bodily micro-perceptions which, as Merleau-Ponty so brilliantly demonstrated, we forget in distancing the lifeworld and the scientific world, and the macro-perception of a privileged transcendent view? I would like to suggest that what I am referring to is the sediment of a long practice of *reading*.

Or, in another way of putting it, can there be in our practice of being literate, not only some relation between the world of the text and the lifeworld of the reader, but a deeper implication even for the bodily, perceptual position in which we find ourselves when we read a text, any text? Is the 'god's-eye' view a projected and privileged reading position?

CONCLUSION

There must be some connection between bodily position and perception; its extension and extrapolation into the macroperceptions of a culture has been suspected for some time in phenomenology. When Merleau-Ponty claimed that culture is perceived, I am suggesting that there is something stronger than metaphor involved. But what of the interconnection between reading position and this macro-perception – is there evidence for this reading-perceiving which constitutes our praxis?

My last example will make this suggestion stronger. Ancient Egyptian bas-reliefs often had odd perspectives. They were perspectives which in the same panel combined overhead and lateral perspectives, perspectives which with respect to their implied observer's position could only appear to be 'inconsistent'. Thus in the depiction of a garden, there could be a laterally perceived series of vines being tended by the workers, but in the same scene, the water pool would be depicted from a directly overhead position. Here was a 'doubled' perspective which, when thought about seems odd, yet which must have seemed quite conventional and familiar to the ancient Egyptian.

But, if one now switched to the reading which was practised by the Egyptians, suddenly one discerns the same phenomenon. Hieroglyphics were a mixed or 'doubled' writing, part pictograph, part phonetic. Thus while it might be an ibis or a bull which was depicted, its significance could be either what it represented, or it could be a phoneme sounded within a word or sentence: a 'doubled' text with respect to reading. Thus in both representation and in the written text, Egyptian seeing-reading was doubled, constituting a familiar praxis within which life was ordered.

This was a lifeworld in which the polymorphy of perception took a particular shape, even when unnoticed and even in the midst of one of the early cultures which could be called literate. I suggest that the same praxis, although shaped differently, orders our lifeworld, and thus while it makes a good deal of sense to utilize the reading metaphor widely, it does not make sense to forget its involvement in the unspoken and unwritten domain of perception and bodily action within a material world.

NOTES

1 Michel Foucault, *The Order of Things; An Archeology of the Human Sciences*, New York, Vintage Books, 1973, p. 35.
2 ibid., p. 38.
3 ibid., p. 38.
4 ibid., p. 40.
5 ibid., p. 79.
6 Paul Ricoeur, *The Conflict of Interpretations*, edited by Don Ihde, Evanston, Northwestern University Press, 1974, p. 33.
7 ibid., p. 33.
8 ibid., p. 41.
9 ibid., p. 47.
10 ibid., p. 48.
11 Paul Ricoeur, *Time and Narrative*, translated by K. McLaughlin and D. Pellauer, Chicago, University of Chicago Press, 1984–8, vol. II, p. 160.
12 ibid., p. 160.
13 *Time and Narrative*, vol. I, p. 53.
14 ibid., p. 53.
15 ibid., p. 54.
16 ibid., p. 56.
17 ibid., p. 77.
18 ibid., p. 78.
19 ibid., p. 78.
20 ibid., p. 78.
21 ibid., p. 78–9.
22 ibid., p. 80.
23 ibid., p. 81.
24 Don Ihde, *Existential Technics*, New York, SUNY Press, 1983, pp. 163–4.

9

THE METAPHYSICS OF NARRATIVITY

Time and symbol in Ricoeur's philosophy of history

Hayden White

Recent debate over the nature of historical narrative has been carried out in terms of the adequacy of the story form of discourse to the representation of reality. Historical theorists such as the *Annalistes*, who were interested in transforming historiography into a science, could legitimately point out that the natural sciences had little interest in storytelling as an aim of their enterprise. And indeed, it could be argued with some pertinence that the transformation of a field of study into a genuine science has always been attended by an abandonment of anything like an interest in inventing a story to tell about its object of study in favour of the task of discovering the laws that governed its structures and functions. According to this view, the prevalence of any interest in storytelling within a discipline aspiring to the status of a science was prima facie evidence of its proto-scientific, not to mention its manifestly mythical or ideological, nature. Getting the 'story' out of 'history' was therefore a first step in the transformation of historical studies into a science.

The defence of narrative history by Anglo-American thinkers was based on a similar identification of narrative with the story form of discourse. For the principal defenders of narrative historiography in this tradition, the adequacy of the story form to the representation of historical events and processes was manifest, even if the theoretical justification of that adequacy remained to be provided. In their view, not only was a story a legitimate form of explanation for specifically historical events and processes but it was the *proper* way of representing historical events in discourse, inasmuch as such events could be established as displaying the

140

kind of forms met with in traditional story types. Historical stories differed from fictional stories by virtue of the fact that they referred to real rather than to imaginary events. But 'true' historical stories did not differ from historical events by virtue of their formal features, because history itself was a congeries of lived stories awaiting only the historian to transform them into prose equivalents.

Now, neither the attack on nor the defence of narrative history did justice to the variety of kinds of stories met with in literature, folklore and myth; the differences between the techniques of the traditional novel and the modernist novel; or the complex relation between 'literature' and the 'real world', to which the former undeniably referred even if in the most indirect and allegorical manner. The notion that historical narratives were unrealistic because they were cast in the form of a story implied that literature could not illuminate the 'real world' in any important way. But the idea that historical narratives illuminated the 'real world' because the world displayed the form of a well-made story, with 'characters' engaged in conflicts similar to those encountered in traditional kinds of stories, was similarly untenable. What was obviously called for was an analysis of narrative, narration and narrativity that would take into account the many forms of story-telling met with in world literature, from ancient epics through the post-modernist novel, and a reconceptualization of the possible relations existing between the three principal kinds of narrative discourse – mythic, historical and fictional – and the 'real world' to which they undeniably referred. It was to these tasks that Paul Ricoeur turned in the late 1970s.

The results of Ricoeur's labours are now available in his magisterial *Temps et récit (Time and Narrative)*, which must be accounted the most important synthesis of literary and historical theory produced in our century.[1] Although at the moment of this writing only two of the projected three volumes of *Time and Narrative* have been published, the plan of the whole is discernible [This paper was originally presented in 1982]. The analysis consists of four parts in three volumes. Volume I contains Parts 1 and 2: 'The circle of narrativity and temporality' and 'History and narrative', respectively. Volume II contains Part 3: 'Configuration in fictional narrative'. Volume III, entitled *Temps raconté*, will present 'the threefold testimony of phenomenology, history, and fiction' regarding the 'power' of narrative to 'refigure time' in such a way as to reveal the 'secret relationship' of eternity to death (*TN* vol. I preface and p. 101).

In his work, Ricoeur seeks to sort out the different notions of story, storytelling and narrativity informing the principal theories of narrative discourse set forth in our time. In the process, he redefines historical narrative as a kind of allegory of temporality, but an allegory of a special kind, namely, a true allegory. This is not to say that he denies cognitive authority to other kinds of allegory, such as theological, mythical and poetic allegory. On the contrary, he grants to fictional narrativity a capacity to represent a deeper insight into the 'human experience of temporality' than does either its historical or its mythical counterpart. None the less, historical narrative is assigned a specific task in the representation of a reality that presents itself to human consciousness, in one aspect at least, as an insoluble but ultimately 'comprehensible' mystery. This mystery is nothing other than the enigma of being-in-time. Taken in conjunction with Ricoeur's earlier *The Rule of Metaphor (La metaphore vive)*,[2] which forms what he calls a 'pair' with *Time and Narrative (TN* vol. II, p. ix), we will have, when the latter work is finished, a comprehensive theory of the relation between language, narrative discourse and temporality by which to appreciate the degree of truth to be accorded to any representation of the world in the form of a narrative.

The overarching thesis of *Time and Narrative* is that temporality is 'the structure of existence that reaches language in narrativity' and that narrativity is 'the language structure that has temporality as its ultimate referent'. This formulation appears in Ricoeur's 1980 essay, 'Narrative time', which plainly indicates that his study of the truth of narrative is based on a notion of the narrativistic nature of time itself.[3] The contention is not that historians impose a narrative form on sets or sequences of real events that might just as legitimately be represented in some other, non-narrative discourse but that historical events possess the same structure as narrative discourse. It is their narrative structure that distinguishes historical events from natural events (which lack such a structure). It is because historical events possess a narrative structure that historians are justified in regarding stories as valid representations of such events and treating such representations as explanations of them.

Needless to say, Ricoeur's notion of story differs in important ways from that used by recent Anglo-American philosophers to account for the explanatory effect of narrative histories. It is not enough simply to tell the story of what happened in the past, in the manner of a sports journalist recounting the sequence of contingencies that resulted in the outcome of an athletic contest on a given day. A narrative history is not necessarily, Ricoeur insists, a 'species' of the genus 'story' (*TN* vol. I, pp. 179, 228). Any number of different kinds of stories could be told about any given sequence of real events, and all of them might be equally plausible accounts thereof. We could follow such stories perfectly well and credit them all as possible ways of making sense of the events related in them but still not feel that we had been provided with a specifically 'historical' account of the events in question – any more than we feel that we have been provided with a historical account of yesterday's political or economic events after we have read a newspaper account of them. Journalists tell stories about 'what happened' yesterday or yesteryear and often explain what happened with greater or lesser adequacy, in the same way that detectives or lawyers in courts of law may do. But the stories they tell should not be confused with historical narratives – as theorists of historiography looking for an analogue of historical discourse in the world of everyday affairs so often do – because such stories typically lack the 'secondary referentiality' of historical narratives, the indirect reference to the 'structure of temporality' that gives to the events related in the story the aura of 'historicality' (*Geschichtlichkeit*).[4] Without this particular secondary referent, the journalistic story, however interesting, insightful, informative and even explanatory it may be, remains locked within the confines of the purview of the 'chronicle'.

By the same token, Ricoeur's notion of the historical narrative differs from that of certain formalist or rhetorical analysts of folktales, epics and novels, for whom the essence of a story is contained in its disposition of 'functional mechanisms', which can be put in any order as long as the conventions of the genre to which the story belongs are observed (or, conversely, systematically transgressed). What such notions of narrative miss, in Ricoeur's view, is the logic, or rather the poetics, that presides over the integration of such mechanisms into a discursive whole that means more, because it says more than the sum total of the sentences that it comprises. For him, a narrative discourse is not analysable into the local meanings of the sentences that make it up. A discourse is not, as some would have it, a sentence writ large; any analysis of a discourse carried out on the analogy of a grammatical or rhetorical explication of the sentence will miss the larger structure of meaning, figurative or allegorical in nature, that the discourse as a whole produces.

In contrast, then, to both chronicles of events and what we may call 'dissertative' discourses, the kinds of discursive stories that interest Ricoeur and that he takes to be the types told in narrative histories are characterized by their possession of plots. To 'emplot' a sequence of events and thereby transform what would otherwise be only a chronicle of events into a story is to effect a mediation between events and certain universally human 'experiences of temporality'. And this goes for fictional stories no less than for historical stories. The meaning of stories is given in their 'emplotment'. By emplotment, a sequence of events is 'configured' ('grasped together') in such a way as to represent 'symbolically' what would otherwise be unutterable in language,[5] namely, the ineluctably 'aporetic' nature of the human experience of time.[6]

Historical discourse is a privileged instantiation of the human capacity to endow the experience of time with meaning, because the immediate referent (the *Bedeutung*) of this discourse is real, rather than imaginary, events. The novelist can invent the events that his stories comprise, in the sense of imaginatively producing them, in response to the exigencies of emplotment or, for that matter, of disemplotment, after the manner of modernist, anti-narrativist writers. But the historian cannot, in this sense, invent the events of his stories; he must (in that other, equally traditional sense of *invention*) 'find' or 'discover' them. This is because historical events have already been 'invented' (in the sense of 'created') by past human agents who, by their actions, produced lives worthy of having stories told about them.[7] This means that the intentionality informing human actions, as against mere motions, conduces to the creation of lives that have the coherency of emplotted stories. This is one reason why, I take it, the very notion of a modernist historiography, modelled on the modernist, anti-narrativist novel, would be in Ricoeur's estimation a contradiction in terms.

The meaning of real human lives, whether of individuals or collectivities, is the meaning of the plots, quasiplots, paraplots or failed plots by which the events that those lives comprise are endowed with the aspect of stories having a discernible beginning, middle and end. A meaningful life is one that aspires to the coherency of a story with a plot. Historical agents prospectively prefigure their lives as stories with plots. This is why the historian's retrospective emplotment of historical events cannot be the product of the imaginative freedom enjoyed by the writer of fictions. Historiographical emplotment is, Ricoeur argues, a poetic activity, but it belongs to the (Kantian) 'productive imagination' rather than to the 'reproductive' or merely 'associative' imagination of the writer of fictions, because it is the productive imagination that is at work in the making of distinctively historical events no less than in the activity of retrospectively emplotting, or refiguring, them which it is the historian's duty to carry out (*TN* vol. I, p. 68).

The creation of a historical narrative, then, is an action exactly like that by which historical events are created, but in the domain of 'wording' rather than that of 'working'.[8] By discerning the plots 'prefigured' in historical actions by the agents that produced them and 'configuring' them as sequences of events having the coherency of stories with a beginning, middle and end, historians make explicit the meaning implicit in historical events themselves. While this meaning is prefigured in the actions of historical agents, the agents themselves cannot foresee it, because human actions have consequences that extend beyond the purview of those who perform them. This is why it is wrong, from Ricoeur's point of view, for historians to limit themselves to trying to see things from the position of past agents alone, to trying to think themselves back into the mind or consciousness of past actors in the historical drama. They are fully justified in availing themselves of the advantages of hindsight. Moreover, they are fully justified in using the techniques of analysis developed by the social sciences of their own time to identify social forces at work in the agent's milieu, because these forces may have been only emergent in the agent's time and place and not perceivable to the latter.

Human actions have consequences that are both foreseeable and unforeseeable, that are informed by intentions both conscious and unconscious, and that are frustratable by contingent factors that are both knowable and unknowable. It is for this reason that narrative is necessary for the representation of 'what actually happened' in a given domain of historical occurrences. A scientific (or scientistic) historiography of the sort envisioned by the *Annalistes*, which deals in large-scale, physical and social, anonymous 'forces', is not so much wrong as simply able to tell only a part of the story of human beings at grips with their individual and collective destinies. It produces the historiographical equivalent of a drama that is all scene and no actors, or a novel that is all theme but lacking in characters. Such a historiography features all background and no foreground. The best it could provide would be 'quasi-history', comprising 'quasi-events', enacted by 'quasi-characters', and displaying the form of a 'quasi-plot' (*TN* vol. I, pp. 206ff.).

And, indeed, as Ricoeur shows in his analysis of Braudel's great book, *The Mediterranean*,[9] once a human being is allowed to enter such a scene, inhabited only by forces, processes and structures, it becomes impossible to resist the lure of the narrative mode of discourse for representing what is 'happening' in that scene (*TN* vol. I, p. 25). Even Braudel must tell stories whenever human beings acting as agents are permitted to appear against the background of those 'forces' that he would describe solely in quantitative and statistical terms. This even against his own conscious repudiation of narrativity as the principal impediment to the creation of a scientific historiography.

Historians, then, not only are justified in telling stories about the past but cannot do otherwise and still do justice to the full content of the historical past. The historical past is populated above all by human beings, who, besides being acted on by 'forces', are acting with or against such forces for the realization of life projects that have all the drama and fascination, but also the meaning (*Sinn*), of the kinds of stories we encounter in myth, religious parable and literary fiction. Ricoeur does not erase the distinction between literary fiction and historiography, as I have been accused of doing, but he does scumble the line between them by insisting that both belong to the category of symbolic discourses and share a single 'ultimate referent'. While freely granting that history and literature differ from one another in terms of their immediate referents (*Bedeutungen*), which are 'real' and 'imaginary' events, respectively, he stresses that insofar as both produce emplotted stories, their ultimate referent (*Sinn*) is the human experience of time or 'the structures of temporality'.[10]

Ricoeur's insistence that history and literature share a common 'ultimate referent' represents a considerable advancement over previous discussions of the relations between history and literature based on the supposed opposition of 'factual' to 'fictional' discourse (*TN* vol. I, p. 64). Just by virtue of its narrative form, historical discourse resembles such literary fictions as epics, novels, short stories and so on, and Barthes and the *Annalistes* are justified in stressing those resemblances. But instead of regarding this as a sign of narrative history's weakness, Ricoeur interprets it as a strength. If histories resemble novels, he points out, this may be because both are speaking indirectly, figuratively, or, what amounts to the same thing, 'symbolically', about the same 'ultimate referent'. Speaking indirectly because that about which both history and literature speak, the aporias of temporality, cannot be spoken about directly without contradiction. The aporias of temporality must be spoken about in the idiom of symbolic discourse rather than in that of logical and technical discourse. But history and literature speak indirectly about the aporetic experiences of temporality by means of and through signifiers that belong to different orders of being, real events on the one side, imaginary events on the other.[11]

Ricoeur's conception of the symbolic nature of all discourses that feature temporality as an organizing principle also allows him to make a significant advance over many contemporary discussions of the relation between the history and the chronicle. For him, the chronicle of events out of which the historian makes his story is not an innocent representation of raw facts given by the documentary record and presenting itself, as it were, spontaneously to the eye of the historian, who then 'explains' the events or identifies the story embedded within the sparse chronological account. Ricoeur points out that the chronicle is already a figurated representation of events, a first-order symbolization that, like the 'history' made out of it, has a double referent: events on the one side and a 'structure of temporality' on the other.

There is nothing natural about chronologically ordered registrations of events. Not only is the chronological code in terms of which the events are ordered culture-specific and conventional but the events included in the chronicle must be selected by the chronicler and placed there to the exclusion of other events that might have been included if the time of their occurrence had been the only operative consideration. A chronicle is not a narrative, by Ricoeur's reasoning, because it does not possess the kind of structure with which a plot alone could endow it. But that does not mean that it is not a mode of symbolic discourse, for neither its referentiality nor its meaning is exhausted by the truths of its several singular existential statements taken distributively, in the way that the truth-value of a logical and technical discourse can be determined. While the value of the chronicle considered as a list of facts is undeniable, its value as an instance of proto-narrative discourse is equally great. In fact, Ricoeur argues, the chronicle is the symbolic mode in which the human experience of 'within-time-ness' achieves expression in discourse.[12]

What the chronicle says, then, is not only that so-and-so happened at a given time and then something else happened at another time, but that 'seriality' is a mode or level of organization of a life lived 'within-time'. This double saying of the chronicle provides a basis for distinguishing between well-made chronicles and those more crudely composed and, indeed, between artistic and everyday forms of chronicling, the 'plotless' novel being an example of the former and the diary or register of business transactions being an example of the latter. There is a difference between giving expression to the experience of 'within-time-ness' (as in a diary) and self-consciously affirming that this is the only experience of temporality human beings can know (as the modernist, anti-narrative novel seems to do). This difference also appears in the distinction, often drawn by Ricoeur in his studies of religious myths, between those that locate the origin of evil in the physical cosmos and those that try to 'take the origin back to man'.[13] In the former kind of myth, we have the equivalent of the expression of the experience of 'within-time-ness'; in the latter, that of the expression of the experience of 'historicality'. This difference marks a qualitative advance, within the general category of mythic thought in cognitive self-consciousness and human self-awareness. The difference between a chronicle and a history marks a similar kind of advance in the human effort to 'make sense' of temporality.

If every chronicle is a first-order symbolization of temporality, awaiting the emplotting powers of the historian to transform it into a history, so, too 'within-time-ness' is only a first-order experience of temporality, awaiting a deeper recognition of the level of temporality, which Ricoeur calls the 'experience of historicality' (*Geschichtlichkeit*). Here the crucial difference is between the experience of time as mere seriality and an experience of temporality in which events take on the aspect of elements of lived stories, with a discernible beginning, middle and end. In historicality, events appear not only to succeed one another in the regular order of the series but also to function as inaugurations, transitions and terminations of processes that are meaningful because they manifest the structures of plots. Historians bear witness to the reality of this level of temporal organization by casting their accounts in the form of narratives, because this mode of discourse alone is adequate to the representation of the experience of historicality in a way that is both literal in what it asserts about specific events and figurative in what it suggests about the meaning of this experience. What the historical narrative literally asserts about specific events is that they really happened, and what it figuratively suggests is that the whole sequence of events that really happened has the order and significance of well-made stories.

Here Ricoeur skates dangerously near to the formalism that he wishes to avoid, for when the notion of the well-made story, that is, the emplotted story, is applied to historical narrative, it appears to make historiography a matter of 'style' and internal coherence rather than one of adequacy to what it represents. Ricoeur seeks to avoid this danger by reworking the notion of mimesis in order to account for the fact that historical stories both are 'well-made' and correspond in their outlines to the sequences of events of which they are representations.

Ricoeur reworks the concept of mimesis in order to show how a discourse cast in the form of a narrative can be both symbolic and realistic at one and the same time. His exposition, drawing upon his earlier work on metaphor and myth, is too complex for a brief recapitulation here. His crucial point, however, is that insofar as historical representation is concerned, mimesis has less to do with 'imitation' than with the kind of action (praxis) that properly serves as the subject matter of a history. He challenges the traditional, Aristotelian distinction between mimesis, considered as an imitation of an action in a discourse, and diegesis, considered as a description of events, on which the opposition of fictional to factual discourse conventionally has been based (*TN* vol. II, pp. 36–7). For Ricoeur, this distinction is useful enough for the characterization of the kinds of representations met with in the drama. When used, however, to analyse the narrative mode of discourse, it obscures the fact that a narrative not only describes but actually imitates the events of which it speaks, because narrative, like discourse in general, is a product of the same kinds of actions as those that produce the kinds of events deemed worthy of being represented in a history.[14]

In Ricoeur's view, then, narrative discourse does not simply reflect or passively register a world already made; it works up the material given in perception and reflection, fashions it, and creates something new, in precisely the same way that human agents by their actions fashion distinctive forms of historical life out of the world they inherit as their past. Thus conceived, a historical narrative is not only an icon of the events, past or present, of which it speaks; it is also an index of the kind of actions that produce the kinds of events we wish to call historical. It is this indexical nature of historical narrative that assures the adequacy of its symbolic representations to the real events about which they speak. Historical events can be distinguished from natural events by virtue of the fact that they are products of the actions of human agents seeking, more or less self-consciously, to endow the world in which they live with symbolic meaning. Historical events can therefore be represented realistically in symbolic discourse, because such events are themselves symbolic in nature. So it is with the historian's composition of a narrative account of historical events: the narrativization of historical events effects a symbolic representation of the processes by which human life is endowed with symbolic meaning.

Narrative discourse, then, is as much 'performative' as it is 'constative', to use the terminology of early Austin, which Ricoeur favours at crucial junctures in his discussions of metaphoric language and symbolic discourse.[15] And historical narrative, which takes the events created by human actions as its immediate subject, does much more than merely describe those events; it also imitates them, that is, performs the same kind of creative act as those performed by historical agents. History has meaning because human actions produce meanings. These meanings are continuous over the generations of human time. This continuity, in turn, is felt in the human experience of time organized as future, past and present rather than as mere serial consecution. To experience time as future, past and present rather than as a series of instants in which every one has the same weight or significance as every other is to experience 'historicality'. This experience of historicality, finally, can be represented symbolically in narrative discourse, because such discourse is a product of the same kind of hypotactical figuration of events (as beginnings, middles and ends) as that met with in the actions of historical agents who hypotactically figurate their lives as meaningful stories.

Obviously, any adequate criticism of Ricoeur's argument would have to examine in depth his whole theory of symbolic language and discourse, his revision of the concept of mimesis as it applies to representation in narrative, his conception of the nature of the distinctively historical event, his notion of the different levels of temporality and the ways in which these attain to expression in language, his ideas of emplotment as the key to the understanding of a distinctively historical mode of consciousness, his characterization of the kind of knowledge we derive from our reflection on history and a host of other issues. His conceptualization of each of these matters constitutes an important contribution to literary theory, the philosophy of history, social theory and metaphysics alike. It is difficult, however, to detach any one conceptualization from the others for purposes of analysis, because each is a part of a whole argument that is more 'symbolical' than either 'logical' or 'technical' (to use his own categories for classifying kinds of discourses) in structure.[16] To be sure, Ricoeur's work is always cast on the manifest level as a technical, philosophical discourse presided over by the protocols of literal speech and traditional logic. But as he has said of those mythic and religious texts that he himself has analysed so perspicuously as examples of symbolic speech, Ricoeur's own discourse always says something 'more' and 'other' than what it appears to be asserting on the literal level of its articulation. It is fair to ask, then, what is the something 'more' and 'other' that Ricoeur is saying about historical narrative?

One thing he is saying is that narrative historians need feel no embarrassment about resemblances between the stories they tell and those told by writers of fiction. Historical stories and fictional stories resemble one another because whatever the differences between their immediate contents (real events and imaginary events, respectively), their ultimate content is the same: the structures of human time. Their shared form, narrative, is a function of this shared content. There is nothing more real for human beings than the experience of temporality – and nothing more fateful, either for individuals or for whole civilizations. Thus, any narrative representation of human events is an enterprise of profound philosophical – one could even say anthropological – seriousness. It does not matter whether the events that serve as the immediate referents of a narrative are considered to be real or only imaginary; what matters is whether these events are considered to be typically human.

Historical narratives may, therefore, resemble fictional narratives, but this tells us more about such fictions than about such histories. Far from being an antithetical opposite of historical narrative, fictional narrative is its complement and ally in the universal human effort to reflect on the mystery of temporality. Indeed, narrative fiction permits historians to perceive clearly the metaphysical interest motivating their traditional effort to tell 'what really happened' in the past in the form of a story. There, in narrative fiction, the experiences of both 'within-time-ness' and 'historicality' can be dissolved in the apprehension of the relation of 'eternity' to 'death', which is the content of the form of temporality itself.

Thus conceived, narrative fiction provides glimpses of the deep structure of historical consciousness and, by implication, of both historical reflection and historical discourse. This resemblance between historical narrative and fictional narrative, which is a function of their shared interest in the mystery of time, would account, I surmise, for the appeal of those great classics of historical narrative – from Herodotus' *Persian Wars* through Augustine's *City of God*, Gibbon's *Decline and Fall of the Roman Empire*, Michelet's *History of France*, and Burckhardt's *Civilization of the Renaissance in Italy* down to, yes, even Spengler's *Decline of the West* – that makes them worthy of study and reflection long after their scholarship has become outmoded and their arguments have been consigned to the status of commonplaces of the culture moments of their composition. It is true, as the conventional opinion has it, that such classics continue to appeal to us because of their 'literary' quality; but this quality should not be identified with verbal style or rhetorical eloquence, as if style could be dissociated from meaning, or rhetorical form from semantic content. On the basis of Ricoeur's theory of historical discourse, we are permitted to attribute the timeless fascination of the historiographical classic to the content that it shares with every poetic utterance cast in the mode of a narrative. This content is allegorical: every great historical narrative is an allegory of temporality. Thus, long after its scholarship has been superseded and its arguments exploded as prejudices of the cultural moment of its production (as in Gibbon's contention that the fall of Rome was caused by the solvent effects of Christianity on pagan manly virtues), the classic historical narrative continues to fascinate as the product of a universal human need to reflect on the insoluble mystery of time.

But in suggesting that historical narratives are, in the final analysis, allegories of temporality, what something 'more' and 'other' is Ricoeur saying about allegory itself? As I understand him, he is saying that histories are not *mere* allegories, in the sense of being nothing but plays of analogy or 'extended metaphors', for it is clear on the basis of what Ricoeur has to say about *allegoresis* in other contexts that there are for him different kinds of allegorization, different ways of 'speaking otherwise', and different degrees of responsibility to those aspects of reality about which we can speak in only an indirect or symbolic manner.[17] For Ricoeur, the problem presented by both historical discourse and the interpretation thereof is false allegorization, a speaking otherwise about history that suggests either that it is a timeless, mechanical structure of functions without meaning or that it is a temporal process, the meaning of which can be provided by metaphysical speculation of religious dogma. For Ricoeur, the meaning of history resides in its aspect as a drama of the human effort to endow life with meaning. This universal, human quest for meaning is carried out in the awareness of the corrosive power of time, but it is also made possible and given its distinctively human pathos by this very awareness. In this respect, that manner of being-in-the-world that we call 'historical' is paradoxical and cannot be apprehended by human thought except in the form of an enigma. If this enigma cannot be resolved by pure reason and scientific explanation, it can be grasped in all its complexity and multi-layeredness in symbolic thought and given a real, if only provisional, comprehensibility in those true allegories of temporality that we call narrative histories. Their truth resides not only in their fidelity to the facts of given individual or collective lives but also, and most importantly, in their faithfulness to that vision of human life informing the poetic genre of tragedy. In this respect, the symbolic content of narrative history, the content of its form, is the tragic vision itself.[18]

Historical narratives are true allegories, then, when they display the facts of human existence under their temporal aspect and symbolically suggest that the human experience of time is tragic in nature. But what is the nature of this narrative truth, which is not literal but yet is not merely figurative either? What is being indirectly asserted about historical narrative in Ricoeur's own symbolic speech?

In trying to identify the allegorical meaning of Ricoeur's discourse on historical discourse, I cast about for a way of characterizing a manner of speaking that would be allegorical in its structure but more than allegorical in its meaning. My friend and colleague Norman O. Brown directed me to the late Charles Singleton's commentary on Dante's discussion of the distinction between poetic allegory and scriptural allegory in the *Convivio*. The distinction is different from that offered in *The Letter to Can Grande*, wherein the topic discussed is the relation between the literal and the figurative senses of the language used in the *Commedia*. In the *Convivio*, Dante wishes to distinguish between the 'allegory of poets' and the 'allegory of Holy Scripture'. The difference between the two kinds of allegory, he maintains, stems not from the distinction between the literal and the figurative levels of the two kinds of discourse but rather from the nature of the uses to which the *literal* sense is put in each. Singleton explicates Dante's thought in the following way:

> The 'allegory of poets', which is that of fable, of parable (and hence is also to be found in Scriptures), is a mode in which the first and literal sense is one devised, fashioned (*fictio* in its original meaning) in order to conceal, and in concealing to convey, a truth. Not so in the other (scriptural allegorical) mode. . . . There the first sense is historical, as Dante says it is, and not 'fiction'. The children of Israel did depart from Egypt in the time of Moses. Whatever the other senses may be, this first sense abides, stands quite on its own, is not devised 'for the sake of'. Indeed it was generally recognized that in Holy Scripture the historical sense might at times be the only sense there. These things have been so; they have happened in time. This is the record of them.[19]

This means, Singleton goes on to explain, that although in Scripture 'the historical . . . sense can and does yield another sense', in the same way that the literal sense in poetic allegory does, as when, for example, the Exodus can be read as a figure of 'the movement of the soul on the way to salvation', the relation between the two senses should not be seen as that of a fiction to its moral or anagogical meaning. The relation is, rather, that of a 'fact' to its moral or anagogical significance. In scriptural allegory, events are portrayed, not in order to 'conceal, and in concealing to convey, a truth', but rather to reveal, and in revealing to convey, yet another, deeper truth. For Dante, Singleton writes, 'only God could use events as words, causing them to point beyond themselves' to meanings that must be construed as being literal truths on *all* of their multifold levels of significance. Thus conceived, history, considered as a sequence of events, is God's 'poetry'.[20] God writes in events as poets write in words. This is why any history considered as the human account of those events would be at best a translation of God's 'poetry' into 'prose', or what amounts to the same thing, a merely human 'poetry'. Since no poet or historian possesses God's power, the best either could do would be to 'imitate God's way of writing' – which Dante purported to do in the *Commedia*. But since this writing will always be only an imitation of God's power to write in events, every history will always be something other than the events of which it speaks, both in its form and in its content. It will be a special kind of poetry which, in its intention to speak literally, is always frustrated, driven to speak poetically, that is to say, figuratively, and in so speaking to conceal what it wishes to reveal – but by concealing, conveying a much deeper truth.

Something like this, I take it, is what Ricoeur is saying in his reflections on historical narrative – although he is saying this indirectly, figuratively, allegorically. His is an allegory of allegorization, intended – if I understand him correctly – to save the moral dimension of historical consciousness from the fallacy of a false literalism and the dangers of a false objectivity.

But to reveal the allegorical nature of a discourse that does not know itself to be such is to de-allegorize it. To identify the referent of the figurative level of such discourse is to reliteralize it, even if on a level of signification different from that of its manifest or 'first-order' level of signification. In Ricoeur's view, every historical discourse worthy of the name is not only a literal account of the past and a figuration of temporality but, beyond that, a literal representation of the content of a timeless drama, that of humanity at grips with the 'experience of temporality'. This content, in turn, is nothing other than the moral meaning of humanity's aspiration to redemption from history itself.

This seems right to me, for otherwise I cannot account for the ferocity of all those struggles, between human beings and whole societies, for the authority to decide what history means, what it teaches, and what obligations it lays upon us all. I am not surprised, therefore, that Ricoeur presses on to the discovery of yet another level of temporal experience, what he calls the experience of 'deep temporality', which has as its content the enigma of death and eternity, the ultimate mystery figurated in every manifestation of human consciousness.[21] On this level, which would correspond to the anagogical level in the scholastic fourfold schema, not only discourse but speech itself reaches a limit. But the form in which the experience of deep temporality reaches expression in language is glimpsed in such disemplotted 'fables about time' as *Mrs Dalloway* and *The Remembrance of Things Past (TN* vol. II, p. 101).

The function of the notion of deep temporality in Ricoeur's thought about history, narrativity and time seems clear. It saves historical thinking from its most common temptation, that of irony. In this work of redemption, Ricoeur joins the efforts of Hegel and Nietzsche, for both of whom the overcoming of irony was the central problem of a distinctively human thought. While arguing (or suggesting) that historical thinking is allegorical but not merely such; that is to say, that it has a secondary referentiality in its figurative dimension to a reality that lies beyond history itself, he has escaped the danger that philosophical reflection faces when confronted by any instance of symbolic discourse, the peril of a *merely* allegorical interpretation. But has he escaped the other peril, the one that, by his own account, threatens thought in its speculative aspect, the 'temptation of gnosis', the inclination to repeat 'the symbol in a mimic of rationality', to rationalize 'symbols as such' and 'thereby fix . . . them on the imaginative plane where they are born and take shape'?[22] The answer to his question must await the appearance of the projected third volume of Ricoeur's meditation on narrative. Whether he will escape the danger of 'dogmatic mythology' that threatens the 'gnostic' turn of mind, we shall have to wait and see. It would, however, be the supreme irony if, in his efforts to save historical reflection from irony, he were forced to collapse the distinction between myth and history, without which the very notion of fiction is difficult to imagine.

NOTES

1 This essay is a revised version of an appreciation of Paul Ricoeur's *Temps et récit*, vol. 1, Paris, Editions du Seuil, 1983, which I was asked to prepare for a conference held at the University of Ottawa in October 1983 to honour Ricoeur on his seventieth birthday. I have used the English translation by Kathleen McLaughlin and David Pellauer, *Time and Narrative*, vol. 1, Chicago, University of Chicago Press, 1984. When I originally wrote the essay, vol. 2 of *Temps et récit: La configuration dans le récit de fiction*, Paris, Editions du Seuil, 1984, had not yet appeared. In my revision I have made use of this work, now available in an English version by the same translators, *Time and Narrative*, vol. 2, Chicago, University of Chicago Press, 1985; further references to

this work, below and in parentheses in the text, are to the English translations, designated *TN* with the volume indicated.

2 Paul Ricoeur, *The Rule of Metaphor: Multidisciplinary Studies of the Creation of Meaning in Language*, translated by Robert Czerny with Kathleen McLauglin and John Costello, London, Routledge & Kegan Paul, 1978.

3 Paul Ricoeur, 'Narrative time', *Critical Inquiry* vol. 7 no. 1, 1980, p. 169.

4 By 'secondary referentiality' Ricoeur indicates the twofold nature of all symbolic speech, its saying one thing literally and another figuratively (see *TN* vol. 1, pp. 57–8, 77–82). In the case of the historical narrative, its literal referent is the set of events of which it speaks, while its figurative referent is the 'structure of temporality' which, following Heidegger, he calls 'historicality' (*Geschichtlichkeit*). Two features of 'historicality', he writes, are 'the extension of time between birth and death, and the displacement of accent from the future to the past' (*TN* vol. 1, pp. 61–2).

5 On plot, emplotment, and configuration as a 'grasping together' of scattered events in a symbolic mediation see *TN* vol. 1 pp. 41–2. Later on, Ricoeur writes: 'This highlighting of the dynamic of emplotment is to me the key to the problem of the relation between time and narrative. . . . my argument in this book consists of constructing the mediation between time and narrative by demonstrating emplotment's mediating role in the mimetic process' (*TN* vol. 1 pp. 53–4).

6 The aporias of time reside in the fact that we cannot *not* think about our experience of time, and yet we can never think about it both rationally and comprehensively: 'The aporetical character of the pure reflection on time is of the utmost importance for all that follows in the present investigation.' It is because such reflection is aporetical that the only response to it can be a poetical and specifically narrative response: 'A constant thesis of this book will be that speculation on time is an inconclusive rumination to which narrative activity can alone respond. Not that this activity solves the aporias through substitution. If it does resolve them, it is in a poetical and not a theoretical sense of the word. Emplotment . . . replies to the speculative aporia with a poetic making of something capable, certainly, of clarifying the aporia . . . , but not of resolving it theoretically' (*TN* vol. 1 p. 6).

7 'If mimetic activity "composes" action, it is what establishes what is necessary in composing it. It does not see the universal, it makes it spring forth. What then are its criteria? We have a partial answer in [the expression of Aristotle]: "it is because as they look at them they have the experience of learning and reasoning out what each thing represents, concluding, for example, that 'this figure is so and so' " (48b16–17). This pleasure of recognition, as Dupont Roc and Lallot put it, presupposes, I think, a prospective concept of truth, according to which to invent is to rediscover' (*TN* vol. 1 p. 42).

8 This theme of the historian's task as being twofold, a 'wording' and a 'working', a signifying and an acting, a speaking and a doing, is elaborated by Ricoeur in the introduction to *Histoire et verité*, 2nd edn,

Paris, 1955, p. 9 (*History and Truth*, trans. Charles A. Kelbey, Evanston, Northwestern University Press, p. 5.) This collection of essays introduces many of the problems that will be addressed more systematically in *Time and Narrative*; see especially 'Objectivité et subjectivité en histoire' and 'Travail et parole' ('Objectivity and subjectivity in history' and 'Work and the word', Charles S. Singleton, Cambridge, Mass., Harvard University Press).

9 Fernand Braudel, *The Mediterranean and the Mediterranean World in the Age of Philip II*, translated by Siân Reynolds, New York, Harper & Row, 1972.

10 See Paul Ricoeur, 'The hermeneutical function of distanciation' in John B. Thompson (ed. and trans.) *Hermeneutics and the Human Sciences: Essays on Language, Action, and Interpretation*, Cambridge, 1982, 140–2; cf. *TN* vol. 1 pp. 77–80.

11 Compare Ricoeur's discussion of the relation between history and fiction in 'The fictive experience of time', chap. 4 of *TN* vol. 2, especially pp. 100–1, with his discussion of historical mimesis in *TN* vol. 1 p. 64.

12 Ricoeur distinguishes three kinds of mimesis in narrative discourse. These are produced by symbolizations that effect mediations between (1) random events and their chronological ordering, which produces the chronicle; (2) chronicle representations of events and the history that can be made out of them by emplotment; and (3) both of these and the figures of deep temporality that serve as the ultimate referent of such modernist fables of time as Woolf's *Mrs Dalloway* and Proust's *The Remembrance of Things Past*. See *TN* vol. 2 p. 30, where chronology and chronography are characterized as 'the true contrary of temporality itself', and vol. 2 p. 62, where 'Being-within-time' is viewed as necessitating the impulse to 'reckon with time' and 'make calculations' of the sort that inform the chronicle form of representing time.

13 On the two basic kinds of myth see Paul Ricoeur, 'The hermeneutics of symbols and philosophical reflection', in C. E. Reagan and D. Stewart (eds) *The Philosophy of Paul Ricoeur: An Anthology of His Work*, Boston, Beacon Press, 1978, p. 42.

14 'Without leaving everyday experience, are we not inclined to see in a given sequence of episodes of our lives (as yet) untold stories, stories that demand to be told, stories that offer anchorage points for narrative? . . . The principal consequence of [the] existential analysis of human beings as "entangled in stories" is that narrating is a secondary process, that of "the story's becoming known." . . . Telling, following, understanding stories is simply the "continuation" of these untold stories. . . . We tell stories because in the last analysis human lives need and merit being narrated' (*TN* vol. 1 pp. 74–5).

15 Ricoeur, *The Rule of Metaphor*, pp. 72–3.

16 See especially Paul Ricoeur, 'The language of faith', in Reagan and Stewart (eds), *The Philosophy of Paul Ricoeur*, pp. 232–3.

17 Ricoeur does not, of course, refer to historical narratives, nor indeed to fictional narratives, as 'allegorical' in nature, because this would suggest that their secondary referents, the structures of temporality,

158

were nothing but verbal constructions, rather than realities. He uses the term *allegory* to designate the 'level of statements' in a symbolic discourse, in contrast to *metaphor*, which designates the level of 'figures of speech'. Symbolic discourse can then be seen to use the technique of 'allegorization' at the level of statement to speak about its double referent – events or actions, on the one side, and structures of temporality, on the other (see Ricoeur, *The Rule of Metaphor*, pp. 171–2). But this means, it seems to me, that we can distinguish a proper and an improper use of allegorization in those forms of symbolic discourse that, like historical narratives, seek to 'speak otherwise' about real events, especially when it is a matter of speaking about them in their diachronic, as against their synchronic, aspects.

18 'The question that I shall continue to pursue until the end of this work is whether the paradigm of order, characteristic of tragedy, is capable of extension and transformation to the point where it can be applied to the whole narrative field. . . . The tragic muthos is set up as the poetic solution to the speculative paradox of time' (*TN* vol. 1 p. 38).

19 Charles D. Singleton, *Commedia: Elements of Structure*, Cambridge, 1965, p. 14.

20 ibid., 15–16.

21 Referring to Heidegger's idea of 'deep temporality' (*Zeitlichkeit*), Ricoeur says that it is 'the most originary form and the most authentic experience of time, that is, the dialectic of coming to be, having been, and making present. In this dialectic, time is entirely desubstantialized. The words "future", "past", and "present" disappear, and time itself figures as the exploded unity of the three temporal extases' (*TN* vol. 1 p. 61).

22 Ricoeur, 'The hermeneutics of symbols', p. 46.

10

DISCUSSION
Ricoeur on narrative

The following Round Table discussion of *Time and Narrative* volume
I, and an earlier version of Hayden White's paper (Chapter 9 of
this volume) were originally published in Revue de l'Université
d'Ottawa/University of Ottawa quarterly, vol. 55, no. 4, 1985. The
contributions by Charles Taylor and Paul Ricoeur have been translated by Iain Hamilton Grant.

David Carr

The study of narrative has become a meeting ground and battle
ground of the disciplines, and is fast become a discipline in its
own right. Philosophers, historians, literary critics and theorists,
structuralists and anti- or non-structuralists – not to mention pre-
and post-structuralists – all approach the topic from different
backgrounds and with different ends in view.

Given this diversity of approach, the wide diversity of theories
and accounts of narrative is not surprising. In surveying some of
this literature, however, I find a curious consensus on one rather
important matter. It concerns, broadly speaking, the relationship
between narrative and the real world. Simply put, it is the view
that real events do not have the character of those we find in
stories, and if we treat them as if they did have such a character,
we are not being true to them.

Among literary theorists we find this view expressed by structuralists and non-structuralists alike. Frank Kermode, in his
influential 1966 study *The Sense of an Ending*, puts it this way: 'In
"making sense" of the world we . . . feel a need . . . to experience
that concordance of beginning, middle and end which is the
essence of our explanatory fictions.'[1] But such fictions 'degenerate',
he says, into 'myths' whenever we actually believe them or ascribe
their narrative properties to the real, that is, 'whenever they are
not consciously held to be fictive'.[2] And in his useful recent
presentation of structuralist theories of narrative, Seymour

Chatman, also speaking of the beginning-middle-end structure, insists that it applies 'to the narrative, to story-events as narrated, rather than to . . . actions themselves, simply because such terms are meaningless in the real world'.[3] In this he echoes his mentor Roland Barthes. In his famous introduction to the structural analysis of narrative, Barthes says that 'art knows no static', that is, in a story everything has its place in a structure while the extraneous has been eliminated; and in this it differs from 'life', in which everything is 'scrambled messages' (*communications brouillées*).[4]

As for history, whose concern is presumably with the real world, one might expect such a view from those who believe narrative history has always contained elements of fiction that must now be exorcised by scientific history. But if we turn to Louis Mink, who above all has championed narrative history as a mode of cognition in its own right, we find him invoking, in one article, the same distinction between art and life that we find in Barthes. 'Stories are not lived but told', he says. 'Life has no beginnings, middles and ends. . . . Narrative qualities are transferred from art to life.'[5] And who, among historians, has devoted more attention to the narrative features of historiography than Hayden White? But when White seeks, in a recent article, what he calls 'The value of narrativity in the representation of reality',[6] it is clear that he finds no cognitive or scientific value in narrative.

White's view is conveyed in a series of loaded questions. 'What wish is enacted, what desire is gratified', he asks, 'by the fantasy that *real* events are properly represented when they can be shown to display the formal coherency of a story?'[7]

> Does the world really present itself to perception in the form of well-made stories . . . ? Or does it present itself more in the way that the annals and chronicles suggest, either as a mere sequence without beginning/or end or as sequences of beginnings that only terminate and never conclude?[8]

For White the answer is clear: 'The notion that sequences of real events possess the formal attributes of the stories we tell about imaginary events could only have its origin in wishes, daydreams, reveries.' It is precisely annals and chronicles that offer us the 'paradigms of ways that reality offers itself to perception'.[9]

Many more representatives could doubtless be found of this view, so widespread that we can call it, for purposes of this paper, the standard view. Fictional stories are distinct from 'reality' or 'real life' not just because they are fictional, that is, because they tell of events that never happened, but also because of the way they present those events, or because of the way those events are interrelated as fictionally presented. As for any discourse – like history, but also including biography, journalism or even anecdote – which claims to represent the real: to the extent that it does so in narrative form, that form must alienate it from the reality of the events it relates. Such form is 'imposed upon' reality, to use the most frequent expression. It distorts life. At best it constitutes an escape, a consolation, at worst an opiate, either as self-delusion or – and this is a thought White shares with Foucault and Deleuze – imposed from without by some authoritative narrative voice in the interest of manipulation and power. In either case it is an act of violence, a betrayal, an imposition on reality or life and on ourselves.

Now I think this standard view mistaken, not so much because of its approach to narrative as because of what it says, or rather offhandedly implies, about life. It seems to me an expression more of frustration, pessimism and skepticism than of a genuine insight into the relation between stories and the real world. Given my interest in and uneasiness about this strange consensus it is understandable that I read Ricoeur's *Time and Narrative*[10] with it in mind. After reading the book I must confess that I am not sure where the author stands on this issue. Perhaps it is unfair of me to expect of him an answer to a question formulated in my terms and not his. But I do think the question a crucial one, especially for philosophy, and in fact I think Ricoeur *is* interested in this question in his book. It is just not clear to me how he answers it.

Consequently I shall adopt the following strategy: I shall state in my own terms why I am opposed to what I have called the standard view. In particular I shall contend that narration, far from being a distortion of, denial of or escape from 'reality', is in fact an extension and enrichment, a confirmation, not a falsification, of its primary features. After presenting those views I shall turn to Ricoeur's book to explain why I think his own position unclear, and end with a series of questions to its author.

Returning now to the standard view, what is it that narrative is supposed to distort? 'Reality' is one of the terms used. But what reality is meant? Sometimes it seems that the real world must be the physical world, which is supposed to be random and haphazard or, alternatively and contradictorily, to be rigorously ordered along causal lines, but in any case totally indifferent to human concerns. Things just happen in meaningless sequence, and any value or structure ascribed to the flow of events is not inherent in them but projected onto them by our concerns.

This may be true, but it is of course irrelevant, since it is not primarily physical reality but human reality, including the very activity of projecting our concerns, which is portrayed in stories and against which narrative must be measured if we are to judge the validity of the standard view. Can we say of human reality that it is mere sequence, one thing after the other, as White seems to suggest? Here we would do well to recall Husserl's theory of time-consciousness. According to Husserl even the most passive experience involves tacit anticipation or what he calls protention, as well as retention of the just past. His point is not simply that we have the capacity to project and to remember. His claim is that we cannot even experience anything as happening, as present, except against the background of what it succeeds and what we anticipate will succeed it. Our very capacity to experience, to be aware of what is – 'reality as it presents itself to experience', in White's words – spans future and past.

Husserl's analysis of time-experience is in this respect the counterpart of Merleau-Ponty's critique of the notion of sensation in classical empiricism and his claim that the figure-background scheme is basic in spatial perception. The supposedly punctual and distinct units of sensation must be grasped as a configuration to be experienced at all. Merleau-Ponty concludes that, far from being basic units of experience, sensations are highly abstract products of analysis. On the basis of Husserl's analysis of time-experience, one would have to say the same of the idea of a 'mere' or 'pure' sequence of isolated events. Perhaps we can think it, but we cannot experience it. As we encounter them, even at the most passive level, events are charged with the significance they derive from our retentions and protentions.

If this is true of our most passive experience, it is all the more true of our active lives, in which we quite explicitly consult past experience, envisage the future and view the present as a passage between the two. Whatever we encounter within our experience functions as instrument or obstacle to our plans, expectations and hopes. Whatever else 'life' may be, it is hardly a structureless sequence of isolated events.

Now it might be objected that structure is not necessarily narrative structure. But is there not a kinship between the means–end structure of action and the beginning–middle–end structure of narrative? In action we are always in the midst of something, caught in the suspense of contingency which is supposed to find its resolution in the completion of our project. To be sure, a narrative unites many actions to form a plot. But the resulting whole is often still designated an action of large scale: coming of age, conducting a love affair, solving a murder. The structure of action, small-scale and large, is common to art and to life.

What can the proponents of the standard view possibly mean, then, when they say that life has no beginnings, middles and ends? I fear that they are taking these to be merely temporal notions, and that they are lapsing into a highly abstract, and again perhaps non-human conception of events. Are they saying that a moment in which, say, an action is inaugurated is no real beginning, simply because it has other moments before it, and that after the action is accomplished time (or life) goes on and other things happen? Perhaps they are contrasting this with the absoluteness of the beginning and end of a novel, which begins on page one and ends on the last page with 'the end'. But surely it is the interrelation of the events portrayed, not the story as a sequence of sentences or utterances, that is relevant here.

But a further objection may be framed as follows: it may be that many actions and sufferings arrange themselves into larger actions or projects, rather than being lined up in a row. But in a good story, to use Barthes's image, all the extraneous noise or static is cut out. That is, in a story we are told just what is necessary to 'further the plot'. A selection is made of all the events and actions a person may engage in, and only a small minority finds its way into the story. In fact, if actions and events that don't further the plot are included in a story, we consider the story cluttered and its presentation inefficient. But life differs from stories just because such a selection is not made; all the static is there.

There is another way of putting this point about selection which leads us into a new domain. As readers of a story or spectators at a play we are told or we are shown only what is essential to the action; the selection is made for us. By whom? Behind every story, sometimes in it, is the author or narrator. (These are not always identical, but let's leave this point aside.) Every story requires a story-teller. The narrative voice, as Hayden White likes to point out, is the voice of authority. Though White says this, I think, for the wrong reasons, it is certainly true in the important sense that the narrator knows the story and we (if we are first-time readers or hearers) do not. He/she knows how it will end before it ends, and we have to wait. It is the narrator who makes the selection, indeed partly on the basis of this foreknowledge. Being a reader or spectator is a form of voluntary servitude. To follow a story is voluntarily to submit ourselves to this authority. It decides what and how much we shall know and when.

Perhaps it is here, then, that the standard view really has a telling point; perhaps here life and the narrative art really do diverge. Life admits no selection process; everything is left in; and this is *because* there is no narrator in command, no narrative voice which does the selecting. One further point may be added. Our discussion so far has tacitly assumed that narrative requires not only a story and a story-teller, but also an audience – the reader, hearer or spectator to whom the story is told.

One must of course concede what is valid in these objections. If we have been arguing that narrative structure imitates and thus resembles, rather than distorts life, this is not to say there is no difference. Narratives do select; and life is what they select from. But it hardly follows that in life no selection takes place. Our very capacity for attention, and for following through more or less long-term and complex endeavours, is our capacity for selection. Extraneous details are not left out, but they are pushed into the background, saved for later, ranked in importance. And whose narrative voice is accomplishing all this? None but our own, of course. In planning our days and our lives we are composing the stories or the dramas we will act out and which will determine the focus of our attention and our endeavours, which will provide the principles for distinguishing foreground from background. Now this may be story-planning or plotting, but is it story-telling? Most assuredly it is, quite literally, since we are constantly explaining ourselves to others. And finally each of us must count himself among his own audience since in explaining ourselves to others we are often trying to convince ourselves as well.

But this last remark stands as a warning not to take *this* point – the self as teller of his own story – too far, and gives us a clue as to how much we differ from that imperious autocrat, the narrative voice. Unlike the author of fiction we do not create the materials we are to form: we are stuck with what we have in the way of characters, capacities and circumstances. Unlike the historian we are not describing events already completed but are in the middle of our stories and cannot be sure how they will end. We are constantly having to revise the plot, scrambling to intercept the slings and arrows of fortune and the stupidity or stubbornness of our uncooperative fellows, who will insist on coming up with their own stories instead of docilely accommodating themselves to ours. And the fact that we are ourselves sometimes among that recalcitrant audience, that each of us has his own self to convince and cajole into line, puts paid to any pretensions we might have to anything like being the authors of our own lives: not only do we not control the circumstances, so that they conform to our plans; we do not control our own plans, or even the self who plans, whose very identity is threatened in the internal dialogue whereby we become our own worst enemies.

There is no doubt that in all these ways life does fall short of art, that it fails to live up to the formal coherence and the clear-cut authorship of some stories. But this is because to live it is to make the constant demand and attempt that it approach that coherence. We want things to come out right in the end, with all the threads of the plot neatly tied up, as at the hands of an author which, at the limit, we ourselves become. Narrative coherence does not impose itself upon an incoherent, merely sequential existence, but is drawn from life.

The standard view errs by the kind of exaggeration that results from frustrated expectations. In bitterness that we cannot control every aspect of our lives as if they were fictions, in the sentiment that things are getting out of hand and out of control, it concludes the worst: that our lives are meaningless sequences, one thing after another. Perhaps the proponents of the standard view just read too many stories and lead very dull or cluttered lives. But this is not to say that their lives are not like stories. It may be that they are just dull stories.

Now we turn to Ricoeur's *Time and Narrative*. I have no intention, of course, of trying to touch on all aspects of this important book, which contributes significantly, in my view, to the interpretation of such authors as Aristotle and Augustine, as well as to the theory of literature and the philosophy of history. I shall consider this work only from the perspective of the problem raised in the foregoing remarks, for the purpose of posing some questions to its author. It may be that the author is not the sole or even the best interpreter of his own work, but one can hardly resist consulting him if, as in the present case, he is here with us.

As I said, while Ricoeur does not pose the 'art vs life' question in quite as explicit terms as I have, he is centrally concerned with this question, as I believe any theory of narrative must be. That he is is manifest in two aspects of his book: the first is that, while he speaks primarily about literary and historical narratives, he begins his book with a reading of Augustine's meditation on time in the *Confessions*, a meditation which gradually transforms a cosmological and theological question into a psychological or phenomenological one, and which is nowhere concerned with texts (except of course to cite the sacred ones). The second is that the concept of *mimesis*, derived explicitly from Aristotle's *Poetics*, is a central concept and problem throughout the work.

My question now is: how does Ricoeur stand on what I have called the standard view? Naturally I expected from him, a learned and reasonable man, a large measure of agreement with my own views. To some extent I found it, and indeed at different levels of his discussion.

At a very general level, I find support in certain of Ricoeur's remarks on the temporality of narrative which run throughout his treatment of this subject, in earlier essays as well as in the book. He is opposed to what he calls the tendency to de-chronologize narrative, a tendency exhibited in the structuralist tradition, starting with Propp, but also in the analyses of the philosopher Louis Mink and of the historian Paul Veyne. Such analyses suppose that the temporal is a mere surface aspect of the story, the mere sequence of events, while narrative properties as such are to be found in structural, quasi-logical properties – Propp's functions, Mink's configuration – which are strictly atemporal in character. Ricoeur himself distinguishes what he calls episodic from configurational dimensions of narrative but argues that the latter, far from being devoid of temporality, is itself temporal in its own much more rich and complex way, including its direction toward an ending, its capacity to flash forward and back and the like.

This is an important point, and my only objection is that it might have been made even more forcefully and simply. The beginning–middle–end division, the most basic of all narrative structures, is simply a temporal structure and cannot be reduced to or transformed into any other sort of order, such as logical, hierarchical or configurational in the spatial sense. An argument may have a middle term, but its premises and conclusion are not the same as beginning and end. A spatial design too may have a middle, but between its edges or sides, not its beginning and end. These atemporal structures *may* be deployed in time, as when we think through the argument, or run our eyes from one side of the design to the other. But they need not be. The beginning–end structure *must* be deployed in time. There is no other medium in which it can be realized. In this respect stories are like music. A musical score may have many atemporal properties, but music occurs when it is translated into sounds that unfold one after the other.

In making this point about temporality Ricoeur is, to be sure, not talking about the relation between art and life, but speaking strictly about the nature of narratives themselves. But his point counts against the view that narratives are essentially or structurally alien to the temporal medium in which the events of real life take their course.

Ricoeur's attention to the relation of art and life is more explicit when he turns to the concept of *mimesis* which he extracts from his discussion of Aristotle's poetics but subjects to a radical and highly original interpretation. He looks at mimesis from three points of view, a division based on the relation of narrative to everyday life and activity. The latter is both 'upstream' from literary narrative proper because narratives flow out of it; and 'downstream' from it, since narratives have their effect on life through their reception by an audience. It is under the title *Mimesis I* that Ricoeur shows how narratives have their source in everyday life. In effect they draw on three aspects of life: the semantics of action, the socially symbolic character of human events – their significance in the sense of convention, custom and ritual – and the essentially temporal character of the everyday.

After discussing all three aspects of mimesis Ricoeur considers two related possible objections to his version of the relation between narratives and the real world. One is that narratives are totally alien to it, exhibiting an order it does not remotely have (this is our standard view); the other is that life does have such

168

an order, but precisely as a result of the effect on it of our literary culture, in particular, our stories. To both objections Ricoeur's answer is the same. Life is not alien to narrative structure, nor does it need to borrow from literature to achieve such structure. It has its own structure, which is 'not reducible to simple discordance', not simply chaotic, but is a kind of 'inchoate narrativity', 'prenarrative structure' (*TN* vol. I, p. 74); 'narrativité inchoative', 'structure prénarrative' (Temps et récit vol. I, p. 113). He said earlier that what Mink calls the 'configuration effected by narrative is not grafted onto something figureless, faceless, but upon a life in which narration structure is 'prefigured' (p. 87). Literature 'give[s] a configuration to what was already a figure in human action' (p. 64); 'vient configurer ce qui, dans l'action humaine, fait déjà figure' (p. 100). Ricoeur cites favourably the work of Wilhelm Schapp with its notion that living means being always caught up (*verstrickt*) in stories (p. 114). If these stories are not actually recounted they call for such recounting. '*We tell stories*', says Ricoeur, '*because in the last analysis human lives need and merit being narrated*' (p. 75); '*Nous racontons des histoires parce que finalement les vies humaines ont besoin et méritent d'être racontées*' (p. 115). More strongly still: '*time becomes human to the extent that it is articulated through a narrative mode*' (p. 52); '*le temps devient temps humain dans la mesure où il est articulé sur un mode narratif*' (p. 85).

Now all this I find congenial in the sense that it seems to count against the excesses of the standard view, and in part seems to be directed explicitly against it. All the same, I am puzzled, for in the upstream–downstream flow of Ricoeur's analysis of mimesis I detect a very strong counter-current that seems opposed to the position I have been outlining so far.

In order to get at this counter-current let me return to a passage already cited. Life, says Ricoeur, or more precisely the temporality of real experience, 'is not reducible to simple discordance'; 'ne se réduit pas à la simple discordance'. But it *is* essentially discordant, 'aporetic', as we learn, Ricoeur thinks, from reading Augustine's *Confessions*. For all his passion and his conceptual energy, Augustine is unable to solve the paradoxes of time. And the reason for this, says Ricoeur in effect, is that they cannot be solved conceptually. They can be resolved not in a theoretic but a poetic sense, only by narrative itself as a poetic activity (*faire poétique*). Art transforms the discordance of experienced temporality into a concordance by means of plot and story.

This hypothesis leads Ricoeur to Aristotle's *Poetics*, in which the concept of plot is central. Here the concept of mimesis is also central, but it is clear that Ricoeur cannot simply accept Aristotle's version of that. If lived temporality is essentially (if not completely) discordant, and if art – narration in particular – brings concord, then art cannot be the simple imitation of life, in the sense of mirroring or representing it. Narrative mimesis for Ricoeur is not reproduction but production, invention. It may borrow from life but it transforms it.

It does this by means of plot, and in keeping with his emphasis on the creative, the poetic deed, Ricoeur prefers the active form 'mise en intrigue' (p. 102) – emplotment, also called the 'operation of configuration' (p. 65). Emplotment is an act of mediation, of drawing together. It mediates in three senses: first, 'between *events* or individual incidents and a story taken as a whole' (p. 65). This means, says Ricoeur, that 'it draws a sensible story *from* a diversity of events or incidents' or 'equivalently' that it 'transforms the events or incident *into* a story'. Second, it draws together 'factors as heterogeneous as agents, goals, means, interactions, circumstances, unexpected results, etc.' Third, it draws together different levels of temporality which are also 'heterogeneous', in particular it unites what Ricoeur calls chronological and non-chronological dimensions of time. It moves beyond the merely episodic dimension because (1) the diversity of events come under one thought or theme, (2) they attain a direction toward a conclusion or endpoint, and (3) the temporal order is even virtually reversed, as the end point reflects back upon and determines what leads up to it. As Ricoeur puts it, 'the act of plotting . . . extracts a configuration from a succession' (p. 66). It is here that the Augustinian aporiai of time are resolved, not by argument or theory but by the production of what Gallie calls a followable story. 'The fact that the story can be followed', says Ricoeur, 'converts the Augustine paradox into a living dialectic' (p. 66).

In its capacity as 'synthesis of the heterogeneous' narrative is comparable to metaphor, to which Ricoeur has devoted an equally important study. Both narrative and metaphor are, says Ricoeur, 'semantic innovations'; in both cases 'something new – not yet said, original [*inédit*] – arises in language' (p. ix). In both cases Ricoeur affirms (in response to post-structuralism, of course) not only that there is a world outside language but that language refers to it. In the case of metaphor, there is metaphoric reference

170

as well as metaphoric sense. But the reference is not direct. It is reference by redescription which permits us to see the world in a new way. 'Whereas metaphoric redescription holds sway in the field of sensual, pathetic, aesthetic and axiological values', the plots we invent concern 'the field of action' and are 'the privileged means whereby we re-configure our confused, unformed, and at the limit mute experience of time' (p. xi). Metaphor, says Ricoeur, is the capacity of 'seeing as'. The narrative activity of story-telling opens to us 'the realm of the "as if" ' (p. 64).

It can easily be seen, I think, why I discern in these elements of Ricoeur's theory a version of what I have called the standard view. It is clear that when he speaks of narratives he is speaking of literary texts, whether historical or fictional. To be sure, the category is broad enough to include myth, folktale and epic, which are neither clearly authored nor, in some cases, even written down. But they too achieve the status of repeatable and identifiable sense-artifacts which have a continuing existence in the cultural world.

Now if the essence of such narrative is to introduce something new into the world, and what they introduce is the synthesis of the heterogeneous, then presumably they are introducing it into a world in which without them these are lacking. It unites actions or events into a configuration; it unites agents, actions, circumstances into plot; it unites chronological with non-chronological elements. It invents and brings into the world not just events and characters that do not exist in that world (at least in fiction); it introduces a form of events that the world does not itself have. It operates on the field of action which in itself is 'confused, unformed and, at the limit, mute' and redescribes that field. But this redescription is indeed a radical one if chaos is given form and the mute is made to speak. Hence, presumably, the expression 'as if' – so much stronger than simply 'as'. A metaphor teaches us to see something *as* something. But a story describes a world *as if* it were what apparently, according to Ricoeur, it in fact is not. *Temps et récit* sets out to close the gap opened by the structuralists and other theorists between narrative and time. But in the end it seems that the gap between narrative and life is left open. To the extent that everyday life 'fait déjà figure' – already has structure – it is not, it would seem, narrative structure that it has. Note how radically Ricoeur departs from Aristotle. In the *Poetics* Aristotle says that history 'describes the thing that has been' and poetry, 'a kind of thing that might be'. But narrative seems, in Ricoeur's view, to portray a thing which could never be, because its very form is incompatible with the real world. This is, of course, the essence of the standard view.

In view of my puzzlement over this combination of elements which seem to count now for, now against the standard view, I propose to end my comments with a series of critical questions.

First, consider the three ways in which plot is said by Ricoeur to effect a synthesis of the heterogeneous. (1) It unites a series of actions or events into a larger unity. But do we not do this in everyday life already, whenever we engage in complex and long-term endeavours? (2) Plot is said to bring together 'goals, means, interactions, circumstances, unexpected results, etc.' But do we not do this every day of our lives? (3) Plot unites the levels of temporality by surmounting the merely sequential with the configurational. Have Husserl and other phenomenologists not shown that time-experience is essentially configurational, and that mere sequence is a myth?

There is no doubt that plot does deal in all these sorts of syntheses. But in doing so, is it not mirroring the sort of activity of which life consists? Is life not itself, in fact, already precisely a synthesis of the heterogeneous? To be sure, we are not always successful in effecting the sort of synthesis required. But does it follow that our temporal experience is essentially confused, unformed, mute without the help of literary artifacts? Ricoeur finds this view expressed by Augustine. But I might suggest another reading of the famous passages from the *Confessions*. Rather than describing discordance at the level of experience, is Augustine not contrasting the comprehension of experience with the incomprehension of theory? 'What is time? If no one asks me I know', he says. And, he might have added, I manage perfectly well, I deal with past and future, plan on the basis of past experience and the rest. It's when we try to explain time, when we try to fit it to logical and ontological concepts, that we are at a loss. The word aporia, used by Ricoeur here, originally means a theoretical, not a practical difficulty. It is an *understanding* of what he believes that Augustine so passionately wants, at least at this stage of his confession. Practical experience presents us, to be sure, with many difficulties. But is the paradoxical nature of time itself among these?

In drawing out this aspect of the standard view, and now Ricoeur's version of it, we are not, of course, suggesting that there is

172

no difference between narrative and life, or between life as described in stories and life as lived. But the question is this: has Ricoeur's theory an adequate account of what the difference is? Is it the difference between the chaotic and the formed, the confused and the orderly?

If it were, what would be the fate of the truth-telling narratives such as history, biography and the like? In the standard view they would of course be doomed by their very status as narratives to fail. Does Ricoeur's theory not in the end court the same consequence? I do not think it helps at this point to assert, as Ricoeur does in the second half of his book, that historical narrative is radically transformed by its scientific aspirations. For his very point is that, though its elements change, its narrative form remains, contrary to the views of anti-narrative historians and philosophers.

A final question can be formulated by returning to Ricoeur's statement that 'time becomes human time to the extent that it is articulated in a narrative mode' (p. 52). Does this mean that such articulation must take the form of literary productions or even, more broadly, texts? This would seem to amount to the assertion that life cannot be lived without literature. We obtain an altogether more plausible interpretation of the passage if we take the view that I have been urging that narration is not only a mode of discourse but more essentially a mode, perhaps *the* mode, of life.

NOTES

1 *The Sense of An ending: Studies in the Theory of Fiction*, London, Oxford University Press, 1966, pp. 35f.
2 ibid., p. 39.
3 *Story and Discourse: Narrative Structure in Fiction and Film*, Ithaca and London, Cornell University Press, 1978, p. 47.
4 'Introduction à l'analyse structurale des récits', *Communications*, 8, 1966, p. 7.
5 'History and fiction as modes of comprehension', *New Literary History*, 1979, pp. 557f.
6 In *On Narrative*, edited by W. J. T. Mitchell, Chicago and London, University of Chicago Press, 1981.
7 ibid., p. 4.
8 ibid., p. 23.
9 ibid.
10 *Time and Narrative*, translated by Kathleen McLaughlin and David Pellauer, Chicago, University of Chicago Press, 1984–8. It was originally published in French as *Temps et récit*, Paris, Editions du Seuil,

1983–5. Page references following French quotes are to the French edition; those following quotes in English are to the English edition.

Charles Taylor

I am unable to comment on the whole of this rich volume [*Time and Narrative* volume I] which already provides an anticipation of the principal thesis of the entire work and which embraces an exceptionally large range of philosophical reflections. I will restrict myself to the discussion of just one stage of Paul Ricoeur's argument, one which I believe to be fundamental.

Further, I will not offer a critique. Firstly because I find myself in substantial agreement with Ricoeur insofar as I grasp the major trajectory of his thought, but also because this thought appears to me to be so original and so interesting that the first task it requires of us is a stricter understanding. Criticisms, if there are any, may follow.

I will attempt, then, to outline what I believe to be a thesis of fundamental importance, and which exemplifies an important step in the argument. I will focus on the thesis dealt with in the second section of the book, where Ricoeur attempts to show that historical science cannot be conceived exclusively on the basis of the atemporal social sciences (if there ever are any), but must also take into account that form of intelligibility always associated with narration. Ricoeur attempts to blaze a trail amongst those who aspire to a nomologically hermetic science on the one hand, and those who simply maintain a 'narrativist' stance on the other. The intelligibility of the science of history, or that of historiography, is not that of the narrative (*récit*). Here we gain access to a transformation of narrative intelligibility. The results of this transformation, however, are comprehensible only on condition that we do not cut our moorings from our point of departure. Historiography remains a transformed narration.

This thesis can be divided into two sub-theses. First, a negative proposition, that history cannot be a totally nomological science. Then, a proposition to the effect that what remains irreducible to the nomological is exactly what derives from the narrative. I will concentrate on the first proposition, but I also believe that what I am going to say will have consequences for the second.

I structure this thesis in two propositions in this way because

I believe that our intellectual culture is subject to an immense force of attraction towards an explanatory model which I call *nomologically hermetic* [*nomologiquement étanche*]. This is partially due to the fact that this model seems to predominate in the really prestigious natural sciences, especially in physics. It concerns a form of explanation whereby the phenomenon to be explained is completely absorbed by the law or structure which constitutes its explanation. The *explanandum* is related to the *explanans* as an example, or particular case or partial manifestation of it. What is formulated in the *explanans* constitutes the totality of the real, the *explanadum* of which is only one part, aspect or singular case.

This, obviously, is the type of relation advocated by logical positivist theory, the nomologico-deductive idea of explanation. To be able to deduce the statement of fact from the explanation of the law and from a statement of initial conditions, is to make the sequence 'initial conditions – fact to be explained' a particular case of the law. This conception of explanation was supposed to account for the practice of modern physics. (A set of philosophical analyses, such as, recently, Rom Harré's, have shown that there is no such account, and that explanation in physics needs to be understood in quite another way, but let us continue.) But the great pre-modern model of science, Aristotelianism, offered a similar conception: a phenomenon is explained by integrating it into the form and by showing how it follows from this. Aristotle, however, had the good sense not to wish to deal with human affairs with a science structured in this way.

These days, however, it is not only the positivists who are attracted by this kind of nomological hermesis. The various 'structuralisms' aspire to an *explanandum–explanans* relation that may also be called a relation of subsumption; without requiring general laws to cover particular cases (as in the positivist model), but requiring instead that results be engendered through the transformations of a system. The confused babbling heard over the last few years of the 'death of the subject', and of an explanation through structures having recourse to subjectivity, rests in part on this subsumptive model; being derived from the structure had to suffice to explain the particular events which are the actions of the subject or his decisions. These latter are only manifestations of the underlying structure.

I dare say that the subsumptive model also favoured this strange mistrust of the event which marked an important tendency in

175

post-war French historiography, and which Ricoeur wants to contest. Evidently, historians, not being philosophers, are protected from this monomaniac bent which throws us into these limit situations where the heights of finesse are equivalent to the depths of stupidity. They are incapable of the errors of an Althusser or a Lacan. They instead pursue exceptionally valuable and interesting work. It may indeed be, however, that their meta-reflexions have been influenced by this noxious theoretical climate where 'structuralist' models enjoy a certain prestige.

There is however, another, very different type of relation between structure and event; its paradigmatic example is that of *langue-parole*. A language may be viewed as a structure of rules, or of possible formations and transformations. But this structure has purchase on the real only by virtue of *parole*. It is only through repeated acts of communication by members of a linguistic community that a structure has real existence. But 'events' or 'particular cases', which are speech-acts, are not in a simple relation of subsumption with the rule to which they are submitted. They may be in conformity with it, or they may deviate. This renewal is not however dictated by the nature of things; it is not a mere example, nor is it a particular case of a regularity. Or rather, it need not be.

For it is a matter of human acts aiming (in principle) at the realization of a structure, which may, however, not succeed or which may even be directed against the structures which must (in principle) rule them. Languages live only through successive renewals, each of which is a risk, for it runs the risk of not coming through this renewal unharmed. This talk you are now listening to is a speech-act which claims to be in French. I know that the French language is injured by this and therefore apologize to French speakers. Technical philosophy has already made terrifying ravages into English philosophy; I apologize again to the French for assaulting them with this barrage of jargon.

Languages, however, do not always survive speech. It is a commonplace that language is in perpetual change. It changes a little with the tide, by the effects of errors, tactlessness and thoughtlessness; it changes also through new styles, modes of expression seeking some means of articulation – just as French on the Continent is subject to the pressure of English; and all modern languages are influenced by mathematical modes of expression, through the languages of technology, computers, etc.

It is clear that the relation of act and structure, which could be called a relation of renewal, is irreducible to the relation of subsumption. To the extent that human actions are explained with the help of structures of this kind, our explanation cannot be nomologically hermetic: disparity is always possible, and what happens in this dimension, even in the limit case of a zero disparity, i.e., perfect adequation wth the structure, is not explained by the structure. Practice can never be reduced to a simple manifestation of structure.

What then are the structures of this type, those one could regard in the light of the paradigmatic model of language? In the twentieth century there has been a tendency to make language or linguistic structures into a master-key model, in an indiscriminate way. I do not want to contribute to this way of thinking, but I believe that on this very limited level there is, effectively, an analogy between language and a set of rules, structures, stable contexts, on the inside of which human action is played out. To put it in very general terms, I will say that each time that the structure, the context, etc., evoked in the explanation refers to signfications, or to the meaning of a situation – therefore to significant realities (*réalités de signifiance*; I follow Ricoeur in the use of this neologism, but I don't know if he uses it in the same sense) which the actor must grasp or comprehend in order to integrate it into his action – each time, that is, that structures of this type appear, there is a risk of divergence; the structure is a structure of those (events) renewed in practice, and the relation 'structure–event' cannot be one of subsumption.

This is what Ricoeur clearly shows in his penetrating discussion of Braudel's great work, *The Mediterranean*.[1] The history of this long period is situated at a level which is beyond the event, especially if one considers the quasi-permanent structures, the geographical structures which are dealt with in the first part of the work. But, as Ricoeur points out, to enter into a work of history, the geographical structures require a human meaning (*sens*). These are the pertinent signifying structures. And so, in this discussion of the inland sea, always the same,

we are concerned only with inhabited or inhabitable spaces, including the liquid plains. Man is ever-present here, and with him a multitude of symptomatic events: the mountain here represents refuge and shelter for free men. As for the

177

coastal plains, they are never mentioned apart from colonial-
isation, the work of drainage, the improvement of soils, the
dissemination of populations, displacements of all kinds:
transhumance, nomadism, invasions.

(*TN* vol. I, p. 209, translation modified)

The belief in explanation which leaves out the event, where the
event shows up only as the *explanandum*, as a particular case or
symptom, originates in a confusion between the two very different
ways in which the structure or the rule may intrude in the explanation, where it is a matter of a relation of subsumption or one
of renewal. These two relations are incompatible. A structure
cannot play both roles at the same time in the explanation of a
given field of events. Either it is carried through these in the sense
of being renewed in them, or it is manifest in them as the particular
case. In each case it is a matter of completely different and totally
non-superimposable explanatory modes. It is thanks only to the
immense prestige of nomological hermesis in our culture that it
has been possible to slip from one into the other and to take
structures demanding renewal for structures of subsumption, to
treat signifying structures as if they enjoyed the ontological closure
of the laws of physics.

Hence there are only two ways to employ subsumptive explanations in the human sciences. The first is to invoke those laws
or structures without significance. Certain aspects of the life and
behaviour of men are of course subject to explanations of this type:
if I jump from the top of a building, my fall would be explicable
as for any other body. This would be a particular case of Newton's
laws. To believe that explanations by non-significant structures
can alone suffice for the human sciences is to lapse into a more
or less scatter-brained reductionism – behaviourism is an example
of this.

The other way is to offer explanations according to behavioural
regularity. In certain given cultural contexts, men have a tendency
to react in a certain way. Particular cases may be explained according to this regularity. But the drawback of this type of explanation
is that it is in danger of having a very short range, because
behavioural regularities exist within these signifying structures only
between differences. From the moment that the structures are
pushed into practice, and language or significances change, when
thus a new cultural form is born, one can no longer count on

yesterday's conventions. Those regularities that resist renewal are precisely those founded on non-significant structures. To bank on these is to return to reductionism.

Further, it is not just that cultural regularities have a short range, but also, what interests us most, in history for example, is that there are changes. These are the moments of divergence which capture our attention. They are the French Revolution, the American War of Independence, the Industrial Revolution, etc., which remain the benchmarks of historiography, and rightly so. We have seen how absurd it is to envisage the explanations we offer of these great events as having their basis in the nomological model (*TN* vol. I, pp. 121–143).

I have attempted to isolate what I believe to be Ricoeur's principal thesis in the first volume of his *Time and Narrative*, by using the distinction between structures of renewal and structures of subsumption. I obviously take the blame for this slightly barbarous vocabulary, but I do not believe that I have falsified his thought. It is the argument from the fundamental incompatibility of these two explanatory modes that I think I see in the magnificent discussion he gives us of Braudel's famous work. What the discussion brings out is just the undeniability and insurmountability of the site of divergence where everything is transformed by structures of renewal. This dimension of divergence opens the possibility – or better perhaps, creates the need – for another kind of explanation that would be closely or remotely linked to narrative. This is the second proposition of Ricoeur's thesis, with which I am also in agreement, but my objective here has been to reformulate the first proposition: have I understood well?

NOTES

1 Fernand Braudel, *The Mediterranean and the Mediterranean World in the Age of Philip II*, translated by Siân Reynolds, New York, Harper & Row, 1972.

Paul Ricoeur

It is true that one always learns from one's readers. Living authors are fortunate to have this opportunity. Derrida likes to say that writing is related to death. This is true: when I write, I suppose that my book will survive me, and that there are readers who, as in Plato's expression, 'bring support', without which the author dies.

The question posed by David Carr is absolutely central to me, since the problem he raised concerning the relationship between art and life is closely related to the problem of refiguration, which I myself posed. David has constructed a 'standard' theory and asked me how I situate myself in relation to it. Taken as a whole, according to this 'standard' theory, life itself, not being history [*histoire*: also story],[1] cannot coincide with any narrative; it follows from this fundamental heterogeneity between history and life that the relation of *representation* between history and life can only be one of violence. Now, it happens that I too speak of the 'violence of interpretation', a term otherwise employed by Heidegger as well as by psychoanalysis. So, where do I situate myself? I think that my suggestion of a triple mimesis constitutes an attempt to address this difficulty. If, according to *Mimesis I*, every narrative configuration has a kind of retroactive reference, it is because life itself is an inchoate narrative; this is what I call the pre-narrative character of life. This being so, I do not see what aspect of the circular character that I see between the three mimeses would lead me to the 'standard' theory. At first, I am placed at a stage of human experience which, groping about, seeks a meaning: but this is an ill-wrought history, a history eaten away by discordances. It is only through transformation into well-made fictions that the effect of refiguration survives. I wonder, consequently, if the circularity between prefiguration, configuration and refiguration may facilitate my escape from the dilemma which will surround me, and the terms amongst which I am constrained to choose: history is either a distortion of life, or it represents life.

Now the concept that I proposed of a refiguration which would be at once 'revelatory' and 'transformative' seems to me to introduce a concept of representation which does not imply a mirror relation (I am thinking of Rorty's book, *Philosophy and the Mirror of Nature*[2]). I have attempted to produce a concept of mimesis which escapes the dilemma according to which either history falsifies life, does it violence, or reflects it. I rather wonder if a standard model exists under which one may group every author mentioned and which constrains each to a yes or no answer.

What struck me most in Aristotle, concerning the term mimesis, was its belonging to a family of terms ending in -*sis*, all of which evoke a dynamic operativity: thus *poiesis, sustasis, catharsis*, etc.;

poiesis, then, does not designate the finished poem, but the act of poetic creation; in the same way mimesis designates a kind of production. This is why to translate mimesis by 'imitation' is insufficient. Else, in his splendid commentary on the *Poetics* to which I owe so much, proposes the term 'imitatings' to designate the products of mimetic activity. If then one retains the dynamic range of the term mimesis, I believe that it is possible to avoid the alternative proposed by David and instead embrace both horns of the dilemma: a *life* in search of its own *history*.

What makes me say that history is not life is rather the difference I see between a theory of action and a theory of history: a theory of action may be based on the reconstruction of motives, the agent's deliberations, such that (s)he includes them in his/her situation. But to recount a history is to relate those actions to their non-intentional effects, indeed to their perverse effects. Thus today, when we attempt to understand Lenin, we cannot base this understanding solely on what he thought before the Bolshevik Revolution, but must also take into account the fact that it was this Revolution which produced Stalin. The historian's problem is then to ascertain to what extent Lenin's thought and actions contain the necessary, but of course not the sufficient, conditions for Stalin's emergence. But this is no longer a question concerning the theory of action alone, it also has to do with the theory of history. The historian does not therefore repeat the structure of the actions of Lenin's life, but attempts to relate this structure to effects of which the agent himself could not be aware. 'Doing history' is about constructing a sequence which includes heterogeneous elements, being aware of non-volitional effects, and further, of all the excluded circumstances, which appear only retrospectively to have been the circumstances of the action. History tears itself away from life; it is constituted through the activity of comprehension which is also the activity of configuration.

The problem which worries me most – and I am not sure that I have resolved it – is not so much the one posed by David Carr, that is, to ascertain whether history and life are strangers to one another to such an extent that history constitutes an intrusion, a falsification, or a consolation, to use Frank Kermode's words; it is the objection of *circularity*. But this circularity is not a product of the method employed; it expresses our true situation. It is then asked if life needs to be understood through literature; I would answer in the affirmative – to a very great extent. Because life 'in the raw' is beyond our reach, for the very good reason that we are not born into a world of children, but that, as unspeaking children, we come into a world already full of all our predecessors' narratives. Consequently, as I have said in describing the stage of prefiguration that I have called *Mimesis I*, action is already symbolically mediated; literature, in the largest sense of the word, including history as well as fiction, tends to reinforce a process of symbolization already at work. It is this circularity which constitutes, in my opinion, the real problem. It could in fact be objected that I am bound to include in the notion of prefiguration the result of a previous refiguration – because effectively, for each of us, what is prefigured in our life results from refigurations operated by all the other lives of those who taught us. This circle is not however a vicious circle, because there is nevertheless an extension of meaning, progressive meaning, from the inchoate to the fully determined.

I have just written a long preface for the republication of the French translation of Hannah Arendt's *The Human Condition*, where I take up the same problem once more, with the help of her concepts of *labour, work* and *action*. Action, according to Arendt, makes an appeal to history, because history *discloses the who* of the action. I wonder if, in this notion of the *disclosure of the who*, there is not a means to avoid the alternatives that David Carr has created in constructing his standard theory.

Is not art, in the largest sense, *poiesis*, a function of both revelation and transformation? So that one may say both that *poiesis* reveals structures which would have remained unrecognized without art, *and* that it transforms life, elevating it to another level.

Charles Taylor addressed himself to the strictly epistemological aspect of my work. He asks me, at the end, if he has understood well. I will offer General De Gaulle's answer: 'You have understood me!' But I will be less devious than the General after making this acknowledgement.

My position with regard to the nomological model is exactly as he has indicated. I completely accept the idea that the best way to clarify the discussion is to propose a counter-model borrowed from the *langue-parole* relation. I am entirely in agreement with the idea that the renewal of *langue* by *parole* itself creates a kind of circularity. I am, moreover, in agreement with your argument when I say, with William Dray, that laws are always interpolated into a previous understanding, and that, in so doing, the historian does not *establish* laws, but *employs* them. Thus, in explaining an automobile accident, I must enumerate the events one by one, *seriatim* (the petrol tank explodes, the engine catches fire, etc.). Physical laws intervene one after another, but according to a series which is a narrative series. The insertion of the nomological into the factual is constitutive of what happens, of everything we call an 'event'.

I would like, however, to add two things to this. First, the two models are not simply alternatives, since, in a certain way, they operate together. Here I owe much to Henrik von Wright's analysis, in *Explanation and Interpretation*,[3] where he shows that explanation, in terms of history, contains nomic and teleological segments, which, taken together, make history into a mixed explanatory mode. This is what makes the epistemological status of history so extraordinarily unstable, and it shows this better than does the linguistic model, where the use of language reacting to the same structures of *langue*, but not the production of a mixed model, may be observed.

This leads me to a second question, which takes me back to the part of my argument that has so far not been dealt with in this discussion, but which nevertheless is closest to my heart (for the nomological question is a constant problem for me and, I believe, to a lesser extent, for the whole world).

What has worried me most is the idea that historical explanation is distanced from ordinary narrative by precisely this double sophistication: there is on the one hand the insertion of nomological elements into a narrative framework, and on the other, the combination, in a mixed model, of nomic and teleological segments. Here I am no longer in agreement with the narrativists, for whom history is only an expansion of narration, a narration simply transformed. Now, it is the word 'transformed' which concerns me. Can I give an account of this transformation in a meaningful communicative way? It is in order to address this problem that I have had recourse to Husserl's method in the *Krisis*: applying myself to this method of retrospective questioning, of retrospective derivation, I have attempted to show that there was, between the explanatory level of history – the level reached by modern non-narrative history – and narration, a transitional zone. I have indeed worked extensively on concepts of transition. In particular, I saw in the notion of *singular causal imputation*, developed by Max Weber and Raymond Aron, a transitional epistemological stage between the explanatory level adopted by modern history and the simple narrative, for example the popular tale, a transitional stage able to bridge the gap between *history* and *story* – if it is now true that *history* is no longer a species of the type *story*. The sought-after epistemological connector is just this notion of singular causal imputation. I have a high regard for the range of this notion which not only covers short events, as one may conclude from the case made for factual history by Braudel, but also long sequences of events: it is in fact through a singular causal explanation that one can discover an incitation and a composition of nascent capitalism in certain aspects of the Reformation; for example, the work ethic. This is a singular causal explanation – although it is concerned not with individuals, but with large historical structures – because this sequence happened only once.

There is then an explanatory singularity even at the level of large structures. This is the case with Braudel himself when he explains how the Mediterranean ceased to be the political centre of the world at the time when the discovery of the New World displaced the axis of history towards the Atlantic, while the Ottoman empire was turning towards Asia. One could say that the theme of this singular causal imputation is the history of the death of the Mediterranean as the great political actor. Hence my attempt to introduce a second connector at this stage, that of the quasi-character; I find here a reinforcement of the narrative theory developed by literary criticism. The place of the 'actor' (*actant*) in Greimas's sense, may be occupied just as well by 'talking animals', as in fables, or by ghosts, as in the tragedy of Hamlet, or by collective entities – as in the history of the Mediterranean! The transition between *history* and *story* may thus be assured by that species of artifact from historical methodology, the construction of the quasi-character. And if I could no longer recognize the character in the quasi-character, then I would topple from history to sociology. But if history must remain partially within the domain of the human sciences, it is to the extent that a singular causal explanation is equivalent to a quasi-plot, and that the entities with which they deal can be considered as quasi-characters.

Finally, I have attempted to construct the notion of a quasi-event, in keeping with the notion of event in the sense Braudel had given it, believing that, by definition, the event had to be short and sudden, like a sudden change of fortune. An event however, may be of any dimension. I mention elsewhere the historians like Le Goff etc.; he calls the replacement of monastery bells, which marked canonical hours, by belfry clocks in the Middle Ages, an 'event'. This struggle between bell and clock constitutes a kind of great event in the social calculation of time. Thus an event may be of any duration; what makes it count as an event is its capacity to produce significant change, a 'turning point' in the course of time. What appeared to me to be important was to be able to expand the Aristotelian notion of *peripteia* (event), beyond its brevity and instantaneousness, in order to equate it with the notion of a significant transformation of a course of events.

Was the attempt worth the trouble, seeking to detect a filiation between a history which had broken with narrative, but remained indirectly bound to it, justifying this indirect derivation through the construction of terms or intermediary stages, on the tripartite basis of explanation, characters and events?

Hanging ultimately on this term is my attempt to escape the dilemma: either history is no longer a narrative, or, if it is, it is so under an outdated form of writing. I agree that as it is written, history is no longer a narrative, despite the success of the historical novel. It is however precisely when history is no longer a narrative that it retains the bonds of the indirect derivation which can be reconstructed. This is my epistemological thesis.

I thank Hayden White for his reading, which I find creative. While not completely recognizing myself in it, I acknowledge its receipt.

He has produced another text, for an entirely explicable reason: he has anticipated a problem not dealt with in *Time and Narrative* volume I, concerning the problem of referentiality, and which he has projected back onto the first volume. The result of this is that he has read constantly, in a referential language, a work which rested precisely upon the putting into parentheses of problems of reference. It was this transformation of my work within his reading which intrigued me.

He has read me entirely from the standpoint of tropology, saying that the mimetic relation was fundamentally an allegorical relation, and that one always produces an allegory of the real. I am slightly resistant to this assimilation, because I fear that the distinction between history and fiction may disappear. Of course I am in agreement over the existence of an ultimate intersection between history and fiction; but this is conditional upon having first

185

maintained, for as long and as resolutely as possible, the polarity between history and fiction. It is in this respect that I insisted on the notion of *debt*. The idea that we are indebted with regard to the past very much preoccupies me. We are not only inheritors, we are equally debtors to a debt which in some way renders us insolvent. Curiously, I rediscovered this notion of debt, via Lacan, in Michel de Certeau in his last work on *La Fable mystique*.[4] But I had rediscovered this notion independently, in the course of my own reflections on the notion of evidence (*témoignage*).

If we do not resolutely maintain the difference between history and fiction, how do we answer people like Faurisson, in France, who declares: 'In Auschwitz, however, nothing *real* has happened; there is only what is said about it'. Roland Barthes's idea of the 'effect of the real' could, dangerously, support this kind of discourse which is an insult to the dead: they are killed twice. Now, with regard to them we have a debt, I would say a duty of restitution. There comes to my lips the very beautiful word *rendre* in French, 'to render' in English. We must 'render' what has happened, that is to say, figure it at the same time as returning it to the dead. Just as in Nicaea's *Credo* mention is made of the communion of saints; thus, by means of history, a communion established between the living and the dead. If we are unable to 'fictionalize' the dead, we would have to return their 'having been' to them. No simple capitulation before 'being no more'. The past is not just what is absent from history; the right of its 'having been' also demands to be recognized. This is what the historian's debt consists in.

Having said this, we are justified in reflecting on the fact that, as *readers*, we are at the point of intersection between fictive and historical narratives: we read Shakespeare just as we read Braudel. What happens to us when we become these readers of fiction and history? At the horizon of my work, I evoke the fate of what we call human time: it is in some way the fragile construction resulting from the intersection between, on the one hand, the fictions which make us understand human actions in reconstructing them in an imaginary universe, and on the other, the reconstructions of history placed under the sign of debt. I sometimes suspect that the man of fiction is no less a debtor, but in another way: no longer with regard to the 'having been', but with regard to a vision of the world to which he never ceases doing justice. I take the example – as dear to Theo Geraets as to myself, since we are both indebted to Merleau-Ponty – of Cézanne. Why did Cézanne return so frequently to Mt Sainte-Victoire? When we read his letters we see a man in pain, weighed down by his sense of debt. The artist, in this way, is in all likelihood no less indebted than the historian. But with respect to what is he indebted? With respect to a *vision* which takes on for him the significance of a *logos* which precedes him, which (pre)occupies him. Past deeds are not the only ones to which we are indebted. Added to this, the task of doing justice to the world has the value for us of being a hermeneutic key to the reading of phenomena. Thus Cézanne is seen in his letters speaking of Nature, with a capital letter – as though he never finished 'rendering' Mt Sainte-Victoire, 'rendering unto' Mt Sainte-Victoire.

Perhaps another species of indebtedness exists, one which would lead us back to our point of departure and allow us a way out of the alternative: either you falsify life, or you represent it. Do we fall into a final paradox, between discovery and transformation? It is only through transformation that discoveries are made. Why so? Because, in the historical past, there is what is implicit, what is inchoate; in particular, there are those history has forgotten, the victims of history: it is to them that we are indebted, much more than to the conquerors, whose renown inundates triumphalist history; and there are also those impeded possibilities, all that in history was inhibited, massacred. Here one sees how fiction comes to history's aid; it is fiction which liberates these inhibited possibilities. What has taken place has also prevented something else from happening and existing. This was Emmanuel Levinas's message, that for us to be there is, in a certain way, to usurp a place. It may be said that every event, by the fact that it has been realized, has usurped the place of impeded possibilities. It is fiction that can save these impeded possibilities and, at the same time, turn them back on history; this reverse-face of history, which has not taken place, but which had been able to take place, in a certain way *has been*; only however in a potential mode.

NOTES

1 Ricoeur is also alluding to Carr's reference to 'stories' here, and at various points below.

2 Richard Rorty, *Philosophy and the Mirror of Nature*, Oxford, Blackwell, 1980.

3 Henrik von Wright, *Explanation and Interpretation*, London, Routledge & Kegan Paul, 1971.

4 Michel de Certeau, *La Fable mystique*, Paris, Gallimard, 1987.

11

NARRATIVE IDENTITY

Paul Ricoeur

(translated by David Wood)

My aim in this essay is to examine more closely the concept of narrative identity, that is to say, the kind of identity that human beings acquire through the mediation of the narrative function.

I encountered this problem at the end of *Time and Narrative* volume III, when, after a long journey through historical narrative and fictional narrative, I asked the question of whether there was any fundamental experience that could integrate these two major types of narrative. I then formed the hypothesis that the constitution of narrative identity, whether it be that of an individual person or of a historical community, was the sought-after site of this fusion between narrative and fiction. We have an intuitive precomprehension of this state of affairs: do not human lives become more readily intelligible when they are interpreted in the light of the stories that people tell about them? And do not these 'life stories' themselves become more intelligible when what one applies to them are the narrative models – plots – borrowed from history or fiction (a play or a novel)? The epistemological status of autobiography seems to confirm this intuition. It is thus plausible to endorse the following chain of assertions: self-knowledge is an interpretation; self interpretation, in its turn, finds in narrative, among other signs and symbols, a privileged mediation; this mediation draws on history as much as it does on fiction, turning the story of a life into a fictional story or a historical fiction, comparable to those biographies of great men in which history and fiction are intertwined.

But what was missing from this intuitive grasp of the problem of personal identity was a clear understanding of what is at stake in the very question of identity when it is applied to persons or to communities. Since the publication of *Time and Narrative* volume

III, I have become aware of the considerable difficulties attached to the question of identity as such. I am now convinced that a stronger and more convincing defence can be mounted on behalf of narrative identity if it can be shown that this notion and the experience to which it refers helps to resolve difficulties relating to the notion of personal identity, as it is discussed in wider philosophical circles, in particular in Anglo-American analytical philosophy.

The conceptual framework that I propose to submit to analytical scrutiny rests on the fundamental distinction I draw between two main uses of the concept of identity: identity as sameness (Latin: *idem*; English: *same*; German: *gleich*) and identity as selfhood (Latin: *ipse*; English: *self*; German: *Selbst*) Selfhood is not sameness. My thesis is that many of the difficulties which obscure the question of personal identity result from failing to distinguish between these two senses of the term identity. We will see, it is true, that the confusion is not without cause, to the extent that these two problematics overlap at a certain point. The determination of this zone of convergence will therefore be of the greatest importance.

Let us start with the idea of identity as sameness (*idem*). Many relations are brought into play at this level. First, there is identity in the numerical sense: we say that two occurrences of a thing designated by an invariable name do not constitute two different things, but one single and same thing. Identity here means uniqueness; its contrary is *plurality* – not one, but two, or more. This first sense of the term corresponds to identification understood as a reidentification of the same. Next we find the idea of extreme resemblance: X and Y wear the same costume – that is to say their costumes are so similar that they are substitutable one for the other. The contrary is here *different*. These first two ideas are not exterior to each other. In certain cases the second serves as an indirect criterion for the first, when the reidentification of the same is the object of doubt and of debate. Then one has to try to show that the material marks (photos, imprints, etc.) or, more problematically, the memories of a single witness, or the concordant reports of many witnesses, show such a great resemblance, for example, between the accused now present in court and the presumed author of a bygone crime, that the man present today and the author of the crime are one and the same person. The trials of war criminals give rise to just such confrontations. The risks here are well-known. And it is precisely the weakness of the criterion of similarity when one is dealing with great distance in time which suggests another idea, which is at the same time another criterion of identity: the uninterrupted continuity in the development of a being between the first and last stage of its evolution. Thus we say of an oak that it is the same thing from the seed to the tree in the prime of life. The same is true for an animal from birth to death, and for a man, as a specimen of the species, from foetus to old man. The demonstration of this continuity functions as a criterion supplementary to that of similarity in the service of numerical identity. The contrary to identity taken in this third sense is *discontinuity*. But what has to be taken into account in this third sense is change through time. It is through this important phenomenon that the fourth sense of identity arises, that of sameness: *permanence* in time. It is with this sense that the real difficulties begin, insofar as it is difficult not to assign this permanence to some immutable *substratum*, to a substance, as Aristotle did, and as Kant confirms in his own way by displacing from the ontological to the transcendental plane the substratum of the categories of the understanding, i.e., the primacy of substance over accidents: 'All phenomena contain something permanent (substance) when considered as the object itself, and something changing, when considered as a simple determination of this object, that is to say as a mode of the existence of the object.' (*CPR*, A182/B224) This is of course the first Analogy of Experience, which corresponds in the order of principles, that is, of first judgments, to the first category of relation, which is called, precisely, substance, and the scheme of which is 'the permanence of the real in time, that is to say, the representation of this real as a substratum of the empirical determination of time in general, a substratum which remains thus while all else changes' (*CPR*, A143/B183). It is very exactly this fourth determination which is problematic to the extent that selfhood, the self, appears to cover the same space of meaning. But this fourth determination is irreducible to the earlier ones as the difference in the contraries verifies. The contrary of numerical identity is plurality; the contrary of permanent identity is diversity. The basis for the discontinuity in the determination of the identical is that identity as uniqueness does not thematically imply time, which is not the case with identity as permanence. But this is what we have in mind when we affirm the identity of a thing, of a plant, of an animal, or of a human being (not yet considered as an irreplaceable person).

190

How does the concept of self, of selfhood connect with that of sameness? We can begin to unfold the concept of selfhood by considering the nature of the question to which the self constitutes a response, or a range of responses. This question is the question *who*, distinct from the question *what*. It is the question we tend to ask in the field of action: looking for the agent, the author of the action, we ask: Who did this or that? Let us call *ascription* the assignation of an agent to an action. By this we certify that the action is the property of whoever committed it, that it is his, that it belongs to him personally. Onto this as yet morally neutral act is grafted the act of *imputation* which takes on an explicitly moral significance, in the sense that it implies accusation, excuse or acquittal, blame or praise, in short appraisal in terms of the 'good' or the 'just'. It will be said: Why this awkward vocabulary of the self, rather than the me? Quite simply because ascription can appear in every grammatical person: in the first person in confession, the acceptance of responsibility (here I am) – in the second person in the warning, advice, the commandment (thou shalt not kill) – in the third person in narrative, which is precisely what will concern us shortly (he said, she thought, etc.). The term self, selfhood, covers the whole range of possibilities opened up by ascription on the level of personal pronouns and of all the other deictics which depend on it: possessive pronouns and adjectives (my, mine; you, yours; his, hers, etc.), adverbs of time and of place (now, here, etc.).

Before marking the point at which the question of self intersects with that of the same, let me insist on the break, which is not just grammatical, or even epistemological and logical, but frankly ontological which separates *idem* and *ipse*. I agree here with Heidegger that the question of selfhood belongs to the sphere of problems relating to the kind of entity that he calls Dasein and which he characterizes by the capacity to question itself as to its own way of being and thus to relate itself to being *qua* being. To the same sphere of problems belong such concepts as being-in-the-world, care, being-with, etc. In this sense, selfhood is one of the existentials which belong to the mode of being of Dasein, just as the categories, in the Kantian sense, belong to the mode of being of entities which Heidegger characterizes as ready-to-hand and present-at-hand. The break between self (*ipse*) and same (*idem*) ultimately expresses that more fundamental break between Dasein and ready-to-hand/present-at-hand. Only Dasein is *mine*, and more generally self. Things, all given and manipulable, can be said to be the same, in the sense of sameness-identity.

Having said that, the self intersects with the same at one precise point: permanence in time. It is indeed quite proper to raise the question of what sort of permanence is appropriate to a self, whether, pursuing ascription, one takes it to be a character defined by a certain constancy of its dispositions, or whether, pursuing imputation, one sees it in the kind of fidelity to the self which is expressed in the form of keeping one's promises. And yet, as close in appearance as this deportment of the self or self-maintenance [*ce maintien de soi*] (to use Martineau's translation of Heidegger's expression *Selbst-Ständigkeit*) may be to the permanence in time of the same (*idem*) there are still two meanings which overlap without being identical.

The problem which concerns me from now on arises precisely from the superimposition of the two problematics which has occurred since we became engaged with the question of permanence in time. My thesis consequently is double: the first is that most of the difficulties which afflict contemporary discussion bearing on personal identity result from the confusion between two interpretations of permanence in time; my second thesis is that the concept of narrative identity offers a solution to the aporias of personal identity.

Rather than undertaking a necessarily schematic review of the difficulties involved in the problems of personal identity and in the solutions which have been offered since Locke and Hume in English-speaking philosophy, I have chosen as a strong opponent Derek Parfit, the author of the important work *Reasons and Persons*.

The force of Parfit's work lies in the fact that he pursues to its logical conclusion a methodology which allows only an *impersonal* description of the facts whether relating to a psychological criterion or to a bodily criterion of identity. According to the view which he calls 'reductionism' and which is his own

the fact of personal identity through time consists only in taking account of certain particular facts which can be described without presupposing personal identity and without explicitly supposing that the experiences in the life of this person are possessed by them or without even explicitly supposing that this person exists. One can describe these facts in an impersonal manner.[1]

What I dispute in Parfit's position is not the coherence of this impersonal position, but the affirmation that the only other alternative would be 'a pure Cartesian ego or a pure spiritual substance'. Parfit continues

> My thesis denies that we are entities existing separately, distinct from our brains and our bodies and our experiences. But the thesis claims that although we are not separately existing entities, personal identity constitutes a supplementary fact, which does not consist simply in physical and/or psychological continuity. I call this thesis the thesis of the supplementary Fact.

What I essentially dispute is the claim that a hermeneutic of selfhood can be reduced to the position of a Cartesian ego, which is itself identified with a 'supplementary fact' distinct from mental states and from bodily facts. It is because mental states and bodily facts have at the outset been reduced to impersonal events that the self appears to be a supplementary fact. The self, I will claim, simply does not belong to the category of events and facts.

Parfit himself touches on the decisive issue on two occasions. First, when he outlines the strange feature of what he calls the experiences constituting a personal life, of being possessed by this person. The whole question of ownness which governs our use of personal adjectives relates to the question of selfhood insofar as it is irreducible both to the impersonal description of an objective connection and to the fantastic hypostasis of a pure ego taken to be a distinct supplementary fact. The second occasion is more remarkable. If the connection, whether psychical or physical, is the only important thing about identity, then, says Parfit, personal identity is not what matters. This daring assertion has important moral implications, to wit the renunciation of the moral principle of self-interest and the adoption of a sort of quasi-Buddhist self-effacement of identity.

But, I would ask, to whom does identity no longer matter? Who is called on to be deprived of self-assertion if not the self that has been put in parentheses in the name of impersonal methodology?

But I have a more important reason to take Parfit's book seriously. This has to do with the systematic use made of puzzling

PAUL RICOEUR

cases, drawn for the most part from science fiction, which are given a considerable role in this investigation. It is the use of these imaginary cases which will lead us shortly to the narrative interpretation of identity that I oppose to Parfit's solution. I will propose in particular a confrontation between the puzzling cases of science fiction and the difficult cases proposed by literary fiction, in my elaboration of the notion of narrative identity. The important point here is that these puzzling cases are posed for the most part by an imaginary technology applied to the brain. Most of these experiments are at the moment unrealizable, and will perhaps always remain so. What is essential is that they are conceivable. Three kinds of experiments are imagined: brain transplants, brain bisection, and – the most remarkable case – the construction of an exact replica of the brain. We will pause for a moment to consider this experiment. Let us suppose that a replica is made of my brain and of all the information contained in the rest of my body, a replica so exact that it is indistinguishable from my brain and from my real body. Let us suppose that my replica is sent to the surface of some other planet and that I am myself 'teleported' to a meeting with my replica. Let us suppose, further, that in the course of the journey my brain is destroyed and that I do not meet up with my replica, or else that only my heart is damaged and that I meet up with my intact replica, who promises me to take care of my family and my work after my death. The question at issue is whether in either case I survive in my replica. Clearly, the function of these puzzling cases is to create a situation such that it is impossible to decide whether I survive or not. The effect of the undecidability of the answer is to undermine the belief that identity, whether in the numerical sense or in the sense of permanence in time, must always be (able to be) determined. If the answer is undecidable, says Parfit, that is because the question itself is empty. The conclusion then follows: identity is not what matters.

My conception of narrative identity can be contrasted term by term to that of Parfit. But this disagreement would be uninteresting if it did not give rise to a confrontation between two sorts of fiction: science fiction and the literary fictions that the narrativist thesis itself deploys.

That narrativity offers here an alternative solution is already anticipated, or, if you will, presupposed by the way in which we talk in everyday life about a life-story. We equate life with the story or stories that we can tell about it. The act of telling would seem to be the key to the sort of connection to which we allude when we speak with Dilthey of the 'coherence of life' (*Zusammenhang des Lebens*). Are we not concerned here with a fundamentally narrative unity, as Alasdair MacIntyre asked, when he spoke in *After Virtue*[2] of the narrative unity of a life? But while MacIntyre draws mainly on stories recounted in the course of, and in the very texture of life, I propose to make a detour through the literary forms of narrative and more precisely through those of fictional narrative. Indeed the problematic of coherence, of permanence in time, in brief of identity, is found there elevated to a new level of lucidity and also of perplexity not attained by those stories in which the course of life is immersed. There the question of identity is deliberately set forth as what is at stake in narrative. According to my thesis, narrative constructs the durable properties of a character, what one could call his narrative identity, by constructing the kind of dynamic identity found in the plot which creates the character's identity. So it is first of all in the plot that one looks for the mediation between permanence and change, before it can be carried over to the character. The advantage of this detour through the plot is that this provides the model of discordant concordance on which it is possible to construct the narrative identity of the character. The narrative identity of the character could only correspond to the discordant concordance of the story itself.

The confrontation with Parfit becomes interesting when literary fiction produces situations in which selfhood can be distinguished from sameness. The modern novel abounds in situations in which the lack of identity of a person is readily spoken of, exactly the opposite of the sort of fixity of the heroes found in folklore, fairy tales, etc. One could say in this respect that the great novel of the nineteenth century, as Lukács, Bakhtine and Kundera have interpreted it, explored all the intermediate combinations between complete overlap between sameness-identity and selfhood-identity and the complete dissociation between these two modalities of identity that we shall now consider. With Robert Musil, 'the man without qualities' – or rather without properties – becomes at the limit unidentifiable. The anchorage of the proper name becomes so derisory that it becomes superfluous. The unidentifiable becomes unnamable. That the crisis of character is correlative to the crisis in the identity of plot, is amply demonstrated by Musil's novel.

One could say generally that as the novel approaches this annulling of the person in terms of sameness-identity, the novel also loses its properly narrative qualities. To the loss of personal identity corresponds a loss of narrative configuration and in particular a crisis of its closure. Thus the character has a reciprocal impact on the plot. It is just such a schism – to use Frank Kermode's expression – which affects both the tradition of identifiable heroes and the tradition of configuration with its double valency of concordance and discordance. The erosion of paradigms strikes both the figuration of the character and the configuration of the plot. Thus, in the case of Robert Musil, the disintegration of narrative form parallel to the loss of identity of the character exceeds the limits of narrative and draws the literary work closer to the essay. It is thus no longer by chance that so many modern autobiographies, that of Leiris for example, deliberately stretch narrative form and come to resemble that least configured literary genre, namely the essay.

We should not misunderstand the significance of this literary phenomenon: it must be said that even in the most extreme case of the loss of sameness-identity of the hero, we do not escape the problematic of selfhood. A non-subject is not nothing, with respect to the category of the subject. Indeed, we would not be interested in this drama of dissolution and would not be thrown into perplexity by it, if the non-subject were not still a figure of the subject, even in a negative mode. Suppose someone asks the question: Who am I? Nothing, or almost nothing is the reply. But it is still a reply to the question *who*, simply reduced to the starkness of the question itself.

We can now compare the puzzling cases of science fiction and those of literary fiction. The differences are many and striking.

First of all, narrative fictions remain imaginative variations on an invariant, the corporeal condition assumed to constitute the unavoidable mediation between self and world. Characters on stage or in a novel are beings similar to us – acting, suffering, thinking and dying. In other words, imaginative variations in the literary field have as their horizon the inescapable terrestrial condition. We are not forgetting what Nietzsche, Husserl and Heidegger have said on the subject of the earth, understood not as planet, but as the mythic name of our being-in-the-world. Why is this so? Because fictions are imitations – as errant or aberrrant as one might wish – of action, that is to say, of what we already

196

know as action and interaction in a physical and social environment. By comparison, Parfit's puzzling cases are imaginative variations which reveal as contingent the very invariant condition of a hermeneutic of existence. And what is the instrument of this circumvention? Technology – not actual technology, but the dream of technology. Imaginative variations of narrative fictions bear on the variable connection between selfhood and sameness, the imaginative variations of science fiction bear on a single sameness, the sameness of this thing, of this manipulable entity, the brain. An impersonal account of identity thus seems to be dependent on a technological dream in which the brain has from the start been the substitutable equivalent of the person. The real enigma is whether we are capable of conceiving of alternative possibilities within which corporeity as we know it, or enjoy it or suffer from it, could be taken as a variable, a contingent variable, and without having to transpose our earthly experiences in the very description of the case in question. For my part, I wonder whether we are not violating something that is more than a rule, or a law, or even a state of affairs, but the existential condition under which there exist rules, laws, facts at all. This violation may be the ultimate reason why these experiments are not only unrealizable, but, were they to be realizable, they ought to be prohibited.

A second difference strikes me. In all the experiments of science fiction mentioned above, the subject who undergoes them lacks relations, lacks the other in the sense of the other person. The only things present are my(?) brain and the experimental surgeon. I undergo the experiment alone. The other plays the part of the grand manipulator, hard to distinguish from an executioner. As to my replica, it is in no sense an other. In fictional narrative, on the other hand, interaction is constitutive of the narrative situation. In this respect A.-J. Greimas is right to claim that the conflict between two narrative programmes is a semiotic constraint ineliminable from the narrative field.[3] In this way narrative fiction continues to remind us that sameness and alterity are two correlative existentials.

But I am eager to get to the main difference between the use of science fiction in the treatment of the problem of personal identity in analytic philosophy and that of literary fiction in the hermeneutics of narrative identity. Novels and theatrical productions have in fact their own puzzling cases, especially in modern literature. But they are not puzzling in the same sense.

Compared to Parfit's 'impersonal conception', the kind of indeterminacy, or undecidability, that literature provokes does not lead to declaring the question itself empty. The question *who* is moreover exacerbated as a question by the evasion of the answer. If it is true that the answers to the question *who* – typical of the problem of the self (*ipse*) – borrow their content from the problematic of the same (*idem*) (the question *who*, the answer *what*), the puzzling cases posed by literary fiction tend to separate the question *ipse* from the answer *idem*. Who is 'I' when the subject says that (s)he/it is nothing? Precisely a self deprived of assistance from sameness – (*idem*) identity.

This suggestion that I am formulating at the level of narrative configuration is not without repercussions at the level of the refiguration of the everyday concrete self. In the course of the application of literature to life, what we carry over and transpose into the exegesis of ourselves is this dialectic of the self and the same. There we can find the purgative virtue of the thought-experiments deployed by literature, not only at the level of theoretical reflexion, but at that of existence. You know what importance I attach to the relation between text and reader. I always like to quote the beautiful text of Proust in *Time Regained*:

> But to return to myself, I thought more modestly of my book, and one could not exactly say that I thought of those who would read it, of my readers. Because they would not according to me be my readers, but the real readers of themselves, my book being only like one of those magnifying glasses offered to a customer by the optician at Combray. It was my book, and thanks to it I enabled them to read what lay within themselves.[4]

The refiguration by narrative confirms this aspect of self-knowledge which goes far beyond the narrative domain, namely, that the self does not know itself immediately, but only indirectly by the detour of the cultural signs of all sorts which are articulated on the symbolic mediations which always already articulate action and, among them, the narratives of everyday life. Narrative mediation underlines this remarkable characteristic of self-knowledge – that it is self-interpretation. The appropriation of the identity of the fictional character by the reader is one of its forms. What narrative interpretation brings in its own right is precisely the figural nature of the character by which the self, narratively interpreted, turns out to be a *figured* self – which imagines itself (*se figure*) in this or that way.

It is here that I locate what I have just called the purgative virtue, in the sense of the Aristotelian catharsis, the thought experiments offered by literature, and more precisely the limit-cases of dissolution of sameness – (*idem*) identity. In a sense, there is a point at which we must be able to say, with Parfit: *identity is not what matters*. But it is still someone who says this. The sentence 'I am nothing' must be allowed to retain its paradoxical form: 'nothing' would no longer mean anything if it were not imputed to an 'I'. What is still 'I' when I say that it is nothing if not precisely a self deprived of assistance from sameness? Is that not the meaning of many dramatic – not to say terrifying – experiences in respect of our own identity, that is the necessity to go through the trial of this nothingness of permanence-identity, to which nothingness would be the equivalent of the null case of the transformations dear to Lévi-Strauss. Many conversion narratives bear witness to such dark nights of personal identity. At these moments of extreme exposure, the null response, far from declaring the question empty, returns to it and preserves it as a question. What cannot be effaced is the question itself: who am I?

NOTES

1 Derek Parfit, *Reasons and Persons*, Oxford, Clarendon Press, 1984, p. 210.
2 Alasdair MacIntyre, *After Virtue*, London, Duckworth Press, 1981.
3 See A.-J. Greimas, *Du sens: essais sémiotique*, Paris, Editions du Seuil, 1970; and *Maupassant: la sémiotique du texte: exercises pratiques*, Paris, Editions du Seuil, 1976. Ricoeur expands on his discussion here in *TN* vol. II, part III, section 2, 'The semiotic constraints on narrativity', pp. 29–60 [Editor's note].
4 Proust, *A la recherche du temps perdu*, Paris, Gallimard, Pléiade, vol. III, p. 1033. David Wood's translation.

INDEX

action 6, 10, 16, 21, 26, 28, 29, 47, 49, 85–86, 98, 149, 191; bodily 139; historical 145; human 17, 50, 117, 129, 131, 144, 150, 177, 186; perceptual 131; refiguring of 6; semantics of 28; structure of 164

actors 21, 145, 177

Adorno, Theodor W. 14, 102–123; *Negative Dialectics* 102, 122n1

aesthetic, aesthetics 16, 997, 103; and feeling 35; and ideas 40; Kant on 106; of reception 129; reversal 91; *see also* art, excess, Kant

agents 86, 150, 191; of History 181; Lenin and Stalin as examples of 181

d'Alembert, Jean le Rond 79

Anaximander 1

Annalistes 15, 140, 145

anthropology 28–29, 34, 42–43, 47, 48–49, 51

aporia 4, 5, 6, 8–9, 10, 13, 85, 86, 87, 147; *see also* time

Arendt, Hannah: *Between Past and Future* 63–64; *The Human Condition* 182

Aristotle 1, 22, 23–24, 28, 31, 34, 85, 149, 157n7, 167, 175, 190; on *catharsis* 198; G. F. Else's commentary on 181; definition of *mimesis praxeos* 28; on *muthos* 21;

on *peripteia* 185; on *phronesis* 11, 23; on plot 31; on time 3

art 14, 16, 17, 38, 104, 113; Adorno on 102–123; and knowledge 107; and life 16–17, 161, 164, 166, 168; standard view of 161–162, 163, 166, 169, 171–173, 180, 182; Lyotard on 102–123; modern, modernist 103, 105–106; pictorial 98; work of 87, 88, 105

Aufhebung (sublation) 55

Augustine, St 34, 48, 167; *City of God* 152; *Confessions of St Augustine* 31, 167, 169, 172; on time 3, 167

Austin, J. L.: constative/ performative distinction 150

author, the 23, 32, 75, 81, 129, 165, 179, 191; of fiction 166

Bach, Johann Sebastian 10

Bakhtine, Mikhail 195

Barthes, Roland 147, 161, 164; on 'the effect of the real' 186; 'Introduction à l'analyse structurale des récits' 161

de Beauvoir, Simone: *Memoirs of a Dutiful Daughter* 75

Beckett, Samuel 63

Bedeutung see reference

being 2, 42; being-in-the-world 49, 51, 153, 191, 196; being-in-time 47, 50, 142; being-there 7; being-towards-death 12, 14, 46,

innovation 58; of the self and the same 198; of self-consciousness 15, 121; *see also* consciousness, Hegel, identity, sedimentation
Dickens, Charles 82
Dilthey, Wilhelm 76, 194
discordance *see* concordance
disemplotment *see* emplotment
Dray, William 182
Durkheim, Emile 114

economy, economics 10; economy of Being 2; economy of 'time-shelters' 9; *see also* being, time
ego; narcissistic 11
Eliot, George 82
emplotment 10, 17, 21–25, 59, 85–87, 92, 98, 144–145, 151, 157n5, 170; disemplotment 144, 156; *see also* configuration, narrative, plot
Enlightenment, the 14, 61, 76, 103, 105
Entwurf see projection
epistemology, epistemological 23, 36, 42, 68, 76, 78, 183–184, 188, 191
epoché 3; *see* Husserl, Edmund, phenomenology
ethics 23, 47, 68
event, events 4, 21, 26, 32, 82, 86, 88, 94, 117, 121, 149; historical 15–16, 140–141, 145, 151; historical/natural distinction 150; human 168; imaginary 141, 144, 147, 151; *vs* real 144, 147, 151; past/present 150; quasi-146, 184; real 143–144, 160–161; revelatory 127; structure and 176–178
excess 14, 103, 105, 107–8, 109, 112–13; aesthetic 105; and signification 110; metaphysics of 108; Nietzschean 132; and self-determination 121; *see also* aesthetics, Kant
existence 2, 46, 48; authentic/inauthentic 119; existential analysis 30; human existence 43;

mediated by semantics 119; *see also* being, Dasein
Exodus 154
explanandum/explanans see explanation
explanation 17, 41, 45, 175, 177–178, 185; *explanandum/explanans* 175; ideological 69; scientific 153; and understanding 153; *see also* interpretation

fate 32, 46, 116, 117, 118; articulated by narrative 14
Faurisson, Robert: on Auschwitz 186
fiction 13, 15, 16, 17, 20, 28, 48–49, 59, 85, 86, 87, 114, 130, 146, 151–152, 156; as action 196; distinction between history and fiction 185; explanatory 160; narrative fiction 16, 31; and stories 141; *see also* history, narrative
figuration 85, 92, 98, 196; of temporality 16, 155; *see also* emplotment, narrative, plot, prefiguration, refiguration, transfiguration
formalism, literary 20, 143
Foucault, Michel 76, 125, 126; and *epistemes* 124; 'Nietzsche, Genealogy, History' 107–108; *The Order of Things* 124; and 'primal text' 125–126
Freud, Sigmund 58; *Totem and Taboo* 67
futural *see* future
future 5, 12, 31, 42, 47, 50, 57, 63, 64, 65, 85, 88, 94, 99, 116; futural 44; *see also* past, present, projection

Gadamer, Hans-Georg 26, 60, 62; on 'fusion of horizons' 26, 58–59; in opposition to Habermas 61
Galileo 76, 131
Gelven, Michael: *Commentary on 'Being and Time'* 43–44, 53n27

38, 46–47, 50, 51, 104;
associative 145; creative 11, 12,
24, 34, 35, 39, 41, 51; critical 66;
narrative 39, 42; ontological 42;
productive 4, 5, 6, 11, 25, 34, 35,
36, 42, 145; reproductive 35, 36,
38
Ingarden, Roman 88
intention: conscious and
unconscious 145; referential 128;
unity of 31
interpretation 10, 27–28, 42–43,
44–45, 47, 59, 66, 69, 107, 108,
111, 122, 173; allegorical 156;
conflict of 70; and
deconstruction 131; excessive
111; Heideggerian 51, 53n23;
infinity of 125; narrative 80, 198;
violence of 180; *see also*
explanation, understanding
Iser, Wolfgang: *The Act of Reading*
75, 86, 91, 100n3

Joyce, James 63
justice 110, 111

Kant, Immanuel 3, 4, 5, 9, 11, 34,
35–41, 51, 61, 71n3, 103–105,
145, 190; *Critique of Judgement* 11,
38; *Critique of Pure Reason* 24,
35–36, 42; determinant
judgement 38; genius 11;
judgments of taste and beauty
104–106; reflective judgment 11,
35, 38–39; schematism 4, 24,
35–39, 40, 41, 42; and the
sublime 14, 104, 105–106, 113,
114
Kearney, Richard 12, 14, 55–73
Kermode, Frank 196; *The Sense of
an Ending* 160, 181
Kierkegaard, Soren: *Diary of Soren
Kierkegaard* 82–83
Kockelmans, J. J. 19n6
Kundera, Milan 195

Lacan, Jacques 186
language 3, 7, 45, 59, 80, 98, 115,
125–126, 128, 129, 170; change

178; figurative 40; language
games 108–109, 110–112, 114; in
narrativity 142; natural 59;
pervasiveness of 2; philosophy of
44; poetic 35, 44; recreation of
68; referential 185; symbolic 150
langue/parole 176, 182–183
legitimation 103; critique of 119;
de-legitimation 103, 106–107,
110–111
Leibniz, Gottfried Wilhelm 79
Leiris, Michel 196
Levinas, Emmanuel 4, 7, 19n10,
187
Lévi-Strauss, Claude 199
Lewis, David 136
life as biological phenomenon 11,
20, 28; and fiction 25, 33; human
20; and literature 87; pre-
narrative capacity of 28–30; *see
also* art, fiction, history,
narrative, world
linguistics 23, 26–27
literature 3, 5, 17, 26, 33, 40, 48,
51, 160, 169, 173, 181, 198; and
history 146; and music 125; and
voice 125; *see also* fiction, novel
logos and *muthos* 12, 69–70, 187
Lukács, Georg 195
Lyotard, Jean-François 14,
102–123; *The Postmodern Condition*
102, 122n1; *see also* Adorno, art,
narrative, sublime

MacIntyre, Alasdair 76; *After Virtue*
66, 195
MacQuarrie, John: *An Existentialist
Theology* 43, 53n25
McTaggart, J. E. 5
Mann, Thomas 74; *Der Zauberberg*
86
Marx, Karl 58, 67, 68
meaning 2, 60, 62–63, 68, 80, 82,
87, 104, 105, 106, 107, 112, 114,
115, 121, 129, 147, 152, 154, 177;
of aesthetic modernism 109;
allegorical 153; closure of 6;
historical 58; *Sinn* 146; of stories

144; symbolic 150; and tradition 59

memory 4, 31, 64, 78, 87, 88, 89, 90, 117, 120; conscious and unconscious 92; historical 58; involuntary 87, 88, 91, 94–95, 98

Merleau-Ponty, Maurice 15, 131, 137–138, 163, 186

metaphor 6, 8, 40, 83, 87, 88, 89, 95, 96, 98, 99, 100, 128, 130, 170; and allegory 152–155; of the book 124–125; and metonymy 6–7, 8; and myth 149; mythological 97; of reading 139; as semantic innovation 170; sense and reference of 171; of the text 126; of the written 124–125

Michelet, Jules: *History of France* 152

Mill, James 79

Mill, John Stuart 13, 78–81; *Autobiography of John Stuart Mill* 79; *System of Logic* 79; and utilitarianism 80

mimesis, mimetic 6, 7, 17, 50, 85, 97, 149, 150, 167, 168, 169, 182, 185; mimesis I, II and III, distinguished 50, 58–59, 85–86, 180; and diegesis 149; mimetic activity 157n7; mimetic imperative 7; narrative 170; *see also* configuration, emplotment, prefiguration, refiguration

Mink, Louis 117, 161, 167, 169

modernity 63, 66, 76–78, 80, 102, 103, 104, 106; crisis of 69

Musil, Robert: *The Man Without Qualities* 195, 196

myth, *muthos* 12–13, 15, 25, 128, 146, 148, 160; anthropological 64; creation myth 64; hermeneutics of 55–70; and history 156, as ideological distortion 12, 69; as narrative; utopian function of 69

narcissism 33

narrative *passim*; anti-narrative 77, 78, 80, 109, 144, 172;

configurational aspect of 12; fictional 12, 15, 58, 128, 130, 151–152, 188, 197; narrative form 91; grand narratives 14; as guardian of time 4, 102–103; historical 15, 121, 128, 130, 140, 149–153, 155, 173, 186; narrative identity 4, 9, 11, 14, 18, 32–33, 99, 188–199; and life 10–11, 20–33, 173; mythic 15; order of 10; personality 82; philosophy's ressemblance to 75; repetition 116–117; structuralist theories of 161; structure of 164–165, 168–169; time 9; understanding 23, 24, 33; voice 13, 16, 30, 75, 78, 82, 165–166; *see also* emplotment, time

narrativity; metaphysics of 140–159

narratology 23–24

narrator 30, 32, 79, 80, 81, 85, 88–89, 91, 94, 96, 98, 165

nature; and freedom 35, 36, 38, 40

Nietzsche, Friedrich Wilhelm 18n2, 58, 67, 108, 111, 156, 196; and genealogical hermeneutics 67; and will to power 67; *see also* hermeneutics of suspicion

noematic/noetic 129, 134

nomological 17

nomologically hermetic 17, 174, 175, 177, 178

novel, the 32, 74, 75, 80, 87, 143, 197; and anti-novel 25, 27; and history 143–156; modernist 141, 144, 148; plotless 148; post-modernist 141; traditional 141

Ong, Walter 76

ontic, ontological 1, 44, 112, 115, 172, 191; ontological closure 178; distinguished 43; historical–ontological 129; ontology 41, 42, 44–45

Parfit, Derek 199; *Reasons and Persons* 18, 192–194, 196–197

paronomasia 7–8; *see also* Schöfer

past 5, 12, 31, 42, 50, 56–57, 59,

pervasiveness of 1;
phenomenological approach to 1;
and possibility 46–51; read 91;
see also configuration, history,
narrative, prefiguration,
refiguration, temporality
totemic thought 127
tradition 3, 11, 12, 24–25, 32, 39,
46, 120; hermeneutics of 55–64;
literary 33; living 57; of
metaphysics 113; narrative 45;
Old Testament 127;
philosophical 110; and utopia 12,
55–73, dialectic between
tradition and utopia 62–63; *see
also* history, utopia,
sedimentation
transfiguration 27, 49
truth 2, 18n2, 45, 60, 66, 67, 80, 83,
94, 102, 105, 109, 113, 142, 147;
figurative 153; literal 153–154;
moral 79; narrative 153;
presumption of 12, 62

understanding 10–11, 14, 23, 24,
26, 30, 35, 36, 42–43, 45, 46–47,
51, 59, 66, 82, 85–6, 104, 172,
182; conceptual 113; historical
62; human 102; and
interpretation 50; phronetic 28;
and reason 113; self- 27, 31, 32,
48, 65; *see also* explanation,
interpretation
utopia 55, 62–63, 64, 65, 103; and

ideology 29; symbolizations of
68; *see also* tradition

Vanhoozer, Kevin 11–12, 14, 34–54
Verstehen (understanding); *see*
Heidegger
Veyne, Paul 167

Wellmer, Albrecht: 'On the
dialectic of Modernism and
Post-modernism' 122n2
Whately, Richard 79
Whewell, William 79
White, Hayden 15–16, 17, 140–159,
161, 163
will 5, 108; philosophy of 11
within-timeness 16, 148, 152
Wittgenstein, Ludwig 34, 82
Wood, David 1–19, *The
Deconstruction of Time* 19n9;
Writing the Future 19n10
Woolf, Virginia 34, 63, 74; *Mrs
Dalloway* 86, 156, 158n12
world 47, 48, 129; of action 86; of
capital 110; relationship of the
human to 127; human lifeworld
128; possible 65, 68; of the
reader 26, 48, 128, 130; of the
text 26, 48–49, 50, 76, 128, 130;
and text 129
von Wright, Henrik: *Explanation and
Interpretation* 183
writing 127; primacy of 126; and
speech 126